THOU SHALT NOT
UNCOVER
THY
MOTHER'S NAKEDNESS

THOU SHALT NOT UNCOVER THY MOTHER'S NAKEDNESS

An Autobiography

GEORGE HAYIM

Quartet Books
London   New York

First published in Great Britain by Quartet Books Limited 1988
A member of the Namara Group
27/29 Goodge Street
London W1P 1FD

British Library Cataloguing in Publication Data

Hayim, George
Thou shalt not uncover thy
mother's nakedness.
1. Great Britain. Male homosexuality.
Personal observations.
I. Title
306.7′662′0924
ISBN 0 7043 2690 6

Typeset by AKM Associates (UK) Ltd
Ajmal House, Hayes Road, Southall, London
Printed and bound in Great Britain by
The Camelot Press PLC, Southampton

Acknowledgements

My thanks to: Gore Vidal, who told me how to do it twenty years ago; Andrew Harvey (*Journey in Ladakh*), who saw a fragment in my house two years ago, and made me write nine hundred pages; Jacob Vromen, a Dutch neighbour in Sydney, who collected and corrected the scattered pages as I wrote them; and Ros Becker, who tore the finished version from my hands and made several thousand corrections, thank God.

1

My shoulders were too wide. There was nothing to be done. Everything came to a halt, but it did give me time to think. Out there I could hear guttural shouts in Arabic, blessings in Hebrew, a Russian dirge and some Chinese. They were waiting. What were they waiting for? For me. Me – the star, the chosen one, the Capricorn, the goat that makes its way to the top. (Years later I learned I had not been chosen at all. I'd been an accident.) A fire-cracker went off, another, another and another. This was my entrance cue. I could not let my fans down. I had to appear. With determination and a wriggle I hurtled down into life – into larger than life. Eleven and a quarter pounds of me. What was done could not be undone. The fire-crackers had nothing to do with me – it was a Chinese feast.

Should I have shut up and stayed where I was? I can never shut up, and I never stay anywhere for long. So what is to be expected of one born in Shanghai on 30 December 1920? I did know, but I cannot remember whether it was the Year of the Rat, the Pig, the Tiger, the Monkey, the Dragon, the Ox, the Dog or the Rooster. Under the title 'Strong Capricorns', my astrology book says: 'ambitious and capricious'. Some manuals say I'm a goat who knows where he is going, that I sit in the background and watch. Others say the opposite. I haven't found the right manual yet. Mine says 'lively, talkative, snobbish and ineffectual. A desire to direct, protect, persuade, wheedle, needle, meddle, mother and smother'. Under 'Health' it says 'weakness in bones and joints' and then adds the word 'warrior'. A warrior? (A warrior I am not.) Now, twenty years later, I looked at that book again: I was a 'worrier', not a 'warrior'.

Ten years ago, when I was living in Paris, I picked up the evening

1

paper and under 'Capricorn' I read, 'You have a pain in the left knee.' Yes, I did have a pain in my left knee. I took the article down to the old porter of my hotel and asked him what he thought I should do. 'You should take the paper every day until it says "Capricorns no longer have a pain in their knee." '

My father, on learning that I weighed eleven and a quarter pounds, rang up his chum at the Club to cash in on a bet he had made that I would weigh more than the other man's expected baby. Mother was huge. The other man's wife was like a hairpin. Her baby shot out of her like a dart and weighed a quarter pound more than I did – no way to start a father–son relationship. Poor Mother had tried her best. She'd drunk gallons of milk, which she hated, from our own cow and became enormous and milkless, eventually having to call in two greedy, giggling Chinese swollen-breasted milk-sisters, wolfing Chinese cabbage and garlic all day. I could smell it, I could taste it. I still can today. But I was hungry. Mother cursed them in pidgin English.

'Whatting you eat tiffin time?'

'Nothing. We no lie.'

'You chow garlic, cabbage fry. Baby burpy, cry.'

Much was against me from the start. Unwanted child (they wanted a girl). One thing was in my favour – I was born blond. Not only do gentlemen prefer blondes, nearly everyone does. For a family from Baghdad to have a blond-haired child was a miracle. Not that we were Arabs, we were Baghdadian Jews, Babylonians. In those days the word 'ethnic' was never used. We were all proud to be Jewish, not proud to be Baghdadian. (How silly when there's Ali-Baba! The Flying Carpet! The Hanging Gardens! Much more fun than being Jewish.) We claimed to be Sephardim, as opposed to the other race of Jews known as Ashkenazim. *Sepharad* is, in fact, a Hebrew word for Spain. At the time of the diaspora many Jews left for Greece, Rhodes, Egypt and North Africa, then on to Morocco, and, finally, to Spain, where they settled till they were thrown out by the Inquisition. Thus, they were known as Sephardi Jews. (They were snobbish about the Ashkenazis, which means German in Hebrew, and their accents.) We were neither. My family didn't leave Babylonia till the late nineteenth century and had nothing whatever to do with Spain. The other race of Jews whose trials and tribulations drove them to success in music, theatre, medicine, law and New York, are Ashkenazis. I don't think they are Jews at all. It is almost certain they were a tribe from somewhere in South Russia called Khazars who converted themselves to Judaism about AD750. I'm

2

against converts. People are always converting to something: Buddhism, Hinduism, Scientology, Hare Krishna or vegetarianism.

Did I know my brother was around when I arrived? Yes. And I immediately wanted to upstage him because he was a black-eyed whizz-kid. I can prove this with photos, and the camera did not lie in those days. Dick was a black-haired beauty with a fringe, not unlike Claudette Colbert as the Empress Poppaea in *The Sign of the Cross*. He not only had this flashing beauty, but also a big ding-dong (also rather black). What use after my theatrical entry into the world that people should look at Brother Dick, swoon, then turn to me in pity and say: 'And you are very nice too.'

When Dick was eleven months old and some old woman was fussing over him, he looked her straight in the eye, sighed, and said 'Beat it.' He was now a star. I had to take my revenge. A couple of years later I was walking down the garden with him, when I plucked something red from the bush that I knew was forbidden. 'Look, Dicky,' I said. 'Cherry.' Dicky looky cherry, eaty cherry. But Dicky, in fact, eaty chilli. Mouth swelly. People said 'What a lovely big mouth Dick has, twice the size of yours.' I felt remorse. Dicky was a Pricky, but he was never consciously spiteful and nasty like I was. I made up for that over the next twenty years. I lied and pimped for him, until . . . .

Father was born in Baghdad in 1894, the last of three children. His father died almost immediately and according to Jewish law Granny was supposed to marry his brother. They were all living in the same house and one day in a temper he grabbed Father's only sister Maisie by the hair and dragged her screaming across the room. Granny blew up. She left for Bombay, where her brother, a friendly, rich, round man, called Benjamin Sassoon, had an import-export business with Shanghai, where he also had an office. Eventually, Uncle Benjamin sent Granny and the children to England where they settled. Uncle Benjamin also had a stockbroking business in Shanghai, called Benjamin and Potts, Potts being a distinguished Christian and an old Harrovian. This was to alter our destiny: I was named George after him; my father became an Anglophile and joined the firm in Shanghai. Father had drive and ambition. The stock exchange was small and when six or seven Baghdadians yelled out in Arabic and no one else understood, they made a killing. Within a few years of his marriage, Father had become a millionaire.

Mother was born in Shanghai. Her fair and beautiful mother

3

accompanied by her seven sisters had all fled from Kiev after a terrible pogrom. They crossed the whole of Russia with all their belongings in a caravan like one sees in a Western. But instead of visualizing them all as babies playing amidst violins, French horns, cellos, harps and drums (their father sold musical instruments), I see them aged seventy, eighty and ninety, in an open wagon, all wearing black-rimmed glasses, black shawls around their shoulders.

The bitter Siberian winds blow and the old girls hobble off the caravan at Tomsk, Irkutsk, Harbin and Vladivostok for a coffee. There is Great-aunt Rosie, Great-aunt Sarah, Great-aunt Fanny and Great-aunt Lily-of-the-Valley – the one who was always putting her finger in her mouth, lifting it to the winds and saying: 'Le fond de l'air est froid' (which sounds much better than 'Oh, what a wind').

But what did they all look like? Was it one caravan or were there two? Did they change horses? How did they pay? With gold coins, or paper money? What was to stop brigands from robbing them? Did Great-aunt Lily-of-the-Valley stick her head, her black-rimmed glasses and her shawl out of the window and ask some *moujik* where they could buy hay for the horses? Did they tell anyone they were Jewish? Could you tell by looking at them? Did Russian-Jewish great-aunts wear heavy-rimmed glasses, even if they were all babies? Above all, did Great-aunt Lily-of-the-Valley look like a whale in those days? She talked the whole way over the Urals, over the steppes and round Lake Baikal, constantly repeating 'Le fond de l'air est froid', whatever season it was. Many years later, could I forget her palpitating entrance into Grosvenor House where we all lived in London? She had arrived from Hampstead wearing the same black shawl I imagined she had worn sixty years earlier. Beginning with that thing about the cold air, she went into her last harrowing adventure all of which she related in detail.

'. . . so I left No. 32 – that's where I live – and I walked down the hill on the left-hand side of the road as far as Fitzjohn's Avenue, then I realized that I had left the key in the porch. So I had to go back to see if I had or hadn't, and I found I hadn't because I found the key in my bag – not exactly my bag, you see, it was a basket. So when I finally got back to the bus I was waiting for, they told me it had gone. So I had to wait for another and while I was waiting there was a lady next to me carrying a basket just like mine, so I asked her where she had got hers and told her how I meant to bring mine but had left it at home when I returned to get the key. She was such a nice lady – her son is in Johannesburg . . .'

Mother's grandfather, Hamovitch, first settled in Vladivostock, one of the towns where Jews were allowed to live, and opened a shop there selling musical instruments; but after a few years the whole lot of them ended up in Shanghai. There is no account of how my mother's Russian mother met her husband, Baghdadian Grandpa Elias. Did he wander into their Shanghai shop to buy a piano? Did they belong to a social set? It certainly was not a result of a wild night, and both parties must have hesitated. Did rich Baghdadian Grandpa think he was better than Russian Grandma? Shanghai standards were money, in which case Grandpa was better. On the other hand, he knew nothing about arpeggios and violas, Borodin or Tchaikovsky; and if he had heard of Rachmaninov, he would never have believed that sixty years later the great composer would come to his daughter Mimi's house in London and sign her piano.

Maybe the success of their marriage was due to the fact that neither spoke the other's language. They did not even speak English well enough to fight. Marriages had to work in those days, anything else was unthinkable. Funny that scandal and divorce are so abhorrent to Jews when there is a thing in the religion called 'The Get'. You stand in front of your poor little wife, point to the door and yell 'Get' three times, just like some old farmer in Wisconsin. I don't know if the wife can tell the husband to 'Get', but if she has to marry her dead husband's brother, it would seem that 'The Get' is good for the gander but not for the goose. Dick and I asked Mama once how Grandpa Elias had made his money. She replied, 'Little boys should not talk about money.' We could now spend anything we liked so long as we did not talk about it. Dick was braver than I and cross-examined Enrica, Mother's Italian dressmaker who had been living with us for years and with whose ways I identified.

'When the war with Russia and Japan, your Nonno [Grandpa] he sell one uniform to one Russian soldier and he sell one uniform to one Japanese soldier.' She stopped talking and smiled mysteriously as if she had explained everything.

'That's only two suits,' Dick replied. 'You can't make money selling two suits. How much was each suit?'

She finally explained that 'Nonno' had supplied both armies with uniforms, so next time Dick and I were in town we went into a shop in Nanking Road and asked the price of some material. Dick asked Mother for an *Encyclopaedia Britannica*. Next morning my rich parents, believing they had two genius sons, bought us twelve brand-new volumes. We then got someone else to multiply the quantity of soldiers involved in the Russo-Japanese War by the price of the material in

5

Nanking Road. The sum was gigantic. We threw in a few more millions for buttons, braid, medals and thread (very remarkable for two small boys). As a result, we could all live in Grandpa's huge house in the best part of Shanghai. If China had not gone Communist in 1948 we would have been worth 500 million US dollars today.

Mother was born in this house. She was the star while her younger sister, Vera, who resembled her, looked as if she'd been dipped in bleach. There were five brothers, none of them interesting.

Freddie, the eldest son, was a handsome playboy although he did work as a stockbroker. He loved being the centre of attraction, wore dazzling shoes and flashy clothes. He won at the races and communicated perfectly with the Chinese who helped him win. He frequented visiting film-stars and liked small boys who Mama thought were girls, and Shanghai was full of small boys.

Near us lived the Kadoorie family. Before I was born Mrs Kadoorie perished in a fire that razed their grand house to the ground, so they all moved into our house. When in his eighties and enjoying the generosity of those Kadoories who paid all his hospital bills, Freddie always explained, 'Well, they all stayed with us after the fire.'

Eddie, his brother, was a kind bore who read Robert Service. Freddie didn't read at all.

David was always peculiar. He'd take endless trouble changing the faces of all the clocks in the house so as to be able to prove he wasn't where he said he had been or that he was where he had not been. He caught syphilis, lied, cheated, plotted, but he had one great godly gift. He could heal. One might be walking along the road with him when he'd stop and say, 'You're having trouble with your left ear.' He was always right and always took away the pain. One sometimes suspected him of inflicting it in order to cure it.

Just before the war, a young Polish girl, victim of Dick's infidelities, lay in agony on Mother's boudoir couch in London. Uncle David threw open the windows, bent over her, did his special passes and then dragged the pain out of her, which he then threw out of the window giving Dick and myself a momentary splitting headache as it passed through our heads into the street. Eventually he was pensioned off and lived in Nottingham where he spent all his money on horses. He could heal, but he couldn't back a winner.

Reggie was fat and friendly and worked in London, after finishing his schooling in England. He was unpretentious and a *schnorrer* but he knew all about gardens.

6

Ronny, the youngest, was deep into Chinese girls. He was generous and arrogent and after the war married a young Chinese girl who had befriended him in the camp where the community lived under Japanese rule in Shanghai. We called her 'Yvonne' but her real name in Chinese was Soo, Sue or Sough. If you didn't pronounce it right it meant pig.

My father had a brilliant older brother who never married. He also lived in Grandpa Elias's house with us. He travelled the world over ordering exotic sweets and specialities from distant lands for shop-girls, children or secretaries. On occasions, an immense block of chocolate would arrive, to be hacked to pieces by Uncle using a great sword that stood in the corner of the dining-room. Bottles of white plaited cheeses swimming in salt water, would arrive in large jars from Bombay. Uncle would take them out and the whole room would smell of vomit. He'd then slice them into small pieces and drop them into boiling water, which killed the smell. I've done this with Fetta cheese and it works. Every morning, after brushing his teeth, he'd take out a long thin piece of celluloid, like the things that stiffen collars, stick out his tongue, bend the celluloid strip, and, with a flicking movement, scrape the fur off it. He had our tailor sew little caps into the toes of his socks to avoid getting holes. Fifty years later when my book *Obsession* was published, the family were so ashamed of it that Uncle Albert bought a shredder and shredded every copy he could find in Hong Kong.

Aunt Maisie, father's sister, was strong, silent and austere. And if her uncle had not dragged her by her hair, in Baghdad in 1901, where would I be today? Mother and Maisie never liked each other. Mother was soft, loving and tender; Maisie, hard and religious.

And Father. What did he look like? Average height and sallow skin, a huge beak of a nose, which he claimed had been broken playing hockey. He looked like some forbidding Arab sheikh. His eyes were hard, black and fine; the whites were blue. He was austere, aloof, noble, menacing and contemptuous. His stare was hypnotic and crucifixorious, and if that word does not exist it does now. His mouth was a sharp, thin tear, showing cruel, white, unsmiling shark's teeth. Every word, every gesture, even his swaying walk was studied. He would tell us never to make personal remarks although he, himself, made them constantly and intentionally to unnerve, humiliate or excite, depending on the circumstances. He never gossiped and never apologized. Anglo-Saxon women were mad for him. Every middle-class colonial wife ached to be a second Lady Hester Stanhope, jerked off her British pedestal and thrown into a tent by the tenebrous Ellis Hayim. The richer he became, the more power he had. Only Mother stood up to him, and then only over trivialities like carpets or curtains. People feared Father. I was both terrified of him and at the same time excited by the hairy chest, his darkness.

I always looked forward to getting into bed with him in the mornings, when he twisted my arms and made me helpless. But, at any moment, one glare from him and I would freeze. Later I would dream of him screwing me or my killing him; but I was never strong enough to kill him, nor did he every screw me.

During the period that Mother had offered the park she owned in Shanghai to billet the British Volunteer Corps, we came into contact with the army. One day at home she caught a British officer leaning right over Father, who was in his bed, something she couldn't explain but which worried her. (She'd have had a far greater shock if she had seen how many soldiers have leaned over my bed.)

Punishment was a word Father adored. Once, at a garden party, silly Great-aunt Lily-of-the-Valley knocked her head on something. She made a great farty sound and flopped down like an emptying balloon.

'Aunt Lily, you look like a dead whale,' Dick said gaily.

Father overheard, and that was the end of the party. 'The Princes' were taken away for punishment.

'I said nothing,' I pleaded.

'You both will be punished. No favouritism.'

'What can't we both be forgiven, no favouritism?' I asked. But no one was ever forgiven. Father would clear his throat and that alone was like on-coming thunder. The waiting paralysed me with fear. He decided to belt us. Why didn't he just give us a quick slap? But no, it was to be slow, sinister and inexorable. He was going to belt us on the feet. All children think of a beating as whacks on the bum. What did this feet business mean? Did Auntie Maisie beat her children on the feet? Where was Mother? Who could I go to for protection? Now I was made to scream with pain, and the only place I could go to for protection was into the arms of the very man who was beating me. After each such beating, I would rush hysterically into his arms. (Great-aunt Lily-of-the-Valley *did* look like a whale!)

Father's no-favouritism rule was broken on one occasion, with deadly results for me. To this day no one has ever told me what I did wrong. As I was only four or five when it happened, how could I have known what I'd said? As I remember it, Father, looking darker and more sinister than ever, walked towards me. I walked backwards till I fell into a chair. Hypnotizing me with those powerful black eyes, he looked for something in the lapel of his coat.

'I am going to punish you, so you will always remember it. And if ever you say such a thing again, you know what will happen to you.'

With that he pulled a pin from his lapel and put it to my lips. I cannot absolutely swear that he stuck it in or how far he stuck it in or if he drew blood. With time, a picture evolved of this creature I thought was there to protect his babies from the howling winds, the beating rains, the cold and hunger of this world. Instead he became the monster who drew out from beneath a big black cloak a sword, which he stuck through my face. Dear God, dear God, is this my father who protecteth me from the storm? Please, dear God, protect me from him.

I've since learned that the skin on the lips is hard, and Father was not much good with his hands anyway. He probably didn't puncture the skin. Thirty years later, I had it out with Mother.

'What a lousy son-of-a-bitch, Mother, to let that evil bastard stick pins into your baby's mouth?'

'He only did it once,' she said. To make up for it she added, 'Oh, how much I wept.'

'Wept?' I screamed. 'You wept? Why didn't you pick up something and throw it at him?'

She was right: he did do it only once, but for the next twelve years, every time he wanted to frighten me, he'd say with gentle, mocking concern: 'Wouldn't this help?' and he'd fumble in his lapel, even if he was wearing pyjamas. Today, sexually I am totally oral. All my pleasure comes from the mouth. Who knows, perhaps I would never have enjoyed kissing those millions of people, cats and dogs, marble horses, wooden tables, had it not been for Father. Maybe Father knew best after all.

2

Throughout the first years Dick and I were as one. We would hold hands, hug in bed and follow each other about. It was a love affair. We would play endless games and take on various roles. He was always Hercules, Sinbad the Sailor, D'Artagnan, or some other hero. I invented my own roles, always female. I was the helpless Princess Tangerina, or the dying Russian actress Runerova, or Wanda, the abandoned fairy (because we knew fairies had wands – but I have no clue about Tangerina or Runerova). Dick, my protector, always saved me. I was beautiful, dramatic, loving and unhappy. We both loved our roles but when we reversed them, the game folded. We would go on searches, climb out of bed at night, tiptoe down to the hall, sniff the hats of the visitors and know who had come home. We did not go to school and knew no other children except our cousins. We feared the word 'Christian'. No one had ever told us it was bad, but we thought Christianity might infiltrate and we would get hooked. When Mother, determined to upstage Shanghai, managed a private audience with the Pope in Rome (he blessed the locket she carried with our photos in it), Maisie and Granny were shocked.

Grandpa's house was always busy, like a city. We were three generations and two families, though we never had guests. I don't think we knew anybody. Everyone shouted 'boy' all day long. Sometimes we would wander off to the tailor's quarters at the end of the house where he sat with a round hat and a pigtail, his small fingernail an inch long. The washer-woman also lived in the house. Anything lying on the floor was whisked away, soaked in suds,rolled into balls and whacked on to the stone yard again and again until it shed its dirt or disintegrated. We had our own cow, which was very special considering we lived in a town. But what with eating kosher and the danger of contracting consumption (Mother's favourite word), we had to have our own cow. We had gardeners, but they did no weeding. This was done by a bevy of women who arrived once a month and took positions on their little wooden stools, going right across the lawn like locusts, never missing a weed.

Bang in front of the french windows in the sitting-room was the tennis court. Mother loved tennis and for a huge woman was surprisingly agile. As time passed, she got bigger and bigger and when she ran for a ball, we were sure she would crash through the windows and flatten us. In Victoria, BC, where we went in summer to escape Shanghai's terrible heat, Mother would take us riding. Today, when I see pictures of her sitting on a horse, I wonder how she got up there, how the horse could take it, and why the RSPCA allowed it.

One summer, Mother went to Europe and Granny took us to Japan instead, to a village called Unzen built on hills of sulphur. It rained all the time and we were bored to death. Granny also brought a rabbi with her. We thought he was going to bless something in Japan, but he was there to teach us Hebrew. We had only a few lessons, thank God, because of the rain. It seeped through every roof and every ceiling in every building. We lived under open umbrellas in the rooms until we left.

As if Father had been reading my thoughts and understanding my needs, he made a decision soon after the pin incident that was to bring me hysterical happiness. There had been a series of burglaries and people started to have guard dogs. We could have got hold of a couple of hounds, but Father ordered a string of Great Danes from London. One day all hell broke loose. The door opened: in pranced Pasha, Sultan, Caliph, Prince, Rajah, Marquis, Chicken and Blintz. In one minute my life changed from misery to ecstasy. Kiss, kiss, hug, hug, lie, feel, push, roll, tug, bark, bite, lick, lick, brush, wash. I loved them, I tortured them, I hid from them, they sat on me. I smelled dog, talked dog; I became a dog. Father gave the dogs one of those threatening speeches like he gave us (he didn't fumble with the pin). They should be noble, attack everything, refuse meat thrown over the wall. Blintz thought it was because the meat was not kosher, but Sultan and Pasha yacked through Father's speech and heard nothing. They attacked nine small dogs, ate the poisoned pies thrown over the wall and died. I had nothing left to kiss. Another batch was sent out from London, another speech given. This time they bit the postman, the rickshaw-man, the

11

washer-woman. No letter, no rickshaw, no laundry. We paid compensation, so they sent their relations to get bitten too. The Danes became affected, dejected, infected, rejected and died. Again, I found myself with no one to kiss.

Something new was taking place. There had been much telephoning and whispering for some days. It seemed we Princes were about to be sent to boarding-school in England. I didn't mind as the dogs were all dead and Father would be staying in Shanghai. Aunt Maisie was against it. She made some snide remarks about mother buying clothes in Paris when Chinese silk had been famous for years and cost a quarter the price of French silk. 'But they don't know how to weave here,' Mother said. With her weight, Mama needed dresses made from a fabric that hung properly. Granny cried over the coming separation. For Father, it meant freedom at last: army wives, counsuls' wives, Tai Pans' wives, relatives and cousins all became possible victims. Although he constantly referred to Mother as 'Our lovely Mimi', I know today that he never loved her or wanted to marry her. He probably did it because she was rich and respectable. Mother had caught him dragging one cousin into her own bed within a year of their marriage. She dashed into the bathroom and picked up a bottle of ammonia and drank it. Father came to her once she was over the danger. 'I am sorry for you,' he said, and walked away. Yet in 1926, he took her to Paris and bought her a huge square diamond-ring and perfect pearls. Even that bliss was interrupted when Mother caught him trying to enter another cousin's 'wagon-lit' on their way to Monte Carlo.

In the end they returned to Shanghai and the old life: father in the office, Mama crying and Granny making jam. There were feasts and fasts and constant reminders about being Jewish, which had nothing to do with God, only with customs. *Succoth* was the feast I liked best. It is the one where you put up a tent in the garden, hang fruit and flowers, light candles and skip round, dipping the bread into salt, sipping wine and kissing the elders on their hands. It was bound to end in tears. Everything did. Dick grabbed the grapes, I grabbed the bananas, the candles set fire to the tent and the feast came to an end. But nothing changed our lives like the Day of Atonement. We thought fasting was silly but we thought it would be grown-up to fast. The family explained that it all had to do with sinning. Dick promised he'd never sinned and my only sin had been to put a chilli into Dicky's mouth. We had nothing to atone for. Obviously our parents had sinned, that's why they were fasting.

12

'If we can't eat, Mama, can we drink?'

'No.'

'Can we brush our teeth?'

'Yes.'

'What if a drop slips down while brushing our teeth?'

'Close the door and leave Mummy alone, we want to pray.'

But they didn't. They opened books and mumbled. They read the *Financial Times* or *Vogue*. Besides how could our parents, our holy parents ever sin?

'Perhaps Mother wants to get thin,' Dick said.

'Why don't they say prayers in English?' I said, 'I can't understand Hebrew.'

Eventually Dick asked: 'Can we read the prayers in English?' and surprisingly Father agreed.

That evening we all gathered together and prayers were read in English.

Dick whispered in my ear: 'God's awfully like Father. All he says is "don't" and "mustn't". They both keep punishing people all the time. Maybe Father is Father *and* God.'

Don't, mustn't, shalt not, won't. Thou shalt not steal or take a life. Thou shan't goose thy neighbour's wife. Now what on earth was Father reading, right out loud?

'Thou shalt not uncover thy mother's nakedness, nor shalt thou uncover thy father's nakedness. Thou shalt not uncover thy sister's nakedness. (That, obviously, referred to me since we did not have a sister.) Thou shalt not uncover thy grandmother's nakedness.'

I imagined Grandpa arriving home from the office in his trap, a servant opens the door and we whip off his clothes. He runs into the kitchen and there is Granny, starkers, long, straight, grey whisps of hair falling into the bubbling saucepans of jam. And Mama, poor fat Mama, naked, roll after roll of pink fat covering the floor. Of course God was right. Thou shouldst not uncover anybody's nakedness, but at some stage someone must have done it, or God would never have had to forbid it.

No sooner was the Day of Atonement over than news came that Uncle Freddie and Uncle Eddie had been kidnapped by Chinese bandits. The train taking them to Peking had been derailed . . . just like Marlene Dietrich and Anna-May Wong in *Shanghai Express*. They were being held for ransom. This was not unusual in China at that time. We sent their personal boy to discuss terms with the bandits. They paid the ransom. Later on Dick improved on the story. 'To show gratitude to their captors, Eddie and Freddie then invited them to a banquet in Shanghai. Toasts were offered, wine was drunk and all the bandits dropped dead; they'd been poisoned.'

Grandpa's house worked. It had beds, tables and chairs and no one cared what they looked like. If a lamp was needed someone shouted 'Boy, buy lamp.'

Although I was devoted to Mother, I actually felt Enrica, with her singing voice and vague behaviour, was nearer what I wanted to become. Not only could Enrica play the piano but she could accompany Mother, singing to records of Caruso and Melba. Mama had a good voice and moved her arms dramatically, her hands clutching her great pink breasts. When Mimi was dying in *La Bohème*, I'd start crying again.

One evening, after dinner, I was awakened by everyone screaming downstairs. I nudged Dick, 'Wake up. Something's going on. Everyone's shouting and Mama's crying. Please go and see.' It sounded like all the Great Danes fighting. I used to slap them right and left and they'd shut up. Should I try it now with the family? Mama had been different that evening. She'd been crying when she put us to bed and kissed us. I'd felt the wet on her face. I had to help, even by just appearing. Father'd never punish me for that. I'd just go in and scream like the rest of them. Dick had already fallen back to sleep so I started silently down the stairs. Through the banisters I could see Mother distraught on the couch. Uncle Albert walked back and forth across the room, blurting our, 'Enough. I've had enough. We've all had enough. Disgrace. Shame, shame.' Granny upset me more. At one moment she burst into a great moan and thew herself on the floor at Father's feet. She was on her knees, her long straight hair all over her face and falling on to the floor, which she was beating with her palms and with her head, shouting, 'Shame! Shame! Kadamoot, kadamoot.' (I am dying) and other wonderful things in Arabic that I used to imitate later till I was punished. Aunt Maisie sat bolt upright, glaring. Father left the room. Aunt Maisie rose. 'I'll break his back,' she said. But how could she break his back? Could she break his back without killing him? Maybe she could and he'd become a sweet old man and not frighten us any more. I slipped back up to our room and shook Dick.

14

'Dick, Dick, Mummy is crying. Auntie Maisie is going to break Daddy's back, Uncle Albert says Father has disgraced everyone and Granny is sitting on the floor.'

'Jews sit on the floor if somebody is dead,' he explained.

'What about the Great War? Did Christians sit on the floor then when soldiers were killed, or only Jews? Do we know any Christians?'

'Uncle George Potts is a Christian.'

'I want to go to sleep.'

At breakfast the next day Mother looked low. Father said 'Isn't our mama a lovely mama? We are so proud of our lovely mama.' He said it in a funny way. The words were nice, but there was something nasty underneath it all. I thought I'd be brave:

'Daddy, why was Mummy crying?'

'Mummy is sensitive. She worries about us.'

'What is sensitive?'

'Feeling things. Some people feel things more than others. They are known as sensitive.'

I wanted to say, 'I felt your pin in my mouth,' but I didn't know if I felt it more than some other boy and I didn't know any other boys except my cousins. But if Mother's tears meant she was sensitive, then I was sensitive too.

In Shanghai there suddenly flared up some political unrest. Britain sent out a few thousand soldiers to protect their nationals in the International Settlement . . . that was when Father offered the British Volunteer Corps the use of Mother's immense garden in the middle of Shanghai in Avenue Haig. It was in that very garden where Father had moved a dangerous dog we possessed, rather than have it put down. It had bitten several people and when it also bit Mother's niece she told Father if he didn't have the dog destroyed she would poison it herself.

With all these officers and soldiers encamped on our land, we came into constant contact with them and the soldiers adopted Dick and me. I loved playing with them. I was excited by the cleaning and polishing, leather and brass and half-naked tattooed men, even though I was only about six.

When quiet returned to Shanghai the family decided it was time to send us to Europe via Siberia. Dick and I thought that going to Europe would be some kind of freedom away from Father. We even thought school might be fun. Father'd be in Shanghai and Mother would be with us, but what happened was different. All the other Baghdadians in

15

our Shanghai circle wanted to join us. Mother was quite pleased. She could patronize them. After all, she'd been to Europe and had a huge square diamond-ring, pearls like golf balls, and she spoke Russian, so she said. Eventually, an unbelievable thirty-nine sallow-faced Baghdadians, mostly women, agreed on a departure date. To get thirty-nine anything to agree on anything is, in itself, a miracle. But God was with us.

There were endless preparations. The tribe all had to have kosher food. This meant bottling, salting and sterilizing chicken and vegetables for thirty-nine people. Not one mouthful of foreign meat was to pass our lips. First a steamer would take us to Dairen on the North Coast and from there we would travel by train all the way to Berlin.

That's when Enrica announced she was returning to Italy and Mother would be left without a lady's maid. Dr Birt, our lovely German doctor, found Mother a big German woman, whom Mama nick-named 'my Uhlan'. Every time Dick and I looked at her, we imagined an Amazon wearing a German war helmet with a spike on the top. Dr Birt and his wife told us all about Valhalla, Brünnhilde, Rhine maidens and Isolde who died for love. We wanted to give the new maid a nickname of our own. Dick suggested Brünnhilde; I said Brünnhilde sounded like brown and she was blonde, – Isolde was unthinkable. How could that big, blonde, lump die for love? All of which shows how little seven-year-old children know about love. Fat lumps are constantly dying for love. Why look further than poor Mama?

Then another bomb dropped. The firm that was to deliver Mother's rubber bath lining couldn't finish it on time. How could we travel without the lining? It was no magic carpet or secret weapon – it was to protect the 'Little Princes' from the used enamel on the train's bath. They might not have much food on the train but they did have a bath with constant hot water and the 'Princes' were to be bathed every night.

What Father must have gone through at the hint of a delay! Mama would leave all right. Father would see she got her lining. Nobody, just nobody, could stand up to Father. The rubber lining arrived on time.

At this point I must stop and explain who our tribe consisted of. I must also add that we Hayims thought ourselves better than the rest of the tribe. Father had been schooled in England. Mother had been to Cartier and the Pope, and her mother had been blonde. As if that was not enough, we were friends of the Kadoories. The tribe chiefly consisted of four families, none of whom had been to Europe. The Schafiks, the Schuschas, the Sassanems and the Schifkas. All the men

16

had names like Ezekiel, Grrrrrrgee (George) and the women like Farha (Flora), Muzli (Maisie). So many stories were told about them that it didn't matter which one applied to whom. Schafik and Schuscha were brothers and so were Sassanem and Schifka. The first lot of brothers were also cousins of the second lot of brothers. Schuscha explained it quietly to me one day, 'We born Baghdad long time ago. Baghdad different. I not mumber [I don't remember], small name, big name, I not mumber. We have name . . . son of father's name. We go Europe, we make new life, make new name, we begin all born 1st January.' (When the tribe visited Madame La Palma, the famous fortune-teller, she was so undone by this, she jumped out of the window. It was on the ground floor and she didn't want to lose the ten-pound fee, so she came back and told them exactly what would happen, despite each having the same birth-date.)

Schuscha was the first to go off the path. This didn't mean wine, women and song – it was food. 'I am a dietetician,' he would explain, adding an extra syllable to give the word more weight, and when corrected, he replied, 'Desent metter, my way better.' He also put his words into the plural ('I give you garlics and olives oils'). Often he cured his patients. They couldn't refuse his treatment – they were poor relations or servants.

3

The whole lot of us finally boarded a steamer for Dairen, and from there took the train to Harbin where something went wrong and we had to stay in our compartments for the night. Harbin is a huge Chinese city, but had been leased to and developed by the Russians. It had a Russian theatre and international opera. It was almost a Russian town. Mother'd been there before and had brought home fifty wonderful sables on her return from a visit the previous year. We were in her bedroom when she took them out and danced round the room with them.

Later, when a friend came to the house, Dick overheard her say, 'They are Kamchatkas, not Barguzinskis.'

So he ran to me and said, 'They aren't Mother's at all, they belong to a Russian friend called Kamchatka.'

I remained perplexed for forty-five years, till I learned that Barguzinski sables are sleeker, darker and smaller than those from Kamchatka. We were quite bored sitting in the train in Harbin, so we asked Mother to take us shopping.

'There is nothing to buy here,' she said.

'And what about those?' I said, poking her glorious sable cape. A guard came in just before I got a slap. That evening we left for our long journey.

Next day we arrived at Manchuli, a town under Japanese rule. When the train stopped Japanese officials made us take every single thing we carried – all thirty-nine of us – and unpack the lot on the platform. Every bottle of chicken and rice, every tin of of food, every cake of soap. The wind blew across Mongolia and we froze. They were bewitched by Mother's rubber bath lining. They never laughed. Mother was about to

18

kill them all, when the whistle went off. We panicked.

'They'll go without us. I am dying of cold. There is no paper in the loo. Oh, what a wind.' (How well I understood Great-aunt Lily-of-the-Valley.)

'The train will *not* go,' said Mama. 'We *are* the train.'

The month of March was bitterly cold. There was nothing to be seen except snow, snow and more snow. We stopped once in a village and rushed out on to the platform in our short trousers. Mongolians gathered about us, feeling our bare legs. We were startled at first, but just when I was starting to enjoy it, Mother appeared, shouting, 'Dirty, dirty,' and dragged us back to the train, into the bathroom, where she washed our knees.

'Why did the Mongolians like playing with our knees, Mummy?'

'Nobody plays with anybody's knees.'

'I've seen people put their hands on other people's knees. I saw Daddy put his hands on Cousin Nadia's knees.'

After a night's sleep, we looked out of the window.

Nothing had changed. Desolate, white, flat fields of snow everywhere. Nothing moved. For no reason, Dick spun around towards Mother as if he'd been promised something and then not been given it.

'Where are the Cossacks?' Silence.

'Mother, where *are* the Cossacks?' Silence.

Ma Sassanem didn't know what Dick was talking about.

'I want a Cossack,' Dick repeated.

'I buy you one,' Ma Sassanem promised.

And then the scenery changed. The guard came back and pointed. 'Lake Baikal.' It went on forever. Thirty years later, I took an old Russian emigré to see *Doctor Zhivago*. The two lovers sit cuddled in a wagon in Siberia and a lake appears. The old Russian and I both screamed, 'I've been there. I recognize it.' Except that it was filmed in Canada.

What makes people jump with joy when they recognize something – even if they hate it? What makes children thrilled to see their parents even if they hate them?

Next morning, as Baikal disappeared, Dick said: 'I love Cossacks. Why won't Mother talk about them?' So when Mother returned, he asked again.

'There are no more Cossacks. They ended with . . . "Little Father",' Mother replied, wiping away a tear.

'Why did Father have a row with the Cossacks?'

'Little Father, my darlings, was the Tsar of Russia. He was killed by the workers.'

When the conductor returned, Dick asked him point-blank why he'd killed the Tsar. The conductor looked at Mother and Mother gave Dick a kick under the table.

'Why did you kick me, Mother?' said Dick. Mother now came out with a spate of words to resemble 'Tsar'.

First she said, 'The cream is sour,' pronouncing sour like 'Tsar'. Then she suddenly shouted out 'Hurrah'. 'Hurrah for the Hussars,' which didn't cover up anything because that also sounded like 'the Tsar'. The conductor just stood there so Mother said, 'Russia has the finest jewels in the world. The Russian crown jewels are twice as good as the Persian, Turkish, or even the Queen of England's.'

(We didn't know what she was talking about in 1928, but years later I learned she was right. After going to school in England, I brought up the subject again,

'Mother, the Cossacks were sent all over Russia into the ghettos to break into the houses, kill the Jews, and steal the silver, and "Little Father" was behind them.'

'Nonsense,' she replied. 'It was Rasputin, and I met Prince Yousupoff, who killed him, at Korniloff's restaurant in Paris.'

'Rasputin?'

'No. Yousupoff.'

'How did he kill him, Mummy?'

'Prince Yousupoff was young and good-looking, like all aristocrats. He asked Rasputin to tea, and gave him a poisoned bun.'

'Oh,' said Dick, who was standing beside me and not listening.)

The train went on. Nobody argued, and nobody read a book. Dick and I got chapped lips from the dry cold. Mama carried a huge medicine bag wherever she went. She and 'the Uhlan' knew exactly where she kept the cream yet she insisted on painting our mouths with red lipstick.

Finally, days later, we arrived in Moscow where we went for a ride in a tram, though I can't remember why we took a tram and not a taxi. It was an opportunity for Mother to say a few words in Russian, with amazing results. She did have a perfect accent, having heard her mother and Great-aunt Lily-of-the-Valley years ago. Alas, she could only say what she knew and not what she wanted. In restaurants she showed off a bit by ordering 'Shashlik' and 'Stroganoff' but even we knew that.

The trouble occurred while negotiating a sale in a shop. Mother said; 'Khoroshaya sobaka, esh svoyu kost' (Good dog, eat your bone), when

20

she meant, 'Where can I buy a ticket?'

If the salesman asked her something she didn't understand, she'd answer, 'Bozhe moi, ia istekaiu kroviu' (Oh, my God, I'm bleeding).

Once when a dear old man in the street offered to help us in very bad English, Mother replied. 'Nichevo, vse barakhlo' (It doesn't matter, it's all rubbish).

If the Russians didn't understand her, she'd mutter. 'Stupid Bolsheviks. Not like in the Tsar's days.'

Her cousin, Benno Moiseiwitsch, the famous pianist, once meant to say, 'My colleague is a pansy,' but he couldn't remember Russian flowers, so instead he said, 'Moi kollege nezabudka' (My colleague's a forget-me-not). At this time in her life Mother knew nothing about gays and lesbians. She thought that the expression Benno used in Russian was a criticism of the way his colleague played, so every time she went to a concert, when asked what she thought, she would say, 'Nezabudka' in perfect Russian, leaving the English impressed and the Russians perplexed.

She was madly keen on Russian phrases and never stopped using them. In Paris, in the fifties, when Mother was a beautiful matron of sixty, she went up in the lift of the Royal Monceau with a Soviet officer. It was a hot night and the man was in uniform. Dying to show off, and forgetting Stalin and the pogroms, she said in Russian, 'Bozhe moi, takaia zhara, ia umiraiu' (Oh, God, it's so hot, I'm dying).

The lift stopped and they went to their respective rooms. A few minutes later, there was a knock at her door. The officer stood there, bright eyed.

'Mozhno?' (May I?) he said.

'How dare he! I slammed the door in his face,' she told me.

'You silly goose. You're a sixty-year-old woman with grey hair. A glorious officer half your age, and an ally to boot, offers you a night of love . . . and you say "No". Are you mad?'

Glaring at me furiously, she screamed out some phrase she'd remembered. 'Dai zdachiu. Poezd ushol,' and then slammed the door. (It actually means, 'Give me change, the train's gone.')

While in Moscow, Dick and I behaved as if we were royal. I told Dick I'd now found out how to read Russian. We'd been standing in the freezing street looking at something written in a shop window.

'I can read that. It's upside down.'

With that, I stood on my head till I lost balance and my feet crashed through the window, shattering it into a million pieces. Nor was I

21

embarrassed when a circle of angry people formed. Why should I be? Weren't we Princes? Mother dived into her bag, yanked out her crocodile purse and handed out a few notes.

When things had calmed down, Dick asked me,

'Just exactly what was written in the window?'

I said I'd forgotten but was willing to do it all over again in front of another shop window.

Imagine, therefore, after the nightmare of the Russian alphabet, the joy of Warsaw, where we were both able to read perfectly.

'Pzlczcncka cszany!' easy!

Funny how memory plays tricks. I remember Warsaw as a clean town with every woman wearing a grey Persian-lamb coat and hat to match, but Dick swears we never got out of the train. On the following day we arrived in Berlin, where we took a suite at the Adlon Hotel.

We loved Berlin. Mother promised to take us to see the head of Nefertiti. I thought it was a children's fair, and Dick, an Italian football match. We were disappointed when we found ourselves in the Museum with other tourists.

'Was she Jewish, Mama?' I asked.

'No,' she said, 'Queen of Egypt. She was Egyptian.'

'Couldn't she have been Jewish too? We are Iraqi and Jewish, maybe she was Egyptian and Jewish too.'

'Everybody's Jewish,' said a nice old American tourist, patting our heads. And that was the last of Berlin.

Next day we left for the Black Forest. Mother wasn't interested in excursions, she went for a cure at Dr Dengler's sanatorium, *the* fat farm in Europe. Baden-Baden is a beautiful watering-place in the Black Forest surrounded by medieval castles where deer roam the woods, trout fill the streams and berries we'd never seen grew everywhere. We'd never roamed woods before. There is no 'countryside' outside Shanghai. The only place we could compare it with was Victoria BC. The Europaischer Hof hotel was sumptuous. On the menu was blue trout but it wasn't blue and we didn't like it. They served chocolate éclairs that only a German could make, each the size of a French baguette. Dick asked if there were any 'Uhlans' about. At this point in his life one was grateful if that was all he did. No one mentioned 'the war'. You can't talk to two eight-year-old Shanghai-educated boys about the Great War unless you're terribly silly, can you?

We had an inferiority complex about England – most people we knew had it. Nor did it help when we were told that an English governess was arriving at any moment to discipline us. We imagined her as a tall woman in boots, with a whip; but we were far too young to enjoy anything like that. On the eve of her arrival, we were reading a children's book, one of those gruesome affairs about wolves wearing glasses, making passes at Little Red Riding Hood. There was a picture of one with pointed ears in a rocking-chair that squeaked through the pages. She was sitting at a spinning-wheel holding a lamb up by its tail, and under the picture was written 'Dame Frosty Face yet spins'.

'There she is,' we shouted. A door opened, and there she was. She looked like a dried leek, wearing glasses. With a mirthless laugh she said, 'Hello, boys. I'm Frosty . . .'

Of course she didn't say that. She didn't know she was 'Frosty' yet. All I remember about that day was her threat to make us into little English boys.

The first day we had jelly, which I vomited. Next day was custard. I gave such a performance that they had to phone Mama at the sanatorium.

'I love custard,' she replied and didn't come.

That's when I realized I would have to face life alone. I had to be frog-marched down the streets to get over my hysteria and, finally, when we spoke to Mother, she now said, 'I don't like custard, but I love jelly.'

Well did she love custard or didn't she love custard? Grandpa arrived out of the blue, in a Zeppelin, an almost mythical, magical invention and rare at that time. That this old man should step out of the Graf Zeppelin, walk into our hotel and start complaining about a lack of green vegetables, upset the hotel to its foundations and set Baden-Baden agog.

'Nein Nein Keine gemuse Schpring iss late this year.'

So he went to the market one morning, filling a basket with celery, spinach, fennel, peas and corn. He entered the dining-room in the middle of lunch, dropping bits of green in a long winding trail from the door to our table. The manager was called. More 'Nein, nein, nich, nicht', and they asked us to leave.

The staff were forbidden to help us pack, so we sat reading the *National Geographic* while Frosty packed. In it were pictures of black women from Africa wearing endless rings around their necks. The text read:

This is Hana Magumba. When Hana was born, they started putting rings on her neck, adding them progressively till her neck looks like a giraffe's. The neck muscles gradually wither and the rings hold the head up like a scaffolding. If she is an unfaithful wife, her husband takes off the rings, Hana's head falls to the floor and the neck breaks with a snap.

'Frosty, what's being unfaithful to your husband?' No answer. And then again. 'Frosty, our granny's name is Hanna. Do you think she was unfaithful to her husband?'

'Your granny isn't a black, although she could be by the way you whipper-snappers behave.'

By the time we'd given Grandpa our version, Frosty was sacked. Jolly nice of Grandpa. He wasn't even Granny's husband.

Mother stayed at Dengler's another month but got no thinner. Perhaps it was Ramadan and she was eating all night. But why should Mother want to get thinner? Mothers have to look the same as they always have, otherwise they're not mothers. We were used to her being enormous; even later when we went to Harrow and all the boys showed their parents off, it never embarrassed us. Mother weighed herself one last time. She had lost a pound. So we all went to Paris. We lost a trunk on the way and Mother was upset. It was Dick's and my trunk and contained all those velvet smocks that made us look like girls, even though I didn't mind being the Princess Mandarina, Tangerina or Barberina when I was playing games with macho pirate Dick.

We stayed a few weeks in Paris, were taken to the Louvre once, but we did visit every restaurant and couturier in town. Paris was to give Mama time to order clothes and she went for fittings daily. As Frosty had been sacked, what to do with the children? They all made a fuss of us at the dressmaker's. Grey-haired ladies knelt on the floor, pins in their mouths, arranging hemlines. Everything was chic, or else it wasn't chic this year, or else it was never chic at all. Film stars and Princesses rubbed shoulders with Mama, all of which I loved.

When the Hayims left Berlin for Baden-Baden, the tribe all continued on to Paris where they were considering settling. All of them did except the Sassanems who decided to try their luck in England. It was a boiling June day when they crossed the channel and set foot in Dover, all muffled up looking like water buffaloes. They were ordered to be searched. The children rolled out of yards of gold brocade and were promptly fined. Dover looked like a souk. Hanna Sassenem shrieked at her husband in Arabic, and at the Customs man in English, 'France better. We stay France.'

Sassenem took the Customs man aside, 'Why you make us pay? We come to stay.'

'You must pay the duty and pay the fine.'

'Why you make troubles for us? I bring lot "meny" [money]. We make bargain.'

'We don't make bargains in England.'

'You not make bargain, you not get bargain, you no get tax meny, you no get meny, we go.' Which they did.

The Customs man should never have let them leave.

On their return to Paris, Sassanem went back to Claridges in the Champs-Elysées from where he had just come. He stopped the lift at the first floor where his brother was living. It was a hot day and the doors to his brother's apartment were open, the family wandering about in pyjamas. He told his brother what had happened, then went to the second floor where his Schuscha cousins were also wandering about in their pyjamas. Here were smells of cooking – okra, onion, aubergine, incense and myrrh. Nor was it different on the fourth floor, except that Ma Schafik was throwing a fit. What screams, what rage! Ma Schafik had caught her husband once more . . . This time screwing 'Checklet' – not chewing chocolate – right on the bathroom floor. Nor was Checklet some sexy black baby. She was a French girl called Jacqueline, a hired help. Ma Schafik never could pronounce her name right, so she became 'Checklet'. Yelling at her husband in Arabic, and out loud in the hall in broken English, she repeated, 'He make Checklet, he go. I mek alone.'

She was throwing him out, yet again. All he had to do was to land carefully on the other side of the Champs-Elysées at Fouquets, the glamorous café. Five minutes later, he sat there, pencil and pad in hand, sending notes to every pretty woman sitting alone. He could not read or write English, or French. But he could write numbers: 20, 30, 40, up it went till someone said, 'Yes', and someone always did.

Ma Schafik now fussed over her son Salach, aged about thirteen, and tall for his age. She would wander around the hotel, or the Champs-Elysées, approaching anyone with a boy the same age and ask, 'Who is taller, your son or Salach?'

She usually chose someone shorter than Salach, but if there was any doubt Ma Schafik would reply with finality, 'Salach is taller *and* taller,' and walk away.

Salach was mad about cars and ached to drive his mother's Hispano-

25

Suiza which only the chauffeur drove. So he winged and whined for a car of his own.

'Later I buy you Spanno,' replied his mother, never having mastered 'Hispano-Suiza'.

'I will be the fastest driver in the world.'

'I buy you Choffer,' she replied.

At the outbreak of the Second World War, the Schafiks fled to London and settled in Grosvenor House, where Ma Schafik sat covered in jewels in the lounge. One day she was accosted by a red-haired woman who'd been hanging about trying to be friendly.

'I am Mrs Hart, daughter-in-law of Lady Hart of Holland Park,' the woman announced. Then silence.

Mrs Schafik stared, put down the newspaper she held upside down in front of her and replied, deadpan, 'I know Hollan, I been there.'

Taller and taller, Salach joined the British Army, whereupon the rest of the family left for the States, ending up in the lounge of New York's Sherry Netherland Hotel. A year later, an acquaintance met Mrs Schafik in the street dressed in widow's weeds.

'Don't tell me, it isn't Salach?'

'Dead,' replied Mrs Schafik. 'Dead, dead, dead,' she repeated, eyes blazing. 'Not say his name, or I kill him.'

She fumbled in her Hermes bag, dropping it in the middle of Fifth Avenue, the contents all over the road. She clutched an official letter which she shoved menacingly in front of the poor woman's face.

'Awarded to Salach Schafik for bravery in face of the enemy – Military Cross.' She pointed angrily at the word and screamed, 'Cross, cross. Not cross. My son Jew – no cross.' Later, she told people he had won the Military Medal (which is given to soldiers, while officers were awarded the Cross). She had nothing to do with Salach for years, and then, just when the ice was beginning to thaw, she heard he was marrying a Baghdadian in London. Ma Schafik felt the girl's aunt had slighted her in Baghdad years before, besides which the girl's family were dark-skinned. She buried her face in her hands.

'Shem, shem, shem fren the pipple,' which meant she was ashamed in front of the people. Eventually, she found strength enough to say, 'Next time Salach shem me, I kill him before he kill me, next time.'

He did kill her next time. No oedipal 'crime passionel'. He beheaded her. Nor did he stand there in ceremonial robe with a Samurai sword and go 'swish'. He was driving her down to Brighton in an open car on a summer's day, when a truck carrying sheets of iron passed by. A sheet slipped and sliced Ma Schafik's head off – just like that. Her funeral in London meant a family reunion. A fleet of black limousines drove to the cemetery. During the ceremony, Salach's children had a spade fight as mourners shovelled earth on the grave. Then the congregation passed their hands under running water in order to wash death away. A water fight ensued.

'All go coffe-house now,' said Hanna Sassanem, for in Baghdad one must break the atmosphere of death with a visit to a public place. I cannot remember why, but every bar, pub and tea-room was closed. The mourners were in despair. Eventually, at the entrance to an imposing building, Ma Sassanem tapped on the window and brought her car to a halt, bidding the cavalcade to follow. Out they trooped, sallow-faced boiling fowls in black robes, following Ma Sassanem as she led them through a turnstile, and then straight out again. It was the British Museum and it was also closed, but the turnstile worked.

Of all that gang I like Ma Schifka best. She gave to the poor, indulged her staff and spoilt her chauffeur, treating him with such consideration that eventually he went mad. She explained it to my mother.

'We not take car after lunch. We not need early morning. He bad stomach. He not see at night. Now he in mad hospital "New Roses".' He had neurosis.

'He seemed well in October when I came to help design your new sable coat. How did it turn out?' I asked.

'I not wear,' she said.

'What went wrong?'

'Nothing wrong. Very cold winter. We not leave hotel,'

Spring came. Ma Schifka's daughter got engaged to an American. The family flew to New York, settled in a flat and found Ellen, a big bouncy maid from Chicago, who massaged Ma Schifka and coped.

'She like daughter,' she said, looking lovingly towards heaven.

The daughter's reception date was fixed. Exotic foods appeared: cardamon, coriander, vine leaves, mangoes and the famous 'Bak bak Kadrassi' – a glutinous resin from Mesopotamia known biblically as manna. Very shyly, the bouncy maid handed her employer an envelope, 'This is my present to you all.'

Inside there were theatre tickets for the following evening. Ma Schifka didn't want to go, but she didn't want to hurt Ellen's feelings, so all the family went, understood nothing, and hurried home to find the cupboard bare. No bonds, no sables, no manna. The police came and took a statement of everything missing.

'What is your "Bak, bak"? What is it worth?' they asked.

She told them that 'Bak, bak' had no price. They then asked all about Ellen and made a few phone calls.

'I think we will get it all back,' said the kindly officer.

That afternoon the police returned with some photos of a GI sitting on a tank.

'This is your Ellen, lady. He dresses up like a girl, and steals.'

'My God! My bath, my breast, my massage . . .'

More police arrived. bag after bag was emptied on to the floor. Furs, jewels, silver . . . With a yell of delight, Ma Schifka danced about her recovered goods, then let out a scream,

'My "Bak, bak", my "Bak, bak", officer.'

'Gaz,' replied the officer.

'Bak, bak,' corrected Ma Schifka.

'Gaz,' repeated the officer. 'My family is from Iran, it's called "Gaz" there.'

4

The real change for us was England. Mother took a house in Eastbourne, a windy town on the South Coast renowned for its many preparatory schools, the two most important being St Andrew's and St Cyprian's. Granny panicked at the idea of our attending a school named after a Christian saint. It took time to calm her down. She wasn't as strong as Father but, if only to avoid her moaning, we often deferred to her. Mother never thought about being Jewish and if ever she picked up a prayer-book she took nothing in. She was thinking about some princess or her hemlines at Lanvin. In my family no one was devout.

On one occasion, an old family friend, Princeton archaeologist Teresa Goell, was returning from her twentieth trip to Nemurd Dagh in Anatolia, where she was doing work on the origins of the Hittites. She was seriously ill so Mother went to fetch her. It was a hot summer's day. Mother was dressed carefully in a white dress, freshly ironed by her maid. She wore a big Bengal straw hat, white gloves and shining white kid shoes. Majestically, she waltzed on to the railway platform, just in time to see her friend practically tumble off the train – a wreck. Teresa had become as fat as Ma, her hearing was shattered. She wore an aid whose batteries were always flat. One of her eyes kept swivelling around. Her skin was like parchment, burnt by the Turkish sun. Her face was grey. She'd caught a bug. Did dear Mama put her arms round her old friend, saying, 'Don't worry, dear, you'll be all right.'

She did not. 'I'm ashamed of you,' she said. 'What do you look like! To think you used to be such a pretty girl.'

I cringed when Teresa told me, and apologized for my mother.

'No matter,' Teresa replied. 'She did take me to the right doctor. She did have me cured and I owe her my life.'

29

'Did she come and see you in hospital?'

'She sent strawberries . . . with the maid.'

There is a cold wind that blows in Eastbourne and it blew straight into my heart. England was cold and forbidding – like Father. Every time I return to England to this day, I feel there is some invisible shape flying around, its forefinger pointing at me saying, 'Thou shalt not.'

Eastbourne offered us nothing except six-year-old Adrian Foley. I don't know where Mama met his mother, Lady Foley, but one day I was introduced to mother and son. He was dressed in black velvet with a stiff white pleated collar, but memory is suspect and he and little Lord Fauntleroy were the only peers I had ever met. I ran to him, shy and thrilled, put on my most wistful and endearing look, and said, offering my hand. 'I'm Georgie.'

'Adrian Gerald, ninth Lord Foley,' he replied.

We stayed on a few months, Dick attending St Andrew's school as a day-boy. Then holidays in Paris: a suite at the Crillon Hotel, more clothes for Mama, Korniloff's Russian restaurant with Yousupoff, Prince Dimitri, Cole Porter, the Duchess Xenia of Holy Russia, Sir Basil Zaharoff, Lady Deterding. (I am sure mother wore away five of the thirty carats of Lady Deterding's famous Polar star diamond – just by looking at it. In 1984, it sold for four million dollars.

And then to Grosvenor House, London, where mother took a large flat to prepare us for prep school. There were fittings for clothes, all made to order – quite mad when an eight-year-old boy goes nowhere and can't even get in those clothes six months later. Mother had a Rolls and a burly, handsome chauffeur called Turner, who hung about with a lot of other Rolls chauffeurs. No one scolded us when we said, 'Where is the Rolls?' instead of, 'Where is the car?'

Later in life I was ashamed of it, but later still I found that grand people also talked of their Rollses. What I do remember was opening the front door of the Rolls as we were going round Marble Arch and spitting into the street.

'Spitting out of a Rolls!' Mother screamed from the back seat.

But never was I as anguished as on that mournful cold September day on our way to school. Mother sat in the Rolls, muffled up in furs; we sat in our made-to-measure suits and white, stiff collars. We drove through Maida Vale and Kilburn, two depressing suburbs. Later, the traffic grew less and the houses fewer: we were leaving central London. Turner stopped at a suburb called Stanmore, asked for directions and we drove into a magnificent driveway lined with chestnut trees. A large white

30

Georgian house, with rhododendron bushes at the entrance, stood in the middle of a large park. It would have been beautiful had it not been school. Cars were parked everywhere. Suitcases and trunks littered the drive. Each boy also had a wooden hamper with his name written on it. These were for biscuits and fruit one's own family supplied. Boys wearing school caps were waving at one another, talking excitedly about the 'hols'. While Turner was unloading, we were shaken by piercing screams. A large Rolls-Royce (no larger than ours) arrived and a beautiful, over-dressed woman, carrying a Pekinese, got out, followed by an Indian-looking boy of about twelve. Suddenly, the boy started to yell. The tall woman dropped the dog and put her arms around the boy to calm him down.

'Marthando! Stop, stop. Be noble, be graceful, be a Prince. You are a Prince. You are my Prince. Behave like one.'

'I won't, I won't, I won't, I know what it's like, you've never been here. I hate it. I hate it. I hate it. It's full of beastly little English boys.'

'Marthando, I beseech you. Mummy has a ball tonight. Mummy musn't be upset . . .' Then, turning to the Pekinese, she continued, 'must she, Manchu, darling? Look, how unhappy Marthando is making me. Back into the Rolls, Manchu. Come along Marthando.'

'I won't, I won't, I won't,' cried Marthando, grabbing Manchu by the tail. 'If you leave me here, I'll kill her.'

With that he started to twirl Manchu round his head.

'Marthando,' she shrieked, 'You devil of evil. Hindu horror. What would your poor dead father "The Prince" have said?'

What would Manchu's father have said?

Marthando must have won that round, for they all left. I tried to imagine whirling my Great Danes round my head, but even in this scene Mother wasn't looking or listening, while Father glared and looked for another pin in his lapels.

Mother entered the headmaster's study first and a few minutes later Mr Holloway, the Head, and his wife asked us in. They stood whispering in a corner. I know they were ganging up on us by the guilty way Mother kept shooting glances at us. At one moment I saw Mother slip a malachite clock into Mrs Holloway's hands. Suddenly, it was all over. Love, protection, Granny, Shanghai, were all gone. We were abandoned. A gong sounded. Mr Holloway appeared in the great hall, telling us Stanmore Park had to beat all other schools at everything. After that, supper and back to the hall where another gong sounded, this time for prayers. The boys clambered on to the benches, kneeling, with elbows on their desks. I looked at Dick.

'Kneel?' I said. 'how could we kneel? We would be Christians.'

Hadn't mother told them at school we were Jewish. What would God do if we knelt?

'Must we kneel?' I whispered to Dick.

Dick didn't answer.

I pulled my crumpled handkerchief out of my pocket and placed it on my head. The chorus sang but I didn't understand. It sounded like, 'Our Father, charter of heaven.'

'Hear ye Israel,' I mumbled.

'Heroin is they name,' they continued.

'The Lord is one,' I replied.

'Forgive us our trespasses and give us the bread and give us puspuspussy.'

I shouted them down with, 'Hear, Oh Israel, the Lord is one. *Shema Israel Adonai Eloheinu Adonai Ehad.*' That's all I knew. So I continued with the alphabet, 'Alef, Beth, Gimel, Dal . . .'

The whole school stared. I fainted.

What right had the parents to plonk me down in this cold, lonely England? I was miserable. I clung to my misery. I became what the Uhlan had once called me, a *Sorgenkind* (a 'worry child').

I was so alone, I longed to make friends, but they didn't like us. They looked like shrimps and dolls with their red golden hair and blue eyes while we were another colour, and fifty million Englishmen couldn't be wrong. I hated the food. If ever I saw a black speck in my salad, I would take the dish to the master-in-charge, place before him the guilty object and point.

'Yes, Hayim junior, it's a fly.'

But I'd been brought up in a country where a fly in a salad could mean cholera, typhus or death. It was hopeless. We could never belong.

On Sundays, when all the boys were playing, we would be having a Hebrew lesson with a rabbi my parents had hired specially to instruct us. I reacted according to the psychology manual – illness (feigned or real), or toothache, then I'd run to the matron. I demanded to see the dentist – that meant a trip into London – to fix the retainer that was there to straighten out my teeth. When I got back I'd spend hours with the handle of my pen, levering out the brace to get another trip to London. On one occasion, a friend of Mother's drove me back from the dentist in her open car. The door flew open and I fell on to the road. I don't remember having opened the door, but she said she saw me do it.

Nobody bothered to find out why a little boy should want to fall out of a moving car.

Winter dragged on, getting colder and colder. Everyone looked forward to the football match on Saturday afternoon, and the free day on Sunday. I didn't like football, so I didn't like Saturdays. As for Sunday, that dreary rabbi wasn't all. There were the hideous church bells chiming from across the park. 'Tong, tong, totong, totong, tong, tong.' Then they sounded as if they were going wrong. It was as if one clang was going faster than the last, trying to catch it up. Then it was bed. The boys all had to brush their teeth. Dick and I used Pepsodent. Most of the English boys used Kolynos. Ours tasted better, but theirs made a lovely foam all over their faces. The church bells went on ringing and the master would come on his round to see if we'd brushed our teeth and to put out the gas-lamp, a round bulb-like thing made of what looked like gauze. When you turned the gas off the light went out, leaving a slowly dying glow. It was as if all the warmth in the world had come to an end.

Dick and I planned to escape and so we stored biscuits and fruit for the great day. When it was due, we kept each other awake till about eleven and then found our way out of the vast building and on to the drive as far as the fourth rhododendron bush. Dick would have carried on, but I lost heart and started to cry. Besides, we had nowhere to go if we did escape. Father was in Shanghai, Mother was in Paris. We gave up.

I hardly spoke to anyone the first term. The second term, Dick and I returned to school now caught up in a photography craze. We learnt that by letting the sun shine through a magnifying glass, we could burn a hole where the ray landed. For three oranges a class-mate lent me his magnifying glass and I went straight to a corner behind some bushes to practise.

I tried it out on a piece of paper which caught fire.

'I'll burn the school down,' I smiled.

Just as the paper caught fire, a shadow appeared. My God, I have been caught! I looked behind me. It wasn't a master, it was that Indian who had whirled the Pekinese round by his tail.

'Are you new here?' he asked in a smarmy voice.

'Fairly,' I said.

'I've been here for years.'

'I saw you at the beginning of last term,' I said.

'I hate it here.'

33

'Then why does your mother bring you?' I asked, thinking it was normal that my parents should make me suffer, but why his?

'Because Father's will says I must go to school or I don't get the money when I'm twenty-one.'

'My father promised me a hundred pounds if I don't smoke till I'm twenty-one,' I said.

'Did you see our car?' he asked boastfully.

'We have the same,' I retorted boldly.

'Our chauffeur is French, he's a "de".'

'What's a "de"?' I asked.

'If you're a "de" in France, you're a noble,' he said very smugly.

'Well, our chauffeur, our chauffeur . . .' and I was trying to think of something to upstage him. 'Our chauffeur has seen the Prince of Wales . . . naked,' in a whisper.

'I hate cricket,' he said, ignoring my naked Prince of Wales.

'I hate it too.'

'I hate Drack,' he said, mentioning the nickname of our most feared schoolmaster. 'He used to be a vampire before.'

'Before what?' I asked.

'Dracula. Never heard of reincarnation?'

'No,' I said, crestfallen.

'Well, reincarnation is all about who you were before you are who you are today. Take me, for instance. I wasn't always Marthando Tondiman, Prince of Pudokota. I was someone quite different.'

'Who?'

'A queen. Marie Antoinette. Queen of France.'

Long, uncomfortable pause.

'I don't believe that,' I said. I was only eight and a half.

'Well, I was.'

'How do you know?'

'Everyone knows,' he said. 'I don't mean these silly English nobodies, I mean my friends, the international set.'

'Can you prove it?'

'Of course I can. The day I went to Marie Antoinette's bedroom, I said in front of everyone, "Mummy, this is my bedroom," and Mummy said, "Of course it is, dear." '

'And where did this happen?' I asked.

'At Versailles.'

'I've been there,' I said.

'Everybody's been there, but it's only interesting if it was once yours,' he said. 'And do you know why I walked out of history class this morning?'

'No.'

'Because they were on about how darling Mary Queen of Scots was beheaded by that beastly Elizabeth.' He continued, whispering, 'I was Mary, Queen of Scots, too.'

'Oh, you poor Queen,' I said, feeling genuinely sorry for him, her – it. 'Why don't you choose to be somebody else, so you aren't beheaded all the time?'

'You can't choose who you are and who you were, silly.'

'Who do you think I could have been?'

'Nobody anyone has ever heard of,' he said.

'Why not?' I fought back. 'I might have been someone much better than you, I might even have been Jesus.'

'How could you? He was tall and fair and Christian and had a beard.'

'No he wasn't. He was a Babylonian Jew – just like me, and I'm more like Jesus than Marthando Tondiman of Pukokota is like Marie Antoinette.'

'Don't let's argue. You're my friend and I'm yours. They don't like you and they don't like me. We speak French and we're the same colour.'

'We're not, we're not. You're Indian and I'm English.'

'With your name and your face?'

'I'm only dark because I'm Jewish. All Jews are dark.'

'What about ginger Phillips and blond Silverman? Anyway, if you don't apologize I'll tell the other boys that your parents aren't English.'

'Then I'll tell my mother about how you treat me.'

'Your mother doesn't love you, or she'd never have sent you here. You don't have to stay here to get your inheritance like I do.'

'My Mummy cries and tells me all the time she loves me,' I replied.

'Words, words, words . . . "Il n'y a pas d'amour, il n'y a que des preuves." All mothers cry. Now give me your hand.'

'Why?'

'At once, or I'll tell on you.'

Fearfully, I gave it to him. He grabbed it, drew it to his face then pounced, sucking my forefinger vehemently.

'No, no – don't,' I said. 'What are you doing?'

'Pushing back your cuticle.'

'Oh please, I beg you.'

I didn't know what a cuticle was and I was afraid it might be something like *that*. 'You know I am Jewish and we're . . . different.'

'Shut up,' he said, sucking busily. It wasn't painful, so I let him. 'Now you're going to do everything I tell you.'

Just then a master blew his whistle and the boys wandered on to the field. I was saved. Marthando was out to get me and I had to escape. He was devouring me.

My freedom did not last long. It was in the Matron's dispensary that he caught me. I thought I was alone at the time and having a sudden urge to pee, I peed . . . fatally . . . in Matron's wash basin.

'Caught you,' a voice screamed. 'Caught you, caught you, caught you. I'll tell Matron you peed in the basin.' His evil eyes narrowed with his new sense of power.

'Oh, Tondiman, Nomdurman, Homdiman, Banderman, don't. You musn't, I didn't.'

'Call me "sir",' he said.

'Yes, sir, but don't tell, sir.'

'Kiss my toe.'

'Oh.'

'My toe.'

'No, no.'

I threw myself down to kiss it. What would he want next? My oranges? The magnifying glass? Worse: to be my friend. I couldn't go through that again – my cuticle, his toe. No, no, no. I would have to kill myself, or him.

Two days passed and he didn't appear. Then, one afternoon in the changing room came a piercing hiss. I couldn't move, fixed to the floor with fear.

'Follow me,' he ordered.

'I must see the Head,' I managed to stammer.

'He's away. Follow or I'll tell. Hee, hee, hee! Pee, pee, pee! Remember?'

I followed like a lamb.

'Into the bogs!'

And into the loo I went.

'Down with your bags.'

'Oh, no, Tondiman! Please Bondiman! Don't. Don't. Please, please don't.'

'Don't what?'

'Don't nothing! Don't anything! Just don't and I'll do anything. I'll kiss your toe, give you the magnifying glass, dance with you instead of

36

with Holdsworth. Oh, please be nice. Let's be friends. You know how alone I am.'

'Down with your bags.' He glared as I fumbled and wriggled and turned till my trousers fell off, hugging me round the knees. 'And now . . . now . . . we're going to touch . . .' and he whispered the wicked word, 'bums'.

He pivoted me round till I stood face to the wall, my bottom bared towards him. I kept pulling my clothes up and he kept pulling them down. Purposefully, he edged towards me, walking backwards, looking over his shoulder at my behind. My heart stopped. What would happen now? Would they find out? What would Mother say? Would my bottom wither? Would we remain stuck like Siamese twins forevermore? Why Tondiman? If I have to be stuck I'd rather it were Holdsworth. Nearer, nearer, nearer he crept and then . . . woosh . . . and it was all over. Damaged, sullied, soiled and stained; how would I ever escape from this degradation? Only by suicide.

I'd been thinking about that long enough and now the time had come: 'Berries red have no dread, berries white poisonous sight . . .'

I would add ink, eradicator, pee or a combination of all three. I collected some white berries and hoarded them in a box. Next day they went brown and I thought that's what would happen to me. That Saturday afternoon I got all my berries together, one bottle of ink, one of ink eradicator and mixed the lot. It bubbled away in a corner while I wrote my Last Will and Testament and told that family of mine why I was doing it – they who never listened. They'd read it now all right and take me away from school. But what would there be left to take away? A poor, cold, dead thing in a hamper, like those we kept our fruit in? A hamper with my name on it? I'd pay for all the sadness of all the other little boys at school.

Poor me, sad me, what was I doing in this world of pink and white boys? How many times had I said, 'Can't you see, Mama, they're pink and white and we're yellow?' And she'd answer, 'Just because you were born in China, it doesn't mean you're yellow.'

One, two, three – now pee. I peed in it, took a great mouthful and swallowed it down. Then I was taken with fear. I'm going to die, I'm going to die, and I haven't been to Rome! Why Rome, I shall never know, but that's all I could think of . . . I hadn't been to Rome. I started to vomit. Did I really want to die or be sick? Dying seemed to be taking a very long time . . . but . . . then I heard footsteps. It was Marthando.

'What have you done?' he cried.

37

'I want to die,' I said.

'But you can't, you mustn't. I got permission for us to dance together instead of your dancing with Holdsworth and Mummy has asked you to join us in the South of France for the hols. I know all the kings and queens so you need never bother with your parents . . . Matron, Matron, George has killed himself.'

They carried me into the school sanatorium and, there, while retching, I learned the knack of vomiting on command. After every meal I'd vomit everything up. Now they'd have to send me away. I spent a quite night in the 'san' dormitory and the next morning I put my plan into action. After each subsequent meal I threw up by making a kind of long 'Mmmmmmm' noise and sucking upwards. I can't even describe the technique accurately as it's terribly difficult to do and I'm about the only person who can do it at the drop of a hat. But it did get me away from school, if only for a while.

Since sickness had not weakened my parents' determination and death had escaped me. I resigned myself to the misery of school. Every two years, Father came from Shanghai to spend the summer holidays with us. This time the parents took a glorious place near Tunbridge Wells, with swimming-pool, garden, conservatory, six servants and a French chef who boasted he could spend the summer without making the same dish twice. Guests came from London, had lunch, received bouquets of flowers and went home again. It was no holiday for Dick and me. We were still subjected to one discipline after another: French lessons, Hebrew lessons, tennis lessons, golf lessons, boxing lessons, lessons, lessons. Added to which the sun never shone. Only the conservatory was warm. Father enjoyed walks. He would give theatrical sighs about how he would love to spend his life on the lawns of England. (Mother said he wanted to do the same on the fields of Flanders when they went to see the war graves.) Father also made me take walks in the rain, as if going for any walk wasn't tiresome enough. Once he asked me if I'd like to go to a football match, Arsenal versus Aston Villa. I remember the word 'Villa' reminded me of something non-English and England had become anathema to me.

'I hate football,' I replied.

This man who had never mentioned football to me in his life – had never been to a football match as long as I'd known him – was now forcing me to go and in freezing, windy weather. At the game Father was a great audience. He clapped and shouted and jumped to his feet and looked round at the other spectators to be sure they also saw him enjoying it all. I sat and sulked. What was this fifty-year-old Jewish business man, with his sallow Iraqi face, huge beaked nose and green tweed coat, doing in this zoo of wild footfall fans? At one point he screamed his applause right into my ear. I drew back, putting my hand to the poor ear. I got a slap.

Life at the holiday house went on relentlessly. More fabulous meals, to impress more Shanghai friends, more posturing, more pretending. I felt we each had a role in a senseless play. Everyone's behaviour changed according to who was there. Mother was doing her thing as the Frenchified grand English lady, Father was the noble tyrant Sheikh, I was the sensitive worry-child. Only Dick wasn't pretending to be anything in particular, he didn't have to, he just *knew* he was God's choice.

Father was strict over table manners. Dick, who was as sensitive as a piece of wood, had good table manners. Mine were awful. I was all elbows. Father gave us instructions on good behaviour without stopping all through the summer. He insisted we show consideration to women. When he saw me remove fluff from someone's bosom he warned, 'Never touch a woman there!'

Where then should I touch them? *There* instead of there? I never did again. Not *there* or there or there.

We boys were glad when Granny joined us for the summer. Father was less hard on us, but tears flowed. Anyway, when Granny and Mother got together they constantly wept and always about *him*. What else did they have to weep about? I continued to be Dick's adoring younger brother. We got on fine. After the holidays and the winter terms we went off to Switzerland to ski at St Moritz. Out of the blue, Father decided to send us there with a tutor, a master from Stanmore Park we called 'Spike'. The prospect of this provoked such panic in Granny, Mother and me that Father eventually compromised. We would go with Spike and Negie, our nanny, as well. So the two wretches were sent off with two attendants. No sooner did we arrive than Spike disappeared. Luxury had turned his head. He spent his days and nights in the bar putting everything on Mother's bill, including old Lady something-or-other whom he was screwing. When he eventually did reappear he found some excuse to give me a fearful belting. It all stemmed from the previous month's events on the rugger field. Spike had chosen me to tackle him and demonstrate how to ward off a tackle. I was the slowest runner in the school, but he hadn't reckoned with my passion for being noticed. When the time came, a tiger entered my

39

body. I hurled myself at him and he crashed ignominiously to the ground. However, to be belted by a drunken man whom my father had paid to look after me, was too much. I screamed down the phone and summoned Mother from Paris.

'Come and save me and get rid of that man or I'll take off my clothes in front of Ambassador Kennedy and all his children. How will the Hayim family like that?'

Ambassadors! Princes! Mother was there the next morning. Her sleigh could be heard miles away, bells clanging, black sweating horses dragging her to the imposing entrance of Suvretta Haus, where we were staying. Porters rushed to greet her and out she landed, like Catherine the Great, swathed in a tent of sable. Behind her in a smaller sleigh came the maid and the baggage.

Mother fired a broadside and Spike sank.

Two years later we were back in England for the summer holidays – with Father. More milky sun and tutors. How we missed the previous year when Mother had taken us to Biarritz: Barbara Hutton, Daisy Fellowes and Maurice Dekobra who had just written *The Madonna of the Sleeping Cars*, which Mother read and hid from us. This time we took a house in Maidenhead on the Thames, opposite Cliveden, the Astors' estate. We punted up and down the river, watched the boats going through the locks and things seemed better. Mother filled the place with staff; everyone we had ever met was invited down and then sent off with bouquets of flowers from the garden, tomatoes and grapes from the greenhouse. There was a new French chef who also never made the same dish twice all through our stay, and again it was never warm enough to lie in the sun.

One afternoon, Dick and I were lying on the lawn, playing a record of Marlene Dietrich in which she sighed, groaned and grunted, all in French. She was telling her lover to go. The bed was not too big for her alone, she'd had enough.

'Pars,' she says, 'J'aime l'amour et je deteste la cour.'

'I don't see what she means,' I said to Dick, puzzled.

'What it means,' said Dick, 'is that she doesn't like to be asked to dinner and told how pretty her eyes are. She wants to make love.'

I thought that's what making love was. Before Dick could explain (I was only twelve), Father shouted to us to come indoors. But I didn't care, I wanted to know this difference between Marlene courting and making love. So I put the record on again. Out came Father in a cold rage, lifted Marlene shoulder high and smashed her to the ground. I was myself again only when she reappeared six months later in a film with Gary Cooper – *Desire*.

With Father back the atmosphere was always tense. We pretended to be jolly at breakfast, as we ate grapefruit, porridge, cornflakes, stewed fruit and eggs, but nobody was happy. One day, while Dick and I were downstairs eating, we heard Mother upstairs let out a piercing cry. We ran upstairs. Mother and Father were stuggling and Mother was fighting to get away, holding a letter in her right hand. Her cries were hysterical, wounded. Father didn't hit her, they were just struggling for possession of the letter. We both jumped between them, climbing up round Father's neck. Mother finally managed to slip away with her letter into a lavatory, which she locked. The game was up. Father knew she would have had time to read the letter. He returned hopelessly to our room where Dick and I lay panting and sobbing on the bed. He then did the most curious thing – deliberately, almost tenderly, he 'unfolded' me stretching me out flat on the bed, and then lay on top of me, half-soothing and half squashing me.

Mother remained in bed, profoundly affected, for the next few days until Father left for London on business. When he came back he brought Mother a brooch consisting of two thirty-three-carat pear-shaped diamonds pointing outward and a huge baguette in the middle. He told her he would sell something short and buy something else short and get the jewel for her if she wanted it. She showed no interest and kept to her bed. Eventually he gave up. He didn't buy the brooch and he didn't give up the woman who wrote him the letter.

41

5

Hadn't we all gone through this before? Again it was late afternoon. Again light was failing and again I was cold. How could anything good come from a moment like this? Doom and misery filled the air. Mama sat in the far corner of a new Rolls, Turner sat imperturbably at the wheel. The roads were the same. The suburbs were empty and dark. There was something *déjà vu* about it all (except for the new Rolls and the new broadtail coat). In this case I *had* seen it before. The road to Harrow was exactly the same as the one to Stanmore Park, only Harrow on the Hill was a little further and stood ominously on a hill around which the wind blew constantly. An imposing, sturdy red-brick building dominated the place: a building like a judgement hall where they pronounced your fate and then cut off your head.

Anything that reminded me of authority reminded me of Father. School buildings, black print telling you this is forbidden, or that your presence is required. Almost anything of that nature filled me with fear: all due to my ingrained terror at the sound, the sight or the mention of Father, whose burning eyes and gentle velvety voice belied a dry, cruel authority.

I clung to Dick because he had already been at Harrow for a year and knew the ropes. I had asked him much about Harrow during the year we had been separated, but his answers didn't seem to give the information I needed. However, I'd learned that Stevenson was a terrible pansy (which did not mean homosexual, but well-dressed and urbane). Williams senior used 'Honey and Flowers' on his hair, but Carris and Dennis only used Brylcreem. Smithson had actually been with a girl on his summer hols, but hadn't known what to do with his dong, so he peed. Some say she stopped him – others that they peed

42

together. None of this was particularly informative about the school, though peeing instead of screwing was interesting. At thirteen, I didn't even know what a woman's body was. I'd been to the Louvre with Mama and seen the hermaphrodite, which I had thought was fun because it was both, whatever 'both' really meant. But I didn't realize what it did mean. I'd never lived on a farm. I'd never had a sister.

I thought, 'Women are shy and so they don't show their ding-dongs and no one shows them in sculptures or paintings.' So here I was at thirteen: I knew that Smithson had peed, that Carris and Dennis used Brylcreem on their hair, and that was it. Sexually I'd only fiddled around with Dick like many brothers do.

When I left Stanmore Park, I had been head of the school; a position which included no authority. I just happened to be top in work and the Headmaster flipped with pride when I entered Harrow directly into a scholarship form, higher than my brother who was a year older. I couldn't maintain this standard and no sooner was I put amongst other bright boys than I was demoted to a more modest class.

I clung to old Dick as we entered the 'House' at Harrow and as Mama drove off back to London, she looked back and waved. But something deep inside me told me that although she loved us, she was actually dying to get back to Grosvenor House, her dressing-table or her purchases and her desk where she spent hours writing letters. I felt quite alone.

Funny that boys at Harrow gave so much time to hair grease. At Stanmore, it was forbidden. Here there was hair grease everywhere: on the backs of chairs, on towels, on bed-covers. (Who wants to run their loving hands through 'Honey and Flowers' and Brylcreem?)

We trooped into the dining-room and had a typical school dinner. I knew what it was to be, I could smell it an hour before. There's a smell of cooking in England to be found nowhere else, thank God, except in Australia and New Zealand. Basically, English food is all cooked in fat. Fat from the lamb joint is used for the pork joint is used for the beef joint and is often given to children as a treat, spread on bread for breakfast, cold. When the fat has been used nine hundred and seventy-three times it is then thoroughly washed in boiling water to get the impurities out and then used again, until the children of Great Harrovians find themselves using fat their fathers used forty years before.

After supper, prayers and finally bed. I was lucky, my room-mate turned out to be nice, but unfortunately had an accent. Anyone at

Harrow was allowed to have a foreign accent, but to have an accent from the north, south, east or west of England was damnation. No 'gentlemen' in England have accents, wherever they may come from. They just don't, can't and mustn't. My friend had one. He was also a new boy and the day he arrived, all Harrow sneered.

The first assignment new boys had at Harrow was their fagging duties. Fags were those new boys who had to take messages, run errands or work for older boys. One did private fagging for a senior, and community fagging for the committee of seniors. To get a fag, the senior on duty would scream out 'Fag!'. If you were on duty that day, you had to run and stand there to be told what to do. Sometimes one would have to clean something or prepare toast for a senior. In winter there were wood and coal fires and seniors would have toast made for themselves, which juniors weren't allowed; though if they were clever they would hold the bread to be toasted on a long fork and then perhaps drop a slice into the ashes, take it out, shake off the ash, cut off the crust and hand the perfect piece to the senior, munching the ashy crust when the seniors weren't looking.

Sometimes two seniors would each scream out 'Fag!' simultaneously from different corners of the house just to torture the wretched fag. Having been forced to memorize practically the whole of the Talmud by the time I was three, and thereby able to pass into a scholarship form, I was exempt from public fagging, but not from private fagging. To be a private fag was to be a senior's personal servant whose duties included cleaning the leather and brass he used during army officer training, which meant polishing belts and brass buttons until they shone. I didn't mind being a private fag because I was already well on the way to being a masochist and Father's domination had led me to seek slavery as a way of life. I enjoyed brushing the shoes and the buttons; it reminded me of those soldiers in Shanghai. I adored the smell of shoe leather and if I worked for a decent senior it was all quite a relief to be protected from the rest of life at school, just as housemaids and butlers feel protected against the hazards of the world outside.

What I remember most clearly was the eternal cold. There was no central heating and Harrow Hill is a windy peak in a damp, cold country. The only time one ever got warm was in a bath and that was only permitted twice a week and then only for a few minutes. We new boys were allowed a clean bath. One might ask what other bath is there? A second-year schoolboy was only allowed into one used by a first-year boy, while a third-year boy got into the same bath already used by the first two – all this in England's second most prestigious school. It was a consolation to have a good pee into the bath in the hope of getting my own back on some cruel prefect who had bullied me. But even that could go wrong, as when I peed to get even with brutal Carris. He changed his mind at the last minute and Jenkins, whom I loved, got into the bath instead. I later found out that Gibson had also wanted to pee against Waddilove, who also didn't bath that time, so Jenkins got the lot.

Swimming was an exciting summer-term event and for some curious reason this was done naked. The pool was a lake in a field. We would all stand shivering and naked waiting for orders to jump in or not jump in. As English summers were notoriously cold it wasn't all that much fun. There was a boy called Bill Lithgow, with corn-coloured hair, of typically good country stock, who ended up as Harrow's cricket captain. Even at sixteen, Lithgow had such a staggeringly handsome muscular body that to look at him was enough to make me hard. This embarrassed me so much I jumped into the water, which got me into trouble because you were only allowed to jump when you were told to.

The Head of our House was a man called Bostock, married to the daughter of the Headmaster of Harrow. He was a thin, pleasureless man with an inhuman dry voice and no one liked him. They also said he only had one ball. So when we went swimming, boys constantly dared one another to dive down and find out, but no one ever actually grabbed it.

Summer term was the best. The boys waited all year round for the Eton and Harrow cricket match, which took place at Lord's Cricket Ground. I loathed cricket but the occasion was a social must. Mother even went to Paris to have new dresses made for the two days of the match. Families took over tents and everyone one knew was invited to drop in and eat. We ordered a spread from the most expensive caterers, who sent servants with cakes, ices, strawberries, raspberries and other goodies. The ladies with their tents would vie to be the best hostess with the best grub. I attended for two years never watching a single minute of the cricket.

There were a few Jews at school and we were not discriminated against. The odd crack came out and Dick, who was such a good boxer that he became Harrow's boxing captain, had to hit a few blokes. But, for such a school, there wasn't all that much prejudice. Nor were they snobbish about titles. They were brash, rowdy, and slightly vulgar, and on the whole I didn't like them. I hoped Eton would beat them at cricket but didn't tell anyone. When they played rugby against intellectual left-wing St Paul's School, I heard a Harrovian say condescendingly, 'Jolly decent of us to put our heads into the same scrum.'

Unlike prep school, where we were enclosed, Harrow consisted of several houses in the town. We were not forbidden to go to the 'tuck' shops and have sumptuous teas consisting of eggs, bacon, sausages and chips or eggs, sausages, chips and bacon or chips, sausages, bacon and eggs. Whatever one chose was covered with ketchup. Fudge was 'In': chocolate fudge, coffee fudge and plain fudge. Some genteel, impoverished ladies who devoted their last pennies to bringing up their sons at Harrow made a few extra pennies supplying the school with it.

There seem to be two ways of going through life: one where you keep waiting for the next wonderful thing to happen to you, the other where you flee from one misery to the next. After that first disastrous holiday with Father I was glad to get away and back to school. I loathed school but I loathed Father more. It was Mother I loved. I loved her face, I loved her smell, her tiny perfect hands, her clothes, her voice, her order. I loved listening to her when she talked of shopping.

'Chi piu spende meno spende,' she loved to say. 'He who pays more spends less' or 'Never buy anything in a sale, always buy expensively, that's the only way you know you want it.'

I did truly love her but – and there was a terrible 'but' – I knew that in any important matter involving Father, she would fail me. She was like a gorgeous basket with a hole the size of a melon on one side. If only Father didn't exist there'd never be an occasion for her to let me down and I'd have loved her totally.

So here we were, back at school, rugger, boxing and work. At the end of term, Suvretta Haus, St Moritz for skiing. There'd been the year Spike had belted me, the year that Gloria Swanson's daughter – also Gloria – aged twelve, had fallen in love with Dick aged twelve, and the year the Kennedys were there. Suvretta Haus was very grand indeed. Unlike the Palace which catered for smart café society, Suvretta was a family hotel. This doesn't mean a nice little place where nice little families go; it was where families with millions went, taking whole suites and bringing their own linen as well. We ate in the hotel dining-room, but the hotel restaurant cost double. Curious, rather private people stayed at Suvretta, and on one visit the list of guests included a

Russian 'Theda Bara' called Madame Gutman Herzfeld, covered in silver foxes and Brazilian diamonds, just as in the movies, who fed her cat, Natasha, caviar and later killed herself. I got friendly with a young Miss Citroën who was having an affair with a handsome Englishman called Percy Legard.

'He is so . . .' her voice dropped '. . . licentious, don't you know?'

I didn't know, so she told me. I never forgot the word. There was also an odd couple. A tall, white-haired Dr Mabuse of a man, who wore a monocle and looked unkosher, and his dashing young companion. People whispered when they passed. They nodded politely once to me.

One lunch-time I returned for my ski sticks, which I'd left somewhere, when the dashing young man, Axel Viale, came up to me.

'I've got your sticks, I saved them. Come, I'll give them to you.'

Like a little lamb, I followed him into his bedroom. Axel then pounced on little me, covering me with kisses, tearing off my clothes and muttering in German and Danish. I didn't punch him on the nose and say, 'Who do you think I am?' or 'Who do you think you are?' He knew both those things. I burst into tears. I thought Axel Viale was wonderful but I wasn't prepared for rape . . . yet. He cooled down for about three seconds and then tried to bugger me. Although I'd been in love at school and done a few huggy things with brother Dick, no one, but no one had ever tried that. I didn't believe such things existed and when he said everybody did it, I knew it was a downright lie. When I resisted he sulked.

'All right then, I'll go down to the Palace bar and get a joy-boy,' he said.

I heard people say that a certain person was a 'so-boy'. 'Is he "so?"' people would ask, meaning. 'Is he homosexual?' But I'd never heard about joy-boys. Oh, boy! 'So-boy', 'joy-boy'! Perhaps I could go down to the Palace bar and get a joy-boy but, in fact, I couldn't. I was actually nothing but a temporary, unpaid joy-boy myself. It all ended on a friendly note. Axel asked Dick and me down to their villa in Barcelona. I wrote off immediately asking Father for permission to go. Father did not reply.

By the time I returned to school, I was in such an unsettled state that something was bound to go wrong. It all started on a sunny day. I was sitting in my room, a new pair of gleaming white tennis shoes beside me. These shoes were for the holidays and not for school, where only prefects were allowed them. I cannot think what madness made me decide to put them on and go out into the street. It meant certain death yet I did it. Perhaps I wanted trouble, perhaps I thought that with my huge brown eyes, charm and innocence, I could say, 'Oh, I'm terribly sorry, what's wrong? Thanks for warning me,' and get away with it.

Whatever it was, I tripped into the street, convinced I could and would get away with it. I think it's called 'living dangerously'. The sun was still shining and there was no warning cloud as I left the House. Thunder and lightning followed almost immediately in the form of a posse of prefects, tall, white, handsome things their hard-blue eyes filled with rage. I found myself surrounded, questions and threats hurled at me. White shoes, Phil privilege, Phil beating, orders, criminal, marginal, rebel, communist, anarchist.

'What's wrong?' I cried. 'We always wear white shoes in Shanghai. It's so hot in Shanghai. Have you been to Shanghai? If ever you go, I'll give you a letter to my Father. He'll look after you. I'm a Capricorn you see. Are any of you Capricorns? I don't get on with Pisces!' It was not going well. I tried something else. 'What about Abyssinia? The Italians have invaded, you know. The Nazis are sending troops to Spain. I don't know about white shoes. People are getting killed all over the world.'

'Report to the Phil,' was the only reply I got.

I had never taken an interest in the school customs and honestly didn't know what the 'Phil' was. Of course, I knew it stood for something important to do with sports. I tried to remember what it stood for: Phillip, Phyllis, Philistine, philharmonic, philanderer, philatelic, athletic, a Phil beating with a string of postage stamps? It was all a blur in my throbbing head. Suddenly, I was alone in the street, my shoes burning holes into my feet. What was my fate to be and who were these seventeen-year-olds to be allowed to cause me such fear?

The next few days were terrible. I could hardly walk. I had to steady myself by holding on to things. My throat went dry, I couldn't eat. Frighteningly I went down to seventy pounds, then sixty, then fifty. The whole school stared. To start with they sneered, then the sneering stopped and was replaced by whispering. They'd avert their gaze and, by the time I'd gone down to forty pounds, they even looked at me with compassion. The world had become my jail, those people my jailers: doing their duty by strapping my hands to the arms of the chair, preparing me for the terrible moment to come. Someone would switch on the current and I'd go up in smoke. No one should be subjected to this, certainly not a nice boy like me. After all, I'm tender, loving, gentle and I didn't deserve such cruelty. I'd forgotten that I knew I'd been doing something wrong. This time Mother would have to do something. She could easily whiz down in her Rolls. Turner would pack my bags and they'd take me away for ever. After all, when we'd had trouble in Baden-Baden, hadn't Grandpa arrived in a Zeppelin? I ran to the tuck shop to phone. Mother would come at once and save me. Oh, but hurry, hurry, hurry, or it would be too late. I was lucky, she was in.

'Mother, take me away. They're going to beat me. They're going to torture me in front of the whole school. Take me away, please, please, show me you have a heart. Take me away! I implore you! I beg you, I've worked so hard. Please take me away! I can't stand it. I can't! Please, please!'

Silence. I could imagine her sitting at her dressing-table calling the maid to bring her a nail-file. She wasn't concentrating on listening. A long pause, then . . . 'Daddy'll only send you right back.'

Here she was, fiddling with some nail while her son was dying.

'Help me, you're my mother.'

She wasn't paying attention. She was busy with her nails. I left the phone booth and started back to my room, walking erect, with dignity like Brian Aherne as the Emperor Maximilian of Mexico in *Juarez* when Paul Muni orders him to be executed. On the way home a lad I didn't recognize ran up to me.

'Wear two pairs of underpants,' he said with a wink, and disappeared.

Later, another boy told me to put a piece of blotting paper there. Some boys showed concern.

'Don't use a pillow, they'll notice.'

A 'Phil beating' takes place in a huge hall in front of the whole school. It is nerve-wracking to stand up in front of five hundred boys even if one is getting a prize, but to bend down in front of them and get six whacks across the arse is dreadful. I thought that although the pain would be terrible, it couldn't be worse than the mental torture of those hours of waiting. I decided to transport the whole thing into another world. I'd be a famous pianist giving this concert in front of everyone. Everyone would watch. I'd show them how well I could do that Chopin *étude* or the Mephisto Waltz. I concentrated on my star performance. It worked, but only for that second. I imagined the crowds clapping and shouting. '*Bis*! *Bis*! Encore!' I must have lost another ten pounds. The sea of faces, the groggy walk to the dais, the bending over and the six brutal strokes. The strokes seared through my pants like knives, but were bearable. Better than earache, toothache or vomiting. When you vomit you want to die. This couldn't last long and it didn't.

I can't remember what happened next. I just wanted someone there so I could lie in their arms and be comforted. But who? Bennett. Why not Bennett? I'd been doing Bennett's private fagging, but how could I ask him that? I loved Bennett. He was so strong and handsome and had a deep, deep voice. I used to polish his shoes until they almost wore away. I bought the finest brown polish I could find to buff up the leather that officers wear. I am obsessive. How long could I go on, and how long could he go on not noticing? Finally, one morning it came out.

'Why are you . . . ho hum . . . er . . . Why are you . . . well, I mean . . . all this trouble for me?' asked Bennett, red in the face.

I stopped polishing the brass buckle, turned round slowly and gave him my 'soft eyes' look.

'Because I love you, Bennett.'

'Oh, I say.'

I'd got it off my chest. There was no more to be said. I put away his gear and left the room.

I spent most of the following day mooning around. I couldn't sit from the pain from my beating. That night I lay in bed unable to sleep. At about 10 p.m. I got up, went to the landing and stood staring. I had worked out that Bennett's room lay in a certain direction. However, between me and his room there was an immense boiler. I was staring through it. Not that the damned thing was any use: everything in England is always cold. At that moment, who should creep up beside me but Bostock, the Housemaster, on his rounds.

'What are you doing here at this time of night?'

I said nothing.

'What are you staring at, boy?'

Then I thought – what the hell! I'd tell him.

'I was staring at Bennett. I don't want to do anything with him or anything like that. I just love him, that's all.'

A curious look came over Bostock's ferret face. Perhaps a tiny grain of human kindness? If it was, it was leaving him at that very moment. 'Come into my study,' he ordered.

Would he put his arms around me and call me 'Silly Sausage'? He might say, 'Today it's Bennett, tomorrow it's Gibson. Little boys are always getting crushes on bigger boys. Off to bed with you now. Good night.'

Instead, he narrowed his eyes, and he spat. Words came out with hate and venom: perverted, twisted, filthy, depraved . . . How could I be allowed to sleep under the same roof as his respectable wife? I couldn't believe it. I absolutely knew I was terribly nice and something had just gone wrong. He sent me off with dire threats to my room. I made a decision. It took one second. Flight, flight, away, away to London to anywhere, perhaps to death. I only had a few pennies on me. Sullivan always carried money. I'd borrow a pound from him. I crept into his room, woke him. Sullivan lent me a pound.

'Dick'll give it back. I'm going. I'm going away. I'm going to kill myself.'

'Better take two pounds,' he replied and handed me an extra pound.

Two minutes later I was at the ticket office on the railway platform at Harrow Station.

'London please, one.'

'Single or return?'

Return? Return! Was she mad? Return to this?

'Single.'

6

In London, I made for Piccadilly Circus where there was an all-night chemist open. I would buy poison and die that very evening. No one would know until it was all over. Even Dick didn't know. Mother wasn't even in Europe. Father? It was his fault in the first place.

'I would like some hemlock, please,' I said to the lady chemist.

'Some what, dear?'

'Aspirins.'

'Big bottle or small?'

'It doesn't matter,' I said, looking tragic.

I put the lethal dose in my hand, guarding it close to me. Then I went to a Chinese restaurant and ordered sharks' fin soup. Discreetly I emptied the pills on the corner of the table and put four straight into my mouth. When I'd done that, I edged a fifth off the table on to the floor. I repeated this a couple of times, carefully dropping the fifth pill each time. If I changed my mind *en route*, perhaps the pills that I'd dropped and not eaten might somehow permit me to come back to life again. I took out a pencil and wrote on a pad I carried: 'I owe Sullivan two pounds. Somebody please pay him back.'

I put it into the empty bottle of pills and slipped it back into my pocket. I thought that if . . . just *if* Father were suddenly to appear to take me from school, if Mother said, 'I'll stand up for you,' those fallen pills would bring me back to life. Then, I would want to live. But Father didn't appear and Mother was probably having a fitting and Bostock was screaming, 'Unclean! Unclean!'

It was inevitable, I must die. I leaned down and picked up one of the pills from the floor and chewed it. Let it be bitter. I am bitter. That pill

52

was going to send me to my death. The waitress brought my bill, patted my head, and said,

'There love. It'll be all right tomorrow.'

I then went to the London Pavilion to see Eddie Cantor in *Roman Scandals*. It must have been nearly three hours since I had taken the pills. I watched him singing 'Making Whoopie'. It's all right for some, I thought, but I am dying. I looked at Gloria Stuart, her blue eyes, her blonde hair, her sweet innocence. Why didn't God make me a pretty girl like that? I wouldn't have been at that beastly Harrow. And if I were, Bennett would take me up in his strong arms, carry me out to the football field, and then . . . and then . . . I daren't think what would happen then. But I didn't look like Gloria Stuart. Actually, I looked like Eddy Cantor. Besides, it was too late now. My life was over. I'd never see Keith Bennett again.

By the time the film ended, I was breathing heavily. I felt different, and afraid. My heart was palpitating. I staggered into Lyon's Corner House and sat at a table. People looked at me. There was no doubt about it. I was the centre of attraction. By now I was really worried. I noticed a handsome man walking about the café, looking . . . He was as handsome as Bennett, but I thought it was unfair to Bennett to think about a perfect stranger the same way I did about him. I don't know how long I had been sitting there when I felt someone nudging my elbow. It was he.

'Hello,' he said. 'Are you George?'

I looked into his blue eyes: tears formed in mine. 'I'm going to die,' I said. 'Will you stay with me till I get cold?'

'I am a police officer,' he replied.

He put an arm around me and walked me quietly out of the café into Coventry Street and, eventually, to the police station. He patted me on the back and abandoned me. It was like my parents and school. I lit a cigarette and started to smoke. I had to do something drastic, but I can't smoke, I don't know how to smoke, I never could. Somebody snatched the cigarette out of my lips. I think I was losing consciousness, because when he snatched the cigarette it was stuck to my lip and I thought he'd torn my lip off.

I awoke some time later, all tubes and vomit. Beastly Bostock and his scrawny scarecrow of a wife were there to take me back to school. I slept in a room alone for a while. When I woke up, I looked in a mirror. Something had happened to my hair. It had gone flat and died overnight. I was taken before the Headmaster. He said my governess would take me away that afternoon and I would not be returning. I burst into tears. (Poor George, I cried yet again.) Negie, my governess, arrived later and took me away. Mother was on her way from Shanghai. Father was in Shanghai. Uncle Albert was in Paris, staying with the Schifkas. Negie didn't know what to do about my death, so she phoned Uncle Albert.

'I want to speak to George's Uncle Albert,' she said. 'George tried to kill himself, and I brought him back from school.'

'Wait a minute,' they answered, and then, 'I'm sorry, I can't help you. Uncle Albert isn't here, and we don't know where to find him.'

Thirty years later, Salach told me that Uncle Albert had been sitting one yard from the telephone. He did nothing.

A friend of Mama's took me to stay with her in her modest basement flat. All I did was eat bananas, Cadbury's nut-milk chocolates and drink milk. I saw every film in town. But I was depressed and worried, and longed to see Mama. I loved the way she looked and her cleanliness. I missed her huge brown eyes, and her voice like a golden bell. But in this case it was something much deeper that had to be put right. Pretty Mother and her finery did not entirely reassure me.

One day the phone rang. Mother had arrived in Paris and Negie was to take me there. We arrived at her suite in the Royal Monceau Hotel in the early evening. Night was falling. Mother stood there in a magnificent dark-blue velvet robe, arms outstretched, ready to pull her baby to her breast. 'It's all right, darling,' she said hugging me and patting me on the head, 'Mummy's here.' Long pause. ' . . . and Daddy's on his way.'

'Oh, no!'

I spent a month dreading Father's arrival. He couldn't be angry with me this time. I'd done my School Certificate well, I had no debts, I hadn't touched another boy. He must be kind to me.

When he eventually did arrive, he took me into a small room and began a conversation that I cannot believe even today. I remember words like 'floating' and 'merger', 'underwriting' and 'insurance'. It ended with, 'and I had to leave it all and come here for you. It has cost me twenty thousand pounds.' (Twenty thousand pounds in 1936 is equivalent to £800,000 today.) 'Now we must find you another school.'

'Not in England, Father, please. Please send me to Switzerland, to Le Rosey. Very nice people go there. The Emperor of Persia is there and lots of ambassadors' sons, and I don't like England or the English. I have worked well. I can't go through all that again.'

54

'We will get you a tutor . I will take a flat in London and Mama will look after you, and you can go to day-school.'

A tutor? Maybe he'd be nice. Like a strong father, lover, friend. I forgot about Le Rosey. At least I wouldn't have to go back to boarding-school, and the tutor might be . . . like Keith Bennett.

Father did some phoning and eventually we visited a possible candidate at his home in Oxford. We drove down in the Rolls. Turner had been replaced by a little wimp, the only advantage being that since Turner had big broad shoulders you couldn't see out the window, while the wimp took up no space at all. The car stopped in a suburb. We got out and rang the bell. The door was opened by a shapeless old man, the kind that notices he has left his hat in the compartment just as the train is leaving.

'Derek,' he shouted, 'Mr er . . . er . . . and his son have arrived.'

Derek Houghton was another who might have left his hat in the train, bigger and even more shapeless than his father. A ring of sweat showed under his armpits. I couldn't stand him. He had a pig-like face and a turned-up nose with bulbous, rebellious nostrils. I had so prayed for somebody nice, and now this . . . this lump with crinkly hair stuck all over his forehead – six foot of it! Something may yet go wrong, I prayed, but even while I prayed I heard father say,

'Take the boy somewhere in the country.'

'The country is for cows,' someone once said. I've seen the Himalayas, Niagara Falls, Rio de Janeiro, Hong Kong, but I hate the country. It was getting worse, and worse, and worse. Houghton said he knew a little hotel in Buttermere in the hills of Cumberland overlooking a lake, but one needed a car. Father bought a second-hand Ford-V8, a spunky thing, faster than the Rolls, like wearing a T-shirt after a morning-coat.

So it was to be Buttermere! The hotel was tiny, with a beautiful view when it wasn't misty and rainy. It was run by three sisters: Edie, Elsie and Emma. None of them pretty. There was nothing to do except study and walk. The Brits love walking, I hate it. They walk in the rain – I don't. They climb mountains – I don't. I was forced to walk up all the hills in the neighbourhood. Edie would tag along often holding Derek's hand. They vaguely tried to hide their affair, but slowly gave up. Edie would sit in the room sewing, then she'd stop and sit on his knee. All this while Wellington was having a bash at Napoleon. After Napoleon left for Elba they started French kissing. I watched spellbound, wondering how long the bridge of saliva would be when he drew his mouth away from hers. I wasn't jealous, I wished I too had something to kiss and hug.

One day we went to climb a mountain called Great Gable, the highest peak in the neighbourhood. I can't climb. It's not obstinacy or laziness. Houghton and Edie kept on at me, as I lagged behind, and when they reached Gable's summit, they cheered and called me to join them. I sat down.

'It's only three minutes,' they shouted. I didn't answer. 'You'll get such satisfaction.' (My only satisfaction was having saved three minutes' worth of climbing.)

That night, tired and depressed, I wrote to Mother at Grosvenor House, telling her how lonely I was and how I wished I had a dog. Here Father did his little number, ringing up Harrods to hire one. Just as car meant Rolls, so dog meant Dane. And Dane appeared. His name was Bruce. It was love at first sight.

It was almost July and the hotel was filling up, so they moved me to a kind of shack a few yards off, where I slept with my Bruce, hugging and kissing (far better than Houghton and Edie) all through the night. Whatever happened during the day, there was always my Bruce to come back to. But even that came to a quick end. For some reason I no longer remember, Derek Houghton decided to beat me. At least P. M. Studd, who'd given me the Phil beating at Harrow, was a handsome athlete, but this smelly, fleshy whale . . . and anyway, damn it, damn it, Jesus Christ . . . I wasn't going to go through life being beaten and beaten and beaten. I got to a phone and rang home. Father was out.

'Mother, if you don't bring me home and get rid of this foul-smelling slob, I'll not only kill myself but I shall tell everybody that you and Father caused my death!'

Bruce was returned to Harrods, I to my family, Houghton to his.

Father now gave Mother *carte blanche* to prepare a home for me in London. She chose a fifteen-room ground-floor apartment in George Street probably because Wallis Simpson, soon to be Duchess of Windsor, had a flat in the same block.

'She was in Peking, my dear,' said Mama. 'Everyone knew her. She went to a school of Chinese eroticism, you know, those things they teach you in China. That's how she got him.'

How did Mother dare make such a statement when she had neither met Wally, nor ever been to Peking?

They managed to get me into St Paul's School in London while Dick stayed on at Harrow. The boys at St Paul's seemed tawdry and poor after 'glittering' Harrow. Many were Jewish left-wing intellectuals. I went to school daily by bus, carrying the one or two books I needed. Within a year I was carrying a trunk with twenty books, chocolates, film magazines, plaster, aspirin, lavatory paper, soap . . . I'd become a caravan.

Meantime, Mother went to Paris and bought expensive furnishings for the new flat. A friend of Mother's, Betty Joel, did the place in hand-worked sycamore. The wallpaper was silver and Mother's bedroom was pink. The electric fire had moving coloured lights. The dining-room was a board room. Had she bought antiques, she would have been a multi-millionaire today. When we sold up years later, we had to pay to have the stuff removed. We had a staff of five. The butler was a faggot, called Pound. When he got cross with the parlour maid, he hissed rather like a snake.

Once the flat was furnished, Mother got bored and when a travelling salesman passed by and offered her a Hoover that blew out the scent of one's choice, as well as sucking in dust, she bought it. You could smell the flat way down the street. She gave ladies' luncheons, gathering titled women, taking them all to the Berkeley and having it put in the papers. She behaved impeccably and dressed divinely, but never had anything interesting to say. She was at her best making jam, minding someone's baby and being cosy. She wanted to be a society woman, but she wasn't. What finally saved her from boredom was the pianist Benno Moiseiwitsch, who had married her cousin Annie in Shanghai. Benno was going through a bad patch at the time and Mother asked them both to stay. He chose for her the finest Steinway boudoir grand in London and transformed the flat into a musical paradise.

Heifetz, Mischa Elman, Szigetti, Milstein, Segovia, even Rachmaninoff himself came; and they all signed the piano. Rachmaninoff said that Benno played his concertos better than he did himself and Heifetz exchanged his bow for an orange, with which he played Chopin's *étude* for black notes by running the orange up and down the keyboard. Another French chef came and he also never served the same dish twice. Our favourite was his baked Alaska, shaped like a dome with birds in meringue round it, their beaks tipped with caramel.

Mother spent some time courting an old dowager called Lady Barlow, a Quaker. She was grey and pleasureless. But Mother fussed over her because Lady B had promised to have her presented at Buckingham Palace. Mother skipped off to Paris to have a dress specially made and returned with a sumptuous, draped mauve crêpe ensemble which was to be worn with a vast velvet hat to match. When the time came, silly old Barlow found it showy and made her wear something else.

Lady Barlow was into politics, as were her sons, Sir John and Tom, or was it Sir Tom and John, or was it Sir Tom and Sir John? She excited Mama with a mad, but genuine thought that Dick, who was spectacularly handsome at seventeen, would become the new Disraeli, and she, Lady Barlow, would one day wear him on her lapel like a jewel. Dick heard about it and started behaving like Disraeli.

'I see myself on a pedestal, haranguing the crowd,' he told me, which I believed because I was in love with him.

During one of Father's visits to London, Sir John – or Tom – came round for a drink the very evening Dick was taking Lady Barlow to the theatre. Sir J or T noticed Dick, all dressed up in a dinner-jacket, and asked him where he was going.

'Taking that old zombie, Lady Barlow, to the theatre,' he replied.

Father went green, Mother tripped up and landed with her tray of drinks on top of Sir whatnot, Dick smiled amiably and Sir whatnot merely thought he'd missed a joke.

Marlene Dietrich was in London then, making *Knight without Armour*. For years Mother had imitated her singing of 'Falling in Love Again'. Professor Plesch invited Mama and us children to a musical party. Marlene was to be there. I thought of nothing else. I read in a magazine that she smoked Chesterfields. I didn't buy one packet, I bought two. I spent hours choosing a lighter. Then I got hold of Mabel, the parlour maid.

'You be Marlene,' I said. 'You're looking for a cigarette. Now wait.'

Then I'd practise, pulling the packet out of my trousers, offering a cigarette and lighting it. I'd been planning to offer Marlene a brand new packet, but hadn't realized before what a fiddly job it was to open it and pull out a cigarette. So I bought a cigarette case, but almost immediately decided against it. I wanted Marlene to see the cigarettes were her own brand.

The great day came. I had to get to the Pleschs' early, but Mother said it wasn't done. Marlene was already there when we finally arrived. She was sitting deep in a couch, her left arm round Alexander Korda, her right hand holding a cigarette, the famous legs in high-heeled shoes were crossed, and you could see up for miles. I watched and watched and waited. She then put out her cigarette and my heart sank. It was announced that Grisha Goluboff, a child prodigy of fifteen, was about to play Saint-Saëns' Rondo Capriccioso. There was silence. Then . . . I couldn't believe it . . . Marlene started looking about her. She wanted a cigarette – of course I leaped over some bejewelled matrons and proffered her mine. She took one and smiled. Did she smile at me, or did she just smile? Maybe she didn't smile. Maybe she just took my cigarette. I think she did smile. But after what happened next, what does it matter?

I wish I'd never even come. I took out the lighter, held it to her nose, and started flicking the wheel down with my thumb. Wwsh, wwsh, wwsh . . . flick, flick, flick. No flame, nothing. I died. I died a hundred deaths. Everyone was staring. Grisha was furious. Marlene accepted a light from somebody else. The Pleschs would never have me in their house again.

I saw Marlene in Paris twenty years later on a sunny day. I was sitting at Fouquets. From a distance her face looked like a death mask. From six inches away I couldn't see a wrinkle.

Dick's and my social début in London was a non-event. I'd started a puppy love-affair with a pretty sixteen-year-old girl across the way called Celia Lipton. She had a long face, long legs and looked like a young foal.

'She's going to look like a horse,' remarked Hermione Gingold later.

She was the first girl I ever kissed. It didn't do much for either of us. My other friend was Harry Kitson, a year or two older than myself and also a neighbour. He was tall, elegant and rich. His great-grandfather was Lord Strathcona, who started the Anglo-Iranian, Hudson Bay, Canadian Pacific and other companies. At seventeen, Harry would hop over to Paris, stay at the best hotels and go to expensive restaurants. I couldn't believe it!

Meanwhile, Dick brought home a beautiful blonde like Carole Lombard with dark-blue eyes, called Diane. Diane and I would wander around London, wearing dark glasses in the hope someone might take us for film stars. In the meantime, Celia Lipton had become a stage star. She imitated Deanna Durbin and then became one of the Forces' favourites a few years later, and was known as the British Judy Garland. Sometimes we'd take Mother's Studebaker, which had replaced the Rolls (the Japanese had entered Shanghai in 1937 and times were bad), for a drive down to Maidenhead and spend the day punting on the Thames. Once, on our return, we passed the Albert Hall where there was a traffic jam and crowds milling about.

'What's going on?' Dick asked.

Diane shaded her eyes with her hand like just before you shout, 'Ship Ahoy', and said, 'Someone called Messi–Ah's giving a recital. How talented you Jews are.'

Subsequently, Diane brought to Bryanston Court a plausible young man called Sidney Crichton-Stuart. 'Heir to the Marquis of Bute, I understand.' I was impressed. I'd met Adrian Gerald, ninth Lord Foley, in Eastbourne, then Harry, great-grandson of Lord Strathcona, and now a Bute. I was pratically launched. It didn't end there. Sidney dropped some wonderful names – Lord Tredegar, Lord Alington, Prince Hilarian Vorontsov Dashkov and the Princess Olga Dolgorouki. He did know at least some of them. I met big brown-eyed Olga Dolgorouki, who was like a furry rich brown cat, but the nearest I got to the Prince Hilarian Vorontsov Dashkov was overhearing a telephone call made to him by Sidney in which he said, 'Larry, put your arms in hot water.'

So I can't really drop his name, can I? Instead I had an affair with Sidney.

About this time I'd discovered a great outlet for my sexuality: Speakers' Corner in Hyde Park. Every tourist enjoys hearing the speakers and the crowd haranguing one another. What the public didn't know, but I discovered, was that when the speaker left the pedestal and the crowds all bunched up together, what was really going on was a gang-bang. It started as night fell. Usually, those taking part wanted the thing to end there, but I used to be upset when I'd meet someone I liked and they'd refuse to take me home. Mother was fascinated with my new passion for politics. But she'd seen Dick on his way to becoming Disraeli, so why not me? After all, isn't that what Father wanted – that his children should be *plus anglais que les anglais*. Mother told her friends, 'George goes to the Park to listen to the political speakers and returns with dark rings under his eyes. He's so passionate.'

7

I had just received the results of an examination. Unbelievably I had been admitted to Trinity College, Cambridge. All I had done was visit cinemas and dream about Marlene. Father said this was the perfect moment to go back and visit Shanghai. Perfect for whom? We imagined we'd go via New York, lie on Waikiki Beach in Honolulu and arrive in Shanghai all lovely and brown. But Father arranged things differently. We were to go via Montreal and be chaperoned by Sir Victor Sassoon's osteopath.

It was early May and cold with icebergs floating in the ocean. I found a handsome Canadian on board and we spent five days in his cabin. I can't remember what I told the osteopath – maybe he was doing the same in another cabin, maybe with another osteopath.

We passed Quebec at dusk. The Château Frontenac was lit up like a fairy palace. I thought I was back in Mother's womb and that the town was all lit up for me, but they were expecting the King and Queen from England.

The train journey across Canada was endless. I had my hair cut in Calgary and bought a daring pair of blue swimming-trunks with red laces criss-crossed up each side. From Victoria BC we took a dull boat to Shanghai, avoiding Honolulu.

Father no longer lived in Grandpa Elias's house. There didn't seem to be tailors and washer-women and stables here. Father had started up a refugee camp for Hitler's victims who had landed penniless in Shanghai. The austere Aunt Maisie, who had become very fond of me, ran the organization. Father was busy with a brewery he had floated for Jardine Matherson, called Ewo. It was now outside the International Settlement, since the Japanese take-over in 1937.

One day Father took us to a car waiting outside his office and told the chauffeur to drive us to the brewery and show us around. I noticed a Nazi flag hanging on the back window. It must be the wrong car. I turned to see if Father had left. He stood in the distance and signalled us to get in. Weakly and fearfully, I obeyed. I was so ashamed of that horrible thing dangling from the window that I got on my knees and hid. How could Father, who had organized a refugee committee for thousands of Jewish refugees and given them vast sums of money, how could he use a car bearing a Nazi flag? Eventually, I understood. The Nazi flag would have no difficulty entering Japanese territory. If Father had to put up with this degradation, why bring us into it? We didn't want to see the brewery anyway.

Father ordered us white sharkskin jackets and the Shanghai set made a fuss over us, but I was happier with Aunt Maisie's family. They were intensely religious, but did not impose it on us. Her husband, Reuben, was a beautiful old man, the kindness of Buddha in his face. It would have been hard to be married to Maisie Hayim and although Rueben had more class than she did, in the end it was money that counted. She dominated him. He escaped into Chinese art, of which he had a fine collection. He gave me his time and his knowledge, and together we collected some attractive jade, cornelian, malachite and lapis figures for me to take back home. Sometimes Dick and I would go into Father's office. In the past we had always avoided Shanghai at this time by going to Canada or Japan. Air-conditioning was not yet prevalent, except in a few cinemas. To combat the heat Father and Uncle Albert ordered huge blocks of ice which stood in the middle of the office, next to an electric heater, while a fan blew the air around.

One day Father ordered us to come to the office before lunch. He took us into a small private room, where he sat behind a desk in silence. He looked across the desk at us both and then, with a fixed stare, he began with me,

'Have you ever been with a man?'

'What do you mean?'

'I mean, have you ever been with a man? Have you ever lain with a man? Have you let a man touch you?'

'Of course not, Father. What are you talking about?'

'I want the truth. I've been worried sick.'

He started to squeeze his right forearm with his left hand, hitting and massaging it alternately.

'Look at my arm – it's swollen, swollen with nerves. If you tell me that this is the truth, I'll have you sent to a doctor. I'll send you back to England.'

I stopped to think what he could possibly have found out and from whom. I'd been seduced at fifteen by the handsome Dane in St Moritz. Then there was a soldier I brought home to Bryanston Court one night when Mother was away. Mother's maid, Marie, must have told her, but why did Mother tell him? Wasn't she supposed to be on my side?' He couldn't know about the adventures I had had after school ended, or even during the lunch hour. So what did he know, and how?

'No,' I lied, 'never, never, never.' Funny that at Harrow, where there were two boys to a room and most of them masturbated one another, I never did. I was never interested in cock, I liked men.

Dick then started,

'Go on, George, tell Father. Why don't you tell him?'

'Tell him what?'

I could have killed Dick. What had got into him? Or did he just want to use this to get us both sent back to England? I remember once Mother catching me climbing out of the window at Bryanston Court on my way to join a lover. I was sixteen at the time. She began with, 'George, George, *what* are you doing? What *are* you doing?' And ended with, 'What are you *doing*?'

But that was proof of nothing. I could have just been going for a prowl, like any other little boy, hoping to taste some forbidden fruit. Yes, I'd had hundreds of adventures by then, hundreds. I was young, tender, in need of love and available. I found it in cinemas, trains, buses and subways. I'd go from carriage to carriage until I caught somebody's eye. But Father couldn't know that either.

The following evening Father informed us we were to be guests of Vera MacBain at the Cathay Hotel. I should never have accepted.She was the woman whose letter Father and Mother had fought over years before. But I was now eighteen. Mother had stopped pretending and told us how she stood with Father. On her trip to Shanghai the previous year, she called on a woman who was leaving for England, to say goodbye. As she entered the house, she noticed a letter on the hall table, in Father's handwriting: 'Please post contents in England'. She left the house with the letter in her bag and read it in the car going home. It was a passionate letter to a Mrs Morris – the usual English type – worded in Father's own special way.

' . . . and never forget, I repeat, never, never, ever forget. I am not anyone. I am not another person. I am me. I am I. I am Ellis.'

Shema Israel. Adonai Eloheinu, Adonai Ehad. Hear, oh Israel. God is one. I *is* one. Ellis is one.

Why should I go out with this woman, who was my mother's enemy? It was a grotesque evening. Vera was tall, skinny and dry, with no breasts, but fine legs. She'd been a chorus girl and married well. When the time came to dance, she dragged me from a chair, 'I hear you are a wonderful dancer.'

She stuck to me like a Siamese twin, wriggled and snuggled, put her arm around my neck and her scented hair in my face. Perhaps Father had just told her about our meeting in the office and she thought that lurking behind every homo was a hetero lion. In her case, she had the added goal of conquering her lover's son. I must admit that if I love someone, I'm also automatically interested in his brother, his father, or his grandfather.

The following evening was no better. Father had arranged for us to take out his secretary and ordered us to be home by eleven. Mother had told us Father spent afternoons with that girl in Mother's bungalow in her famous garden. She was pretty and vivacious, and enchanted to be with the boss's sons. In the car, taking her home, Dick had his tongue stuck way down her throat and thinking she was going to choke I bashed her on the back. After that, we were driven back to our home. We told the chauffeur to stop outside the house so as not to wake anyone. Then together we crept up the creaky stairs. There was a sudden roar from Father's room, vicious and angry.

'I told you to be back at eleven! You go sneaking up the stairs without your shoes! Scum, both of you.' (It was a quarter-past eleven.)

Why, oh why, could I be so brave on a football field and such a coward in front of Father – with one exception? If he'd dared attack Mother, I'd have killed him, sat on his chest and banged his head against the ground till it split.

Next day I got hold of Dick.

'We must go, go now, quickly. Its getting bad and I'm going mad. We have our return tickets. We'll book, take a few things and no one will notice. We'll leave a note saying we're out riding, anything, and we'll be away.'

I rang the agency and booked. Patiently we waited to leave Shanghai and Father, but the day before the departure, Dick insisted he see Father's secretary again. He must have opened his silly big mouth to her. When Father returned that night he was jolly, menacingly jolly.

64

'Hello, my sons! And are you both going to help me shampoo my hair?'

It was a typical Father thing to do. By getting us to do something for him, we were put into a position of servility. We trotted into the bathroom to help him. As he was drying his hair he spun round and snarled.

'So you're booked to leave, you dirty little cheats? I'm going to beat you.'

With that, he made as if to hit us. Dick stood, ready to punch. I did the same. He backed down. I ran out of the house and went to Aunt Maisie's. I was hysterical. She put her arms around me and we sat till it was over.

'I'm never going back to that house again. I'm leaving Shanghai. I'll break windows, set fire to the house. I'll shame him . . . I'll expose him to everyone he knows in Shanghai. I'll ruin the family and myself. Wait and see.'

'Stay here now. You will have to return to England. This cannot go on.'

It was agreed we take the next ship back home. Maisie must have put the wind up Father. She wanted to avoid a scandal and I'd told her I'd do anything to disgrace the family.

Meanwhile, at Bryanston Court in London Mother set out to get a good husband for Aunt Maisie's daughter, Aziza. We did not belong to the international set . . . not even to a fashionable Jewish set, but when one has a lovely girl with a dowry to offer, one should be able to find somebody suitable. In Europe, Mother considered a Mond, a Seligman, a Goldsmith, a Rafael, a Cholmondely . . . but the war put an end to all that. In Shanghai the choice was restricted, but there was one young man who answered almost every requirement: Lawrence Kadoorie, son of the woman burned in the fire thirty years before. He appeared to be the perfect match. Both from the same background, the right age and already friends.

'The Kadoories do not keep the Sabbath or eat strict kosher. We must find her somebody else.' Maisie had spoken and that was that.

The war came and went. Aziza was now twenty-five and still unmarried. The plan had been to send her to America to study with her brother Isaac, after the war, but during the Japanese occupation Isaac had taken up with an Eurasian girl in the camp they lived in and it had broken up the holy family. So all that was cancelled. Lovely Aziza was

65

practically on the shelf. But not to worry! Didn't my family order those cheeses from Bombay, chocolates from France, Great Danes from England? They could also order husbands from Baghdad.

They wrote to Baghdad and ordered, unseen, a man from a 'respectable religious family', without a job, of course, without money, of course, but from a respectable religious family. The man arrived a few months later: small, uninteresting, unemployed, unemployable and grotesquely older than Aziza. To have imposed this person on a civilized, gracious, lovely, stately woman like Aziza, was one of the most cruel and disgraceful acts ever committed by my family. He lived on Hayim and Abraham money for the rest of his days, but no one dared discuss the situation with Aziza. It was bad enough to have lived it, why talk about it? But Aziza said a beautiful thing many years later,

'He gave me two lovely daughters. They made my happiness complete.'

At the time she said this, Lawrence Kadoorie had become Lord Kadoorie, and one of the world's richest men and most efficient philanthropists, having transformed the New Territories in Hong Kong into a beehive of employment, created schools, hospitals and factories. But 'He didn't keep the Sabbath,' repeated Maisie.

In his youth, Ezekiel showed musical talent and bought himself a saxophone, but it disturbed the family so he stopped playing. After the move to Hong Kong, although he needed a car, the family judged it was safer to take taxis. Little by little they castrated him. All his life he dreamed of going to Israel. In a moment of aberration the family permitted Ezekiel to go there for a month. He was now fifty. After four days they summoned him back to Hong Kong.

'We needed him,' said Maisie.

Many years later, one evening at dinner, at the family house in Hong Kong, when I was fifty and Ezekiel sixty, I suggested going to a movie. Aunt Maisie said,

'No.'

The same year I met an old woman from Israel on holiday in Hong Kong. It was my birthday and I asked her to the house for tea. Maisie made me cancel.

'We don't want strangers in the house.'

After that I had no time for her. Mind you, Ezekiel did need a kick in the pants. Particularly when one of his devoted and wealthy friends died leaving Ezekiel the choice of his most valuable items in a priceless art collection. Ezekiel could be a million dollars richer; he refused. For that

66

alone he should have had two kicks. Today, his brow is furrowed and his walk tragic. Sixty years of giving up everything always for everyone else, fifty years of nursing the old and dying, sleeping in their rooms, washing them alive and dead, has taken its toll. He is a beautiful broken old man.

8

The SS *Canton* was an average P & O liner on the London–Shanghai route. It was empty when we boarded her. War was in the air and people weren't travelling. It was a relief to have all that ocean between Father and me. I didn't jump with joy. I felt I'd been through a serious operation and was just up and walking again. I wanted to have a talk with Dick . . . not necessarily to berate him for telling Father I went with men, I know he didn't do it out of spite. But people like Dick are as dangerous as those who have no sense of smell or who are deaf. If you don't know what you're doing, you're far more dangerous than if you're evil, simply because you're more unpredictable.

'Dick, why do you think Father ever wanted us if he's so bloody mean to us?' I asked him.

'He probably didn't. We're just drops off the old man's tool.'

'You might be a drop,' I said indignantly, 'I'm a love child.'

'That's just what a love child is . . . the drop that got away.'

'I'm the child that was born to remind fathers in offices and mothers at dressmakers to be kind and tender.'

'You're there to remind them not to have another child,' Dick replied.

We stopped talking. Hong Kong had come into view in the distance. As we approached we could feel the peace and the calm of the place, so different from busy bustling Shanghai. It was oh, so British, with Government House splendid and white, a reminder to the world that Britain ruled.

'Dick, you know what? Father *is* Government House, only he's dark, not white.'

We left Hong Kong for Singapore to be welcomed there by cousins

68

who wined and dined us at home in their vast sprawling houses, servants bustling all over the place and lizards all over the ceilings. We were bewitched by wild orchids and introduced to the durrien, a huge fruit that looks like a monster pineapple and smells like shit.

'You just have to get over the smell and the taste's divine.'

But we will never know. We didn't get over the smell. We had chota pegs and Pimms at Raffles Hotel and talked of Somerset Maugham whom I hadn't read, but I had seen Bette Davis in *Of Human Bondage*.

The ship continued to Penang and Rangoon, where I didn't see the famous Buddha with an emerald in its eye or a ruby on its nose. I only remember a fruit, a cross between a strawberry and an octopus. From there, on to India.

We arrived in Bombay on 1st September, the day war was declared. It was exciting. What do two boys of eighteen years know about war? Vimy Ridge, Mons were just names in a history book. What does anyone know about anything at that age if they haven't seen it or been there? We looked forward to fighting. Don't all boys? We didn't give it another thought. We called a cab.

'Take us to the Taj Mahal.' I said, showing off to Dick.

'You are asking very much. It is being a long way, you must be taking a train to Agra.'

'How much will it be?'

'I am thinking perhaps my taxi is not being strong.'

I didn't know where the Taj Mahal was, but I didn't want to look a fool, so I quickly changed the order.

'I meant the hotel, you know, "The Taj Mahal".'

'That will be not so far as Agra. I will be happy to show you the town of Bombay. I will also be happy to recite you a poem.'

At this point he became illuminated and started to chant. I was afraid it would be one of those absurd romantic poems in Indian that drones along like;

> Good day little bee,
> Come out to me.
> Don't be solemn,
> Settle on my pollen.

Instead, he began gravely,

'Indo de bally of death dey came riding.
Dey were shooting five hundred to the lefting of dem
and shooting to de riding of dem
and de lady wid de lamp was waiting for dem . . .

I forgodden what happens den, Sahib.'
He asked for an extra rupee for the poem. I gave him two. He
dropped us at the corner of a derelict street.
'Taj Mahal?' I asked him as he left.
'Taj Mahal,' he answered.
We were now in Grant Road, a street a mile long, full of women, all
sizes and ages behind bars.
'Men always pay wages to women in cages,' I said smartly.
We went to a bar. 'Taj Mahal,' we said clinking glasses.
Then we returned to the ship. There must have been something in
that drink because neither Dick nor I remember leaving Bombay.
After Bombay came the long hop to Cape Town. We took turns to
watch for submarines and were happy to arrive there safe and sound.
After Cape Town and a call at Sierra Leone, the *Canton* finally
berthed in Liverpool. The next morning we arrived home. Mother was
worried, torn between staying and going back to Shanghai.
'Close up the flat and leave for Shanghai. We'll be away fighting and
you'll get bombed. Besides, Father will have to look after you.'
She didn't know what was better: Shanghai and Father, or bombing
and no Father. She chose Shanghai and we found a three-roomed flat in
Hallam Street near the BBC.
'What if they bomb the BBC?' Dick said.
'Then they'll miss us,' I replied. 'It's only if they miss the BBC we
have to worry.'
Mother departed and Negie, Dick and I settled in. Dick and I shared
a room. Negie had hers and there was a sitting-room without windows
in the middle. We didn't care. We would soon be away at Cambridge, in
the Army, the Navy.
No volunteers were taken when the war began. They took names and
told us they'd let us know when they were ready for us. Men already
enrolled at university didn't even have to go to war until they'd finished
their degrees. So I went up to Cambridge where I attended a single
lecture given by Keynes. I understood nothing and left. I went home to
study my own economics. I discovered that by some error I would be
getting twice the allowance I was supposed to get. I had a string of gaily

coloured lights in my rooms and there was always a bottle of sherry for guests. I was grown up at last!

I frequented a bar called the King's Parade and became friendly with a girl who worked there. She told me she was pregnant.

'Take a boiling bath, swallow a glass of gin and take a purgative.' I told her.

It didn't work.

That restaurant served jugged hare and Andrew Cavendish, son of the Duke of Devonshire, used to pour port into his Stilton cheese. I was entering a better circle. I mean, watching the future Duke of Devonshire eating cheese! I picked up a handsome officer in the Air Force, stationed in Cambridge, and his wife, a half-black, half-Jewish girl who had modelled for Epstein, and encouraged them to make love in my flat. It didn't help me get a degree.

The summer term was the happiest time I'd known. It was May. Germany was bombing the country, night and day, and we'd watch the planes having dog-fights in the cloudless skies above. Yet I still had no conception of what war was about. One could still go to Marks and Spencer and buy Brie cheese from France. We'd boil a great dish of asparagus and new potatoes all covered in butter to eat lying lazily on the banks of the river Cam. Occasionally, we'd go up to London for a party. Once, I went to Simpsons in Piccadilly for a haircut. The man wasn't paying attention – he snipped my right chop right off. I went mad, insulted him, tried to lose him his job, called for the manager. I mean, how *dare* they employ a man who did such a monstrous thing in a respectable shop? That millions were dying, bombs were falling and London was burning meant nothing to me. It didn't seem to matter much to the manager of Simpsons either, who thought that it was indeed a terrible thing to chop off my chop.

A few years later at a ski resort in France I went to a hairdresser who asked me how I wanted my hair cut and I replied,

'I don't care.'

He took a razor and shaved my head till I looked like a Buddhist monk, and very interesting too.

I became friendly with Ronald Millar who was running the Footlights Review. We all went to the station when Hermione Gingold came to Cambridge. It wasn't to perform, it was to meet a wonderful-looking man in the Air Force she had had a one-night stand with. Hermione stepped off the train, shook like a dog after a bath and started down the platform on her long shapely legs. Then, with a shout of, 'Fuck, I've lost

71

my eyelash,' she stopped and started scavenging on the floor for the missing lash, which she found and stuck across one of her eyelids. She kept repeating:

'Where's Garith Windsor? I want Garith.'

Garith Windsor finally appeared in sergeant's uniform and the finest blue eyes in the world. Hermione asked us to lunch with Stephane Grappelli, an hour before an exam; by the end of lunch I was drunk. I crashed into the exam rooms, wrote at high-speed. (I think better when I'm drunk, I drive better when I'm drunk and fail better when I'm drunk.)

That evening, I accompanied Gingold and Grappelli to London. Grappelli drank a bottle of Chanel No.5 on the train and Gingold said he was now as delicious inside as out. She then decided to seduce me.

'I know nothing of women and love,' I stammered. 'You must meet my brother.'

'I know all about love,' she replied. 'Where's your brother?'

That Hermione knew about love, Garith had confirmed. Garith was wildly intelligent. He'd left home in his teens first for Australia and New Zealand just before the war, ending up at the Sorbonne in Paris. Due to his looks and brains, he had been wooed by half of Paris and particularly by an influential talented set of rich homosexuals, all of whom had fallen in love with him and whom he in turn loved deeply, but purely. I became yet another of those friends and our devoted love over the years only strengthened the rumour that he was queer. But the facts were otherwise: he had proven himself a great lover and any pretty girl I ever sent him had only praise for him. He was the greatest influence in my life and the friendship continued for years, despite endless rows – for he was demanding, jealous, selfish and spoilt. One had to make up one's mind: did one want this brilliant, witty, wonderful creature or did one want to get rid of this spoilt, selfish, exhausting tyrant? One wanted each alternately.

Once in London, during the bombing, he sat holding me, squeezing my hand, my arm. I thought, 'This is it!' But not at all.

'I'm having an anguish, George. Do you know what that is?'

I didn't know, but I was enjoying it.

In London the bombing grew worse. Harry Kitson and I would meet every evening anyway and do the rounds. Someone could be found

72

propping up a bar while London blazed away. Harry used to say, 'Walk in the middle of the road. You'll get glass splinters from the windows.'

One evening Harry took me along to pick up a girl he was taking out. She was sharing with a girl-friend and was talking to her through a bedroom door when we arrived.

'...and Pamela, please don't forget to give me that cheque. You're a month late and I'm just not going to go on buying you food for ever.'

The voice from inside intrigued me.

'The bastard I went out with last night said he'd give me some nylons if he could put them on.'

'A transvestite,' I said.

'Put them on *me*,' corrected the gruff voice from the dead. She sounded oldish and tired. Socially her accent couldn't have been better. What was Harry's pretty girl-friend doing with this peculiar creature who didn't seem to get out of bed or pay for her food?

Later in the week, at Harry's request, I went round to the flat to deliver a package to his girl-friend. Pamela opened the door. I saw a face, dead white and flat with large brown eyes under swollen lids. She held something wet and dirty to one eye and was not embarrassed when I came in, though she was barefoot and wearing a dirty kimono.

'Hello pretty boy. What can I do for you?'

She didn't give me time to answer. A spate of words came out like a torrent... her father who sat her on his knee when she was twelve, which gave him an erection, her mother who made her dye her hair red while she was still in the convent, the long wet months of reading stuck up in Tanganyika. She talked and talked, occasionally using a word of Swahili as she referred to Kierkegaard and Rilke. I was bewitched.

She ended her breathless monologue with a mirthless laugh but I was already hooked. We agreed to meet again. I didn't know what to offer this bizarre creature so I suggested a cheap soft drink at the Ritz Bar.

I arrived early for the appointment, my eyes fixed on the staircase leading into the bar. I was expecting a dishevelled creature in a dirty kimono, I suppose. There was a sudden hush and in walked this silhouette on shoes with heels a mile high, red hair drawn into a bun behind her neck, large high breasts and wide padded shoulders. She must be a tart, I thought. As if she read my thoughts she said as she came up to me, 'I know I look like a tart. Men like tarts. We have the same ankles with high insteps.' She stuck out a finely shaped foot.

Again the monologue, the man she'd just been living with who'd sold

73

her jewellery and broken her heart, the Irishman in Arusha who tried to strangle her, it never stopped.

'How old are you?' I interrupted. 'I've never met anyone like you.'

She must have forgotten something for she got up and left, not before making me promise to go back to her place the following day.

When I called the following day, she was again lying on her bed, another wet rag covering her eyes. On the table was a note from her flat-mate: 'If you don't give me your cheque, I'm throwing you out.'

I referred to it and she got up to get her cheque book but when she found it, she became involved in a lot of scribbling which took ages. Eventually, she handed me the envelope stuffed with papers and told me to take it to her bank manager. Just then the phone rang and seeing she was settling in for a long chat, I left.

She had written her bank manager a long letter on both sides of the cheque, continued it on two pages torn out of a printed book where she scribbled between the lines, all of which, incredibly enough, was perfectly readable. I handed the lot to the manager.

'She hasn't been in for some time. She told me she'd been ill. How is she?'

'Her hips are tight and narrow, her breast stand high, her stomach's flat. I don't actually know her,' I replied.

'She has money in her account but she'll have to write out a proper cheque, unless I send the money by post.'

When I next returned to see her she was again lying on the bed in the same dirty kimono.

'I'm glad you called. I must get up. An American asked me out to dinner. I haven't eaten for days.'

Half an hour later she looked dazling, dressed in skin-tight black crêpe, her hair in curls down to her waist. She stood in front of the mirror carefully brushing specks from her dress and poking delicately with a pencil to give her eyebrows shape.

'You might lose one of your breasts in that dress,' I said.

'They fall out all the time,' she said without a smile.

Garith would adore her, I thought, so next time he was in London I brought him round to meet her. Now seeing her still in the same kimono, no make-up, hair falling over her face, I felt I'd made a mistake and Garith would hate her. Instead he found her wonderful. They started an affair.

Having coupled Garith and Pamela, I now busied myself with getting Dick off with Gingold. He was tall, dark and handsome and she was a star with turquoise eyes and with fantasy. It worked. Hermione had landed Dick a job doing something mysterious in Turkey through some man she knew in high places. One wonders at the sanity of people in responsible jobs who accept the recommendation of an ageing actress in love with a young man. Dick was handsome and had been a good boxer, captaining Harrow, so . . . ?

In the days that followed, I never saw a Turkish teacher or remember Dick going to Turkish classes. He didn't even mumble Turkish in his sleep. He was, however, playing around with what he claimed were explosives.

He covered the table in our windowless sitting-room with bottle after bottle of liquid, pouring out of this one and into that one, making clouds of smoke and smells such as have to be smelled to be believed. Eyes watered, and we had coughing fits. The place smouldered like a pharmacy after the fire-brigade had been at it. Dick never actually said he was on a secret mission, but that's the message he wanted to give us. While the table smoked and smouldered, Dick repeated Turkish words – *urgu*, *yok*, *kuturoo*, right out loud.

A month later, Dick was on the Simplon Orient Express. After her show, Hermione would often come and spend the night at our place, and the windowless room became a haven for friends. We'd lay mattresses on the floor and whoever came could sleep there. When Dick finally returned to England he had no wonderful reunion with Hermione but went straight to Diane Scott's. That's our Dick.

Now Dick began telling us what he'd done in Istanbul.

'It started in the mosque. I'd just eaten a borek washed down with raki when a shot whizzed past my ear. They were trailing me. Why did I go into that restaurant and watch that belly-dancer when I should have delivered the papers to the Embassy? I dashed home, but as I entered I knew I felt something was different. You know, one gets a sixth sense when one does this sort of work.'

'What happened?' I asked.

'I crept silently into bed, turned off the light and slipped my curved Ramseh from its scabbard.'

'Why didn't you go to the Embassy with the papers?'

'I did. I forgot to tell you.'

'And then what happened?'

'The curtains moved.'

'What did you do?'

'I plunged my curved Ramseh into him. Just one sharp, brutal stroke

75

and he fell at my feet. Not a sound came from his lips. I bent down and removed his dark glasses. It was the German agent who'd been trailing me.'

'How did you know it was a German agent?'

'I can tell a Kraut anywhere. Just looked at his haircut.'

'And then?'

'The Embassy didn't need me after that, people had gotten used to seeing me around Istanbul. They have to change the chaps every so often.'

'What are you going to do now?'

'Marry Diane.'

Telegrams were sent to Shanghai. Telegrams came back from Shanghai:

'Could she be bought off? Was she a Jewish girl?'

'No, she wasn't.'

We heard that Granny sat on the floor to show she was in mourning and cut off some hair. I think she sent a small cheque too.

Eventually, the Diane–Dick love-affair disintegrated and he started up with Moya, a pretty girl with big grey eyes, black hair and a gorgeous figure and at the same time I met a girl called Benedicta. She was thirty and from a world totally new to me. She was pure Bohemian, went on fat-free diets, had visited Corfu, had been painted by Derain in Paris, read Huxley, D. H. Lawrence and Freud and used words like 'basically', 'fundamentally' and 'subconsciously'. She lived frugally, knew Stephen Spender and David Gascoigne and had green-blonde hair. She wore no make-up at a time when girls wore masses. Benedicta looked weird. She loved me and I fell into her ways. Dick and Moya, Benedicta and I all lived together in a double bedroom at Hallam Street and when Dick left on what he took to calling secret missions, which meant he was probably with another woman, our friends would have funny sex games – kissing one another in the dark, blindfolded and guessing who was who; everyone kissed divinely and I never knew who was who. Ronald Millar joined us from Cambridge. The blue-eyed Garith became a fixture.

Benedicta spoke of books, diets, Montessori schools, psychology, fat reduction, conditioning and motivation. None of which I had ever heard of. She never wanted me to make love to her. She wouldn't have stayed if I'd been a normal man. Besides, a normal man wouldn't have liked her much even though she did look like the *Mona Lisa* and had an inscrutable smile.

76

I'd now left Cambridge because I was bored. Dick was hanging around waiting for his Army call-up or another 'top secret' assignment.

One evening I asked Dick a question – some usual matter. I asked again, and then again. Suddenly, he got up and without a word, punched me. We started a fight. I got dressed and went round to Harry Kitson's. I was shattered.

'Harry, I shall never love Dick again.'

I never did.

9

I'd been hanging around London for sometime waiting for something to happen but the Navy still hadn't called me up. Occasionally something would remind me of Mother and Bryanston Court, like Lady Barlow ringing up one September,

'George, is that you? Are you making hay while the sun shines?'

'Oh, yes, Lady Barlow, indeed I am.'

'Where?' she asked, not cross-examining me, just wondering in what part of England I'd been gathering hay. Silly me didn't understand. To her 'where?' I replied, 'Everywhere, my dear! The Ritz, the Berkeley, Pruniers . . . for tomorrow we may die.'

To my parents I wrote that I'd passed my first Cambridge exam: one of the only lies I ever told with intent to deceive, but it was to save them the embarrassment, after I'd drowned, of having to say, 'George failed Cambridge and then drowned.'

I imagined old Aunt Schifka going to Cambridge to check on my exams and returning to say, 'Who pass bettah George or Salach? Salach pass bettah.' But then I remembered she'd gone to America.

I never wanted to join the Navy to kill anyone, or to sink the *Bismarck*. I just thought it would be a turn on: a bunch of hard men bubbling away together in a pot. Also, navy blue is my best colour and I love dressing up. I chose the Navy because I'm sallow and look green in khaki. I hate the rain. I hate standing in the cold. I hate going on runs. In the Army discomfort was inevitable, even if you never heard a shot go off. But in the Navy one was always clean, warm and well-fed, unless, of course, you drowned. But I didn't think of that. What was worrying me was the ruling that anyone entering the Navy must be a British subject or the son of a British

78

subject, and this I truly was not. So who would get me in?

I did know a few who would swear George was a darling and clean and kind and ironed well and was nice to dogs and could sing 'Falling in Love Again', like Marlene, but the British Navy could do without these qualities. Yet, I did know someone . . . maybe.

On my last skiing holiday, coming down the Drostobel at Klosters, a body had hurtled helplessly down on its back, its side, its stomach – the owner – helpless. I sped down to stop her falling over a precipice and saved her. She turned out to be Mary Ashley, sister of Lady Louis Mountbatten. Eventually, through Mountbatten himself, my entry into the Navy was arranged. I used sometimes in my confusion to say Mountbatten was *my* brother-in-law but the sailors didn't listen and besides they were more impressed with my having received a signed photo and letter from Celia Lipton, the English Judy Garland.

What with having discovered wild sex, stage stars and the Ritz Bar, I had totally forgotten the Navy when suddenly I was called up. A kiss for old Negie, a telegram to Shanghai and I was gone. It was a fresh October morning when I left for the training-camp in Essex. It was like going back to school, only this time no mother and no Rolls Royce.

After a few tests and some questioning, young men with education were selected as officer material and though we remained without privileges, we were set apart by a white band round our caps.

I was interesting to the others if only for the fact that I'd been born in Shanghai, a name that conjured up far more magic than Hong Kong today.

It meant Marlene (again) in *Shanghai Express*, Vicki Baum's *Nanking Road* and Russian princesses who were dance hostesses. The sillier sailors would greet me with,

'Where's ya slit eyes? Got a slit arsehole?'

But that didn't last too long and, after all, one must endure some discomfort if one wants to become a hero. When the old hands tired of that, they started on the 'golden rivet'. Everyone had to see the golden rivet if they were going to be a sailor. A lot of winking and giggling went on. One was taken down a passage and when you were all bent down, they'd suddenly crash into your behind and scream with laughter. It was funny the first time, but they did it to the recruits all the time. The constant use of the word 'fucking' drove me mad at first but the French say, 'Comprendre c'est aimer.' To understand is to love. 'Fucking' was the word that replaced the word one couldn't think of: Give me that fucking . . . fucking . . . whatnot.

79

The boys in this particular training-camp were mostly 'townees'. The best were the cadets. So far, I saw little of the real Navy man. Some instructors were strong sergeant types, shouting orders, built like statues, rough and nice. I had a 'pash' on one of them and was wildly happy when he took me into a corner. I would have liked it to happen every day. The fact that he was in control was like Father suddenly putting his arm round me, if only for ten minutes. But he soon found someone else small and pretty and dropped me.

I was also the near victim of a rape when I was sent to the armoury on an errand. After I'd walked in and started looking around, I heard the door being locked behind me. A lanky giant of a marine stood staring at me. I thought I'd break the tension by chatting away. First I gave him a silly salute, then complimented him on keeping the place so clean. Slowly he made towards me and then gave a quick lunge. He chased me round the table but there were guns lying all over it. I didn't want to be shot and although I didn't want to be raped, I minded much more the chance of being beaten up during the exercise.

The mind works fast. I thought of endless solutions: 'Lie down and enjoy it. Tell the rapist, "I want you, I love you. I want to cover you with kisses".' In fact, when you're that scared nothing works and you can't shout. Besides, the only decent rape is the one you can control.

I don't know how many times we chased round the table, but in the end he opened the door and I fled.

The end of the training period was approaching. It was now December. The wind and the cold were bitter and I was always tired. There never seemed to be a moment when we weren't running or working. There was no peace, no respite, no silence, only bugles and orders by loudspeakers.

On Sundays we were allowed 'shore leave'. I would go to a hotel, take a room, buy a quarter bottle of champagne, run a hot bath and lie in it.

Eventually, the course came to an end. We were to be transferred to a fighting-ship. I'd always been told I was intelligent, I'd done well at school – almost scholarship standard – yet here I was no better, in fact worse, than the uneducated boys. I never mastered a knot. I'd have failed the exam to become an officer cadet had it not been that the examiners themselves had never encountered officer cadets in wartime and probably thought we possessed other qualities the common man lacked – that even they themselves lacked.

Before going on shore leave, we were offered a chance to choose the

80

mates we'd like to be with on the ship we were to join. About ten of us were sent to join a brand new anti-aircraft cruiser, the *Cleopatra*, being fitted out with the last touches in a yard near Newcastle.

The ship was beautiful, slim and sleek. Nothing was further from my mind than death and destruction, vomit and blood. The atmosphere on board was bad. Old hands muttered, '*Cleopatra*! Named after a bleeding whore! Whatcha expect?'

The first days were spent learning where things were, setting up hammocks and practising dropping paravanes. These were wire nets dropped from the ship's bows that spread out in the water causing an oncoming torpedo to blow up before reaching the ship. I hoped I'd get along better with this crew than with the boys in the training-camp. I liked talking about 'the will to power', 'Rasputin' and 'the Freudian slip'. I told them how Prince Yussupoff was a beautiful queen, how he'd filled Rasputin with poisoned cakes and that nothing had happened.

The Freudan slip was easy to explain: 'How nice to blow you,' when I meant, 'How nice to know you.'

A confused old regular replied, 'If you want to blow me mate, blow me and shut up.' So I blew him.

I couldn't explain 'the will to power', so I said I would reserve that for a later date.

'Your kind won't be able to face up to naval battles and bombs,' the old hands assured me. (By 'your kind' they meant class, not fags.) Nor was I really considered a fag. I was considered peculiar. The fact that I'd occasionally lean over from my hammock and do a job on my neighbour didn't give me a bad name at all.

In the middle of a seeming lull we were suddenly sent out to sea. 'Get the *Bismarck*' was the cry. The *Bismarck* was an unsinkable German battle-cruiser covered in armour and stronger than most of ours. She was roaming around the North Sea sinking everything, so the Admiralty sent a mass of ships and aircraft. The wind blew, the seas rolled and gurgled, I vomited and vomited and vomited till I fell into a faint. A whistle blew: 'Down paravanes'. I knew if I didn't go I'd be in trouble, but I couldn't. What use could I be to England if I couldn't stand up and fight?

Next day at roll-call, I was on the punishment list. I was scared of the Commander who was dry, silent and humourless. I was going to tell him I was of no possible use to him and that if he persisted in keeping me on that ship I would be a liability. Couldn't the Navy use my talents elsewhere? In the Pacific, perhaps, where the sun shone and the waters

81

were blue and the days balmy and there would be music and madness and mangoes. But when I stood before him, I froze and could only mumble, 'I fainted.'

I did get a small punishment, but remained lost in my fantasies; my posting in the Bahamas, Tobago or Bermuda . . . Was there no other way of getting a medal without vomiting my guts away?

After a fruitless chase we anchored at Scapa Flow, an island off the north coast of Scotland, where the German fleet surrendered in 1918. Ashore I bought anything there was to buy, ending up with dark glasses, Hugo's *Italian in Three Months* and some sunburn oil. No one has yet guessed how any of these items got there.

A whistle went off, then a siren, a smoke-screen; everything came to life. We rushed back to ship. The *Bismarck* was at it again. I didn't care what happened to her or if she sank the whole British Navy. I couldn't bear the thought of another week of vomit.

The sailors said it was all a question of mind over matter. If one was busy and excited one didn't vomit. I said I did mind and it did matter. The wind blew, salvoes were fired, flares flew, smoke filled the skies. The sea started to move, I started to vomit again. As I came to, a sailor passed by and said, 'We sank the *Bismarck*.'

We were then sent to another North Sea port to have shields set up around the pompom guns on deck. These were big protective steel squares to shelter the gunners. As most of the men had never been on a ship before, it was only then that we realized we hadn't had them when we first went out to sink the *Bismarck*.

Before nightfall, we were told we'd be putting to sea next day. Destination: Malta. Parts for Hurricane and Spitfire fighter-planes based there, were desperately needed. Half the crew was offered shore leave and warned not to return late. One of my pompom crew said, 'What about those steel shields? They haven't put them up yet. Fucked if I'm going back. I'm skipping ship.'

'They'll put you in prison.'

'I don't mind going to prison. I'm safe there. You poor buggers might get killed.'

Next morning we were off to Malta. 'Hurrah!' I thought, 'the Mediterranean and sun.' Malta was being bombed night and day. I didn't care. I might escape a bomb, but I could never escape the

82

vomitous North Sea. As we passed through the Straits of Gibraltar, at night, we had time to spare so I studied my Italian book. I already spoke French and knew some arias from operas: 'They Call Me Mimi', 'Your Tiny Hand Is Frozen', like Mama speaking Russian in Moscow. The sailors looked on my studies suspiciously. The Navy is renowned for its superstition and I wasn't quite trusted. I climbed into my hammock and prepared for sleep. I sat glaring at the pipes above me, wondering whether I'd done the right thing by joining up at all. I could have stayed in Shanghai and been surrounded by servants, and Father. The guy in the next hammock lifted his head and gave me a wink. I leaned over and joined him. Yes! I had done the right thing and was going to do it again the following night as well – for tomorrow we might die.

Early next morning the alarm sounded action stations. I took my position on the pompom gun. I wore the earphones and relayed the orders I received from the bridge to the gun crew. They'd chosen me because I spoke proper English. The others came from different regions in the British Isles and couldn't understand one another. Enemy planes had been sighted. We were about to be attacked. We were nearing Sicily and though we couldn't see the coast it felt close. There was a distant roar and a formation of enemy planes appeared.

'That's you and your fucking Italian grammar,' one of the crew accused me.

'They're Stukas – German not Italian,' replied another.

'He speaks German too,' said the first man.

The planes attacked in waves. They shot screaming out of the sky, as we sat there pointing our pompoms at them and going bang, bang, bang. Everyone was missing everything and nothing happened. I gave my orders clearly and calmly till there was a lull and we all relaxed. Then I thought I'd have fun and shouted out orders of my own. 'Off with her head,' I cried. 'Boil the bacon, Shema Israel!'

Just as we came within sight of Malta, dive-bombing Stukas dropped their load, scoring several hits, shrapnel spreading all over. Some of the pompom crew directly behind ours lay dead: blood streaming everywhere. My friends! That's all I thought of, for in our four or five months together we had become life-long friends. I recognized one man lying dead, his insides popping out of his belly like a concertina. It was the gunner's mate, a brute of a man who used to bully me.

I spread it around that I had put an old family curse on him. In the state of superstition in which we all lived, this caused havoc. I told them the curse was rarely used but that I had put it on a number of people and all had had disasters: my Father, my bank manager, a bus conductor, a guard on the Davos train and an employee at Harrods who wouldn't give me credit without proof of identity. What I didn't tell them was that nothing ever happened to any of them.

The attack had now stopped and the wounded were being attended to while the ship limped bravely into Valetta. The dock was next to a huge formation of solid rock. No bomb would ever get through it. Next to us lay another ship, the *Penelope*, known as the 'Pepper Pot' because she'd been peppered with shot and was unable to sail. I asked one of the sailors if he knew who Penelope was. No? I told him that she did tapestry all day to pass the time waiting for her husband to return because she had agreed to marry again if her tapestry was finished before he returned, and how she got up at night and unpicked it. He said his mother was always picking and unpicking things, at which moment he ran to his locker and returned with a piece of home-knitted something which he said his mother had unpicked and remade for him. I asked if she'd be forced to marry again once she'd finished her work and he replied, 'Wotcher talking about? She don't 'ave to marry no one she don't want to. She's my Mum.'

During the day, trucks converged on the port bringing crews to repair the damage we had sustained. In the evenings, if we had leave, we'd go off to the local movies. The bombing continued, those on board manning the anti-aircraft guns. The others would go ashore and barter cigarettes and chocolates with the islanders for a fresh egg and a night's sleep in a proper bed. Two of our cadets were killed in a cinema when a bomb got them. They were young, fair, beautiful. I wept for them. I wrote to their parents, told them how we had loved them, offered to call on our return to England and talk of their sons.

Sometimes I'd spend an evening with the rough boys drinking in the 'Gut', Malta's street of whores. One became the best friend of whomever one went ashore with – one's mate of the moment . . . known as one's 'Oppo'. or Opposite Number. You always ended up sharing a bed.

After a month in port, the *Cleopatra* made a dash for Alexandria. More battles, more smoke, but this time we returned unhurt and laden with stores for poor ill-fated Malta.

Loading and unloading began to be a problem for me. I had felt something go in my back, like the string of a guitar snapping. It gave me a twinge but didn't last long so I took little notice and carried on working. Then I began to limp. I avoided going to the doctor, feeling ashamed to fuss over a pain while others were dying, but it became so serious it was affecting my work. I could no longer carry things. My back seemed to be out of place and my leg to be withering away. I consulted the ship's doctors, who liked me. They had no idea what was the matter. They said they would have me looked over when we returned to Alexandria. In the meantime, I got worse. In the morning I could carry on, in the afternoon I'd try and exchange my job for someone else's, to polish instead of carrying. Standing became impossible. After a few more journeys back and forth to Alexandria, we suddenly left Malta. Trouble was in the air. There was a rumour we were about to confront the Italian Navy.

Soon after, the expected battle started. We occasionally got a glimpse of the enemy and guns fired non-stop, shells dropping around us. Then we got hit . . .

Had we sunk any of them? What had we lost? We knew nothing except that we were now putting up a smoke-screen. We had some wounded, but the ship was unscathed. An order came to take the wounded below. The shelling had stopped. I ran up to the pompom guns, many lay dead, some still groaning. Where were the sailors who were supposed to bring the wounded into the sick bay? The surgeons were waiting to tend the wounded.

'Come on you, the battle's over,' shouted the Medical Officer.

No one came.

'Can't they be shot for that?' I asked the doctor.

My anger against those conscripts knew no bounds. But then what about the regulars? They weren't cowards and they'd come from modest backgrounds.

We returned safely to Malta. We'd had hardly any damage.

I was back on my ship's messenger rounds and to my delight discovered from papers lying on the Captain's desk that I'd been put down to get a medal. After all those toughs teasing me and telling me what a real war was going to be like, I'd wave this medal in their faces. Malta continued to be bombed and we continued to hide under the rocks. The one person I despised was a naval sergeant known as the Chief Buffer.

The Buffer always flew to safety beneath the rocks, almost indecently, his eyes flickering furtively right and left. Well, this rotten coward got a medal and I didn't. I decided to quit. I'd had enough. I wanted to go home. The ship returned to Alexandria shortly for routine repairs and the crew was billeted in shore camps.

If you want the smell and the feeling of Alexandria you must read Durrell, not me. But for a twenty-one-year old arriving on this dry land, far from battle, where the 'white' man was supreme, Egypt seemed a haven. The first thing I noticed was a tin of Ewo beer floating in the sea – the Ewo Company that my Father had floated for Jardines in Shanghai. I had a sudden pang. It's funny that one can wax sentimental over someone one hates, and Ewo beer reminded me of my Father.

In the meantime, I had had my twenty-first birthday one night on board. The Japanese had entered the war and I was now totally cut off from both family and money. I was now a sailor living on my pay in a foreign land. Yet this land reminded me of Shanghai – the white man in the colonies. I had no idea how long I might be staying. I had one concern only – my back. I had to get out of the Navy.

A visit to the Naval Hospital in Alexandria produced good news. They had no idea what was the matter with me and had no intention of keeping me there. I was to be sent home. It was May, the sun blazed away and I lived on water-melon and Turkish coffee. During the months I had spent in London, having a ball instead of staying on at Cambridge trying to pass the exam I'd failed, I had met people who lived a life I never knew existed. The focus of them was Felix Rolo, a tall, elegant thirty-year-old Anglo-Egyptian who lived in Hamilton House, a run-down hotel opposite Green Park. Felix came from a grand Alexandria family, originally Spanish Jews, now British and titled. The family enjoyed an aura of beauty and wealth: Felix's mother had dropped dead while dancing with King Forouk at a ball in Cairo. Felix lived in Europe and was a notorious playboy.

I looked in the telephone book and found a Rolo, perhaps a relation who might befriend a poor young sailor. A warm velvety woman's voice replied, 'Come at once, take a taxi and don't pay him.'

I arrived at a long, low-slung house on the edge of Alexandria, by the sea. I didn't go in for the first few minutes as braided Captains, Commodores and Admirals mingled with fashionably dressed women, all leaving the house. When I entered, I saw that inside was like Ali Baba's cave. There were couches, rugs, exotica everywhere. Servants in white scurried around noiselessly. Yvonne Rolo led me through room after room and out to a rear garden.

'Felix is a cousin of mine but Marie Rose is closer still. I will walk you over to her house at the end of my garden.'

Marie Rose was thrilled to meet a friend of Felix's and took me straight to her heart. Realizing my back problem was serious, she made an appointment with the head of Alexandria's well-known Jewish Hospital. Her friend Dr Katz, a refugee from Germany, examined me and then gave me a local Novocaine injection, which permitted me to stand up straight for the first time since my trouble began. He warned me it wouldn't last.

Marie Rose adopted me. Her house was open to me and all my friends and she even knitted me a sumptuous pair of socks, that smelled of her scent – Chanel's Bois de Îles. God how I missed women! I was instantly brought back to the life I knew . . . drawing-rooms and servants, lifts in Paris loaded with scent. Back to the camp I walked, holding the socks to my nose, enjoying the memories which provoked the sailors to say, 'First 'e learns Italian while they're bombing us. Then we learn they're German Stukas and 'e speaks German. Now he walks around sniffing his socks. Time 'e went home.'

Back in camp, all we did was wait until one day we were told the officer cadets were all to be sent back home at any moment. There were a dozen or so sailors to each dormitory, it was stifling hot and I couldn't always sleep.

One night, lying on my bed, I noticed a sailor tossing and turning on his bed opposite mine. Slowly and carefully I lifted myself on to my elbow and caught his eye. It all took a second. With a flick of his head he signalled me over. The others were asleep. We fell into each other's arms. I felt the whole of Egypt had been thrown in: Felix Rolo, King Farouk and the Sphinx. I felt knocked out on his bed. A few minutes later he dug me in the ribs. Looking towards the man in the next bed, he said to me, 'What about my mate?'

I hesitated. 'He who hesitates is lost.' The moment had gone. I returned, head bowed, to my bunk. Why hadn't I jumped at the chance? I couldn't go back now. I lay on my bed and stared. When I could stand it no longer, I slowly tiptoed across the room, stood by the 'new' mate and slid my hand under his sheets, thinking he, too, would pull me into his bed. He'd been fast asleep and now, feeling a foreign body slipping in to his bed, shot up ready to fight – and he fought. So I fought too. I could hardly say, 'I didn't want to rob you. I wanted to blow you.'

I was a good fighter at that time and quickly got him around the neck so he couldn't do much to me. I couldn't and didn't want to do anything to him either. Nobody accused me of being a dirty bastard or a thief.

They knew it was not a cut-and-dried case, which proves just how wrong they were. It was. I, George Hayim, wanted the sailor next to the sailor I had just had. End of story. The first sailor then joined in.

'He's all right mate. I'm telling ya. 'es all right. He didn't want nothing of yours. He was just ya know, ya know what I mean. 'es all right.'

Eventually, we were separated. I was now back in my bed. I hadn't punched the man but he had punched me. I came off worse because I wasn't trying to hit him. I was battered and bruised and aching, my heart beating like mad. I was humiliated and I couldn't bear that the man should think I was a thief. I lay on my bed inert but ready for anything that might happen. After a while I lifted up my head almost imperceptibly. I noticed the fellow had also lifted himself on to his elbows. I stared straight at him with big, imploring brown eyes. He lifted his head arrogantly. Then purposefully, with no hesitation, he sat up straight. Please God, I begged, bring him over here. The man got straight out of bed and, looking neither left nor right, came over, stark naked, cock high, and fell upon me. After a moment or two he pulled himself together, got up to leave, smiled and winked.

'All right cock?' he said, which I must explain means: 'Was that OK mate?' and not 'Did you like my cock?'

It was now our last shore leave. We were to leave Egypt the following morning at dawn. I rushed to Marie Rose's. The fight, the love, the bruises. Everything hurt, even my love for this woman who had adopted me.

Next day, hundreds of us boarded the *Mauretania*. We were due to go home through Suez and round the Cape of Good Hope, but as we neared Durban our ship received a message that tyhoid had broken out amongst the troops who had arrived at Alexandria on that ship. We all disembarked at Durban and were driven in buses to Pietermaritzburg in the hills. After ten days, the *Mauretania* sailed again. This time we had a load of Italian prisoners cramped into the bottom of the ship. I'd always had a love for Italy and imagined the prisoners would be beautiful, curly-haired, brown Adonises talking of food and singing. Instead, they were a batch of undernourished shaven-heads. It's terrible how people put into positions of inferiority are worn down. But what an opportunity to learn Italian!

We took turns doing sentry duty round the ship. Our sailors were shits. They'd throw all left-over food into the sea rather than give it to the prisoners. I never thought of Italians as enemies. They were friends who had taken a wrong turning. I gave them what surplus food I could and they grew to like me. I'd go my rounds, using my rifle as a walking stick, to screams of 'Ecco la sentinella gentile' (Here's the nice sentry.), and they'd sing Neapolitan songs and make their miserable quarters tingle with warmth. I thought they were having me on when they called me '*la* sentinella'. Sentry is a feminine noun in Italian.

On that long voyage home I got to know our sailors' mentality better, and I liked them less. Good pals might well turn on each other over a matter of seniority. I suddenly took a revulsion to all of them. I must get out. I thought of nothing else.

On arrival back in England we were given ten days' leave. I rang my osteopath, an American who'd once cured an ailing knee by giving me high colonic irrigation.

'There's nothing I can do by manipulation,' he said, 'your condition is too far gone.'

My right leg was wasting away. I had a pain between the fourth and fifth vertebrae which went down the sciatic nerve into the side of the foot. My shoulders were thrown back so that I walked like a dwarf. But I still had a few days before returning to barracks. Naval doctors couldn't cure me and osteopaths were helpless, so I went to the Westminster Hospital where they did a lumbar puncture on me and I fainted. Nothing helped and the ten days came to an end. They sent me to a naval hospital outside London and gave me long wave and short wave. A famous London surgeon who devoted one day a week to the Navy manipulated me under anaesthetic and made me a plaster cast. My vertebrae stuck out into the cast. I couldn't stand it. I hated the Sister who was thin and pleasureless, with a laugh like breaking glass. She always singled me out for attack but I got even with her. She was a passionate music fan and after the pianist Benno Moiseiwitsch's daughter came down to see me she was 'mine'.

While waiting for the surgeon's final decision, I happened to read in the papers that a ship had left Shanghai for Lourenço Marques in Portuguese East Africa with a group of Europeans in exchange for another ship containing Japanese diplomats. The thought that Father might be on that ship, and subsequently in the same country or town or

89

even house as me, filled me with anguish. A little later Negie heard, indeed, that my parents were on the ship and heading for London. What with naval life, my condition, now Father coming, I went into a decline.

I tried to make myself useful in the ward. My neighbour, called Farrel, lay half-paralysed. Every day the nurses washed him but the smell from his bed was appalling. I got the screens, took off the sheets and sniffed out the cause. They hadn't washed under his foreskin. I didn't dare reproach the nurses but I did say to his wife, 'Your husband doesn't smell any more, does he? You have to pull back his foreskin, wash it, dry it every day.'

By now I'd lost track of time. It had been five months since I'd left Alexandria. It was now autumn and getting cold. My glamorous mother was to come and visit that day. She arrived like a Christmas tree, lighting up the dullness of the hospital, the vast mink, the diamond, the sapphire and scent filling up the ward. Father, austere, sinister, histrionic, bent over me, repeating, 'My son, my son, we'll save you even if I have to get you on a Boeing to America.'

He left the room and returned later asking if I wanted a room of my own. How he had managed that, I don't know. Of course, I wanted special treatment, but I refused his offer. Besides, who would wash Farrel's cock? So no Boeing. I was to regret it.

That afternoon was over too quickly. There had been so much to tell. How could I ever guess what they'd been through? Prison, agony, cold, illness. Mother now had to have her gall bladder removed which meant that only Father would be coming to visit me. I wished he wouldn't come at all.

Mother and I were operated on almost the same day. I have never endured such pain and will never forgive the Navy for inflicting it on me. My surgeon did a long and complicated operation on my back, after which I was returned to another uncomfortable plaster cast. I groaned out aloud night and day for three days. I begged for pain-killers. They gave me nothing. I kept the whole ward awake all night. It took ages for the pain to die down and when it did, I could not stop thinking. Return to the Navy or live with Father? Both choices were unthinkable. There seemed no way out.

The Battle of Alamein was now over. People talked of the Flying Fortress that was going to end the war and I was walking again. Was I now to be invalided out of the Navy, or not? It was rumoured that if one gave a large tip to the Petty Officer in charge, he'd arrange it. I believed the rumour, but can you visualize some man on crutches bargaining with a Petty Officer over how much he had to pay to get out of the Navy? I paid him five pounds. I'd have got out anyway.

10

Mother's operation was over. Father had left Grosvenor House and was living in his London club. I returned to the little flat in Hallam Street. One worry was over. With Father in England, there would be money. It is remarkable the way children, or even wives, think that if there once was money from a certain source, there always will be. The fact that China had been overrun by Japan and that accounts the world over had been blocked, made no difference: Father had always been rich, he must have what he needed. On the other hand, perhaps we were not all that silly, for Father being Father probably did have access to money, war or no war.

'How else could he keep us all and pay the bills?' said Mama, and she filled me in on what went on when the Japanese walked into Shanghai.

At the time of the Battle of Britain, when Spitfires and Hurricanes were hailed as the saviours of England, Father and Mother had offered a week's entertainment in Shanghai which they called the 'Follies'. This consisted of seven nights' revelry and took place in Mother's garden during May and June. Tickets were sold and the proceeds sent to the Spitfire Fund in England. The Japanese accused Father of spying.

'I am English. I am at war with Germany. I do all I can for my country, just like you are doing at this moment.'

He insisted that his life and his work were open to any investigation and that the 'Follies' had taken place before Japan had even entered the war.

No one can claim the Japanese behaved correctly, but there occasionally does exist a code of honour between gentlemen that works. This time it worked. It didn't save him from going to prison and being questioned daily, but he stood his ground. There were even times when the Camp Commanders came to Father to ask advice on how certain things should be run. Father consistently played on being Jewish, knowing the Japanese respected religion. In the middle of telling her story, Mother paused. 'Your father always suffered from back trouble. He did not suffer once all the time he was in that damp jail. He put it down to sleeping on a hard floor, but I knew better. He got it when he made love. He had been in jail for six months without pain.'

After some months Father was freed from jail. All the allies were interned in Camp. 'Camp' was a part of Shanghai that had been cornered off: Mother and Father even had a flat and servants there. Here the Jews got together and sent a petition to the Japanese Camp Commander: 'We are practising Jews. We kill our cows our way and we only eat kosher food.'

If anyone wrote that the Japanese Commandant had accepted the petition and agreed to its demands, I'd laugh. Yet, it did happen. The family cows were allowed into the camp and were fed, milked and slaughtered according to Jewish rites.

Mother and Father were on spitting terms during this period and didn't even speak to each other. On a cold December morning the Japanese military arrived and told Father they were taking him back to prison. As he got dressed, they told Mother she was to come too: 'You always wanted to get rid of me,' Mother screamed scathingly, 'but you can't. I'm coming too.'

She was almost glad to be taken. Little did she know what awaited her. While he was put in one prison, she was thrown into a cell with Chinese and foreign crooks and prostitutes. There were no visitors, nor was she accused of anything. Later, Marie came. France was out of the war so Marie was allowed to visit. What she saw was her mistress lying on the floor in her broadtail coat, her face with bites, and lice crawling over her. All mother asked for was a comb and next time, when Marie brought a comb, the women all sat combing lice out of one another's hair. There was no lavatory. Men and women hung around a hole in the floor waiting to do their business. Apart from the shame of having to do this in front of mixed company, Mother was unable, due to her size, to get into the crouch position. She didn't pass a stool for two weeks. Her system stopped functioning, her face went black. She was dying. Marie screamed at the jail commander and got Mother transported to Shanghai's best hospital of which Father was a director. They removed her faeces surgically and saved her life. The morning after the operation they brought her her first cup of tea in a fortnight.

93

'It isn't hot,' she said, returning it to the nurse.

After that the Japanese left her in peace. Father, however, was still in jail.

Quite unexpectedly it was announced that there would be an exchange of certain Japanese in Allied hands with Allied diplomats and others in Japanese hands. Mother applied to the Swiss Consulate in charge of immediate repatriation. When told she could sign to have Father freed and repatriated immediately she asked for a day to decide.

'I got on to my bicycle,' she told me proudly, 'and cycled over to the Abrahams to ask Uncle Albert what I should do about Ellis.

' "I don't know," he replied.

'They all looked shifty and nobody helped. I thought better get Ellis out alive, even if it's not what he wants, than leave him there perhaps to die. It wasn't obvious that Father did want to get out of jail. Perhaps he had other plans which needed his presence in Shanghai the moment things changed, so I signed. They also told me that once I'd opted for repatriation the decision couldn't be reversed. Then Father came home and in front of the family fell on the ground and started kissing my feet and blessing me for saving his life. We were all crying together.

' "I didn't know what you wanted me to do," I told him.

'He turned to Albert snarling,

' "Didn't you tell her what I told you."

'Albert started to shout and then stormed out of the house. We were to be considered full diplomats and could bring out all our valuables, money and jewels, so I asked Uncle Ruby to pack up his famous collection of Chinese porcelains and I would save them. Aunt Maisie foolishly preferred to leave them buried . . .'

Mother showed me pictures of herself walking arm in arm with Father as they boarded the ship taking them away from Shanghai.

'At last, I thought my nightmare with Ellis was over. We had come together again. From the moment we set foot on that ship, Ellis didn't speak to me again. I was frantic. What had I done? Saved his life? Was that a reason for crushing me so brutally?'

She started weeping again and had to stop talking.

'Never mind darling,' I put my arms around her. 'We are all safe. Me in the little flat, you in spendour at Grosvenor House and Father at the club. What better solution?'

'No, no, we must live together. We're not divorced,' she replied.

Live together! 'Mother, what are you saying? He doesn't want to live with you and I don't want to be anywhere near him.'

94

'I don't want people saying we're separated. We're not separated.'

'Stay where you are. Just stay.'

Two months later she had talked Father into taking a flat in Kensington. 'My God, she's going to regret this,' I thought. Our furniture was taken out of storage: case after case unpacked. We were to be one happy family.

The new flat in Melbury Court, Kensington, was a great sprawling thing with several bedrooms. Being a top-floor flat, it was going cheap as people shunned them because of the bombs. Father spent most of his days at his club. We hardly spoke, we were all on edge and we hated the place. When Mother and I were alone, I'd say, 'Is this a family?'

'It's better than being separated,' she replied.

It wasn't long before Father told me I'd have to start looking for a job. I didn't want a job. I'd never work. I'd use my back as an excuse. To myself, I said, 'I can't sit, I can't stand, I can't work. It's Father's fault. Not the war and not the back, just Father's fault.'

Community living is difficult but among people who are unhappy before they start its impossible. Father locked his room, but as Mother had duplicate keys she found out what he was doing, what letters he received and how much money he lent his friends. Father sensed what was going on. His letters stopped arriving at the flat.

Few people came to see us. We had one or two old Shanghai friends to stay, but Father complained, 'I want no permanent guests in the house.'

I spent much of my day out in the open in summer and in cinemas in winter. Once I lay sprawling on a couch in the hall and Father came in and kicked my feet aside so he had a clear passage to walk past. He could have said, 'George, look at you! Lying about the house, not working and your father has to climb over your legs.'

It would have shamed me. By kicking my feet he only made me hate him – but I no longer sprawled on the couch.

One day in the Park I met a man in naval uniform, a Lieutenant-Commander with a grand, hyphenated name, who had joined the *Cleopatra* after I'd left. He gave me his card explaining that gentlemen had them engraved, not stamped.

He was Tony Heckstall-Smith, about thirty-five, and stationed at Southend at a naval barracks. He told me his father had been in charge

95

of King George V's yacht, the *Britannia*, and to prove it showed me snaps of his father with King George. I was with Royalty – at last. I loved his 'poff-poff' way of talking so we made an appointment to meet again. He didn't turn up. I became depressed waiting day after day. I stopped eating. I didn't want to go out and lie in the sun in the Park in case I missed his call . . . so I chose to lie outside the window on a ledge of Melbury Court, so narrow that it was difficult not to fall off. I became obsessed with this man. I thought he was handsome, rich, clever and socially prominent.

Meanwhile Father continued to harass me about getting a job. He got me an interview with London's leading chartered accountants. I was tempted not to go but was too afraid of him, so I went, arriving an hour and a half early.

The manager received me with, 'Fine opportunity, young man. I'd have given my soul for a chance like this when I was young. Twenty-five shillings a week for the first three years. If all has gone well, then your father will be putting up the three million for a partnership.'

I stopped listening but something had slipped through. Partnership, gamesmanship, one-upmanship, three-million-pounds-upmanship. I stumbled blindly out of the office hearing a voice saying, 'Your hat, your hat.'

'Did you say hat? I didn't bring a hat. I don't wear a hat. I don't own a hat.'

A moment's silence as we stared at one another. Suddenly the hat I was supposed to be wearing started to melt and run down my face turning into steel bars. I had become the man in the iron mask. I shuffled out blindly from the interview, lay in the Park in the sun for an hour or two and eventually returned home.

'How was the interview?' asked Father.

'It's not so much the job, or even the man who interviewed me,' I replied. 'It's sitting. Sitting is too uncomfortable. Besides, I have to attend hospital three afternoons a week.'

'You don't have difficulty sitting in a cinema,' Father replied.

'There I sit in soft, padded seats and I get up when I want.'

The atmosphere at home got worse. I had given up hope that Tony Heckstall-Smith would ever telephone me again, let alone whisk me off into a world of duchesses and yachts. I wrote to the Ambulance Corps telling them I spoke French and they might need me now that the Allies had landed in French-speaking Morocco. I had to get away. Oh, oh why, why, why had Mama been such a wilful spoilt fool?

I did not understand at that time the fear Mother had of not having Father to protect her financially. If Father left her, the law could do little to help when no one knew what assets he had. But I couldn't live like this – with fear and hate in my heart. I'd go pale every time I heard Father's key in the door. If only they'd take me in the Ambulance Corps, I might yet become a hero. Death didn't worry me. It wasn't certain, only Father was certain.

My way of coping with life had always been to escape. I'd run away this time as well, perhaps to . . . Morocco? I'd forget bombs and danger and run to the sun to warm my heart and blood, so cold now from years in England because of Father's presence.

One morning he summoned me just after the postman had been. He stood there, an accusatory envelope in his hand. It was printed and I recognized it as coming from the Ambulance Corps. He handed me the letter glaring at me furiously.

Fumbling, I opened it. In a glance I managed to read: 'In view of your physical condition we regret . . .'

I burst into tears, a combination of Father's presence, my helplessness and the fact that I really must have been physically badly damaged. What was to become of me now? When I was more composed I did admit that, of course, I could find some job. But despite this, I continued feeling I was too sick to earn my living. The truth was that I never ever intended to. Father was going to support me for the rest of my life and, if not Father, then somebody else. I was throughly ashamed of myself but not ashamed enough to change my thinking.

Later that afternoon I forgot all my woes when Tony rang out of the blue. Father was out and before I realized what I'd said, I'd asked him to come home and meet Mama.

Tony arrived all freshly laundered in his uniform covered with medals. Mother was impressed and he in turn admired Mother's clothes and jewels. He told us he'd been on a secret mission and promised Mother a souvenir next time he went there, leaving her in no doubt it was France.

When Father entered, instead of the afternoon ending in more tears, it ended well. Father was proud to hear Tony'd been on the *Cleopatra*, where I'd left an unforgettable impression. Tony spoke to me in avuncular terms and never looked at me during the whole afternoon.

We tried to get him to tell us where and how he had got his DSC, which is the best citation one can have in the Navy. He was very British about it all: he said it all had something to do with torpedo-boats in

Crete. In short Mother liked him because she was lonely, Father because of his Britishisms and his bemedalled presence. As a result, Father invited Tony to the Savoy where he was pleased to introduce him to Jardine's Keswicks. Tony said Father's behaviour was effusive and he found Father embarrassing.

As Tony slowly became part of the household he told us many tales of peace and war, of kings and queens, of his property in the country and his antique silver. One time he returned allegedly from France with a hundred bottles of cognac which he had stored in his country place and which he wanted to sell. (I wished he'd sell it and return me the pound he'd borrowed.) He asked Mother and myself out to the Ritz bar which he could well afford as Mother didn't drink and soft drinks cost nothing there. I feared that sooner or later Father'd think of him as just another aristocratic British sponger.

Father cooled off him a bit but the magic of those medals on the uniform still worked wonders. Tony slept in my room when staying with us and one night we were mad enough to make love with Father in the room next door. In the middle of it, Tony heard a click and shot back to his bed. Father flung open the door and to his disbelief – and ours – found each of us in his own bed.

'What is it?' I asked breathless.

Father knew. He knew, he knew. 'I heard something,' he said accusingly.

'Me too, Father. I thought it was in your room.'

'What's up,' shouted Tony. 'Ever since I was sunk I always wake up in a panic.'

Father closed the door and left.

Tony was posted away for a short time and life at home returned to normal, except for a letter for Mother that arrived from Dick in Burma. She took it to her bedroom to read it and then returned to the sitting-room all smiles.

'Oh, Ellis, look what he says. He really is a good boy.' She began reading aloud, ' "I'm in hospital with malaria and ringworm. At least it's kept me away from the Arakan front. By the way, I kept it a secret. I married Moya before I left London. As for Father, I really want nothing from him except his money." '

A deathly silence. Mother turned to Father smiling nervously.

'You see, he wants nothing from you. All he wants is money.'

My mother had gone batty but I knew what she meant. Alas, so did he. Ellis's face was enough to send her blindly back to her room where she did the first thing that came in to her head – put on the radio full blast. It actually saved the day. There was an announcement from an Italian station which Mother understood to mean that Mussolini had fallen. She came back running and gave the news. Father picked up the phone to check but all the lines were busy. The news was broadcast from London a few seconds later and Father gave us another of his great performances. He fell to his knees, groaned and exclaimed in Arabic and Hebrew invoking God all the time, then stood with his arms outstretched like Christ on the cross hitting the back of his hands against the wall, all the while glaring at me because I wasn't doing as much as he was to show my joy.

Father never spoke for the rest of the afternoon but that evening as we sat around the hall in uncomfortable silence he scratched his head and said, 'I'm buying Japanese Bonds.'

Next morning, as usual I opened the door to the milkman when he rang. Mother, Negie or I would always be there to offer him tea and wheedle an extra pint from him. He arrived with another man. Father appeared, to see us drinking tea together. Signing to me to come to the pantry he said accusingly,

'Who's that?'

'The milkman, Father.'

'Who's the other one?'

'I don't know, they came together.'

'Is he the milkman or isn't he the milkman?'

Father had now raised his voice and the milkman got up and disappeared.

'Perhaps he's another milkman. What does it matter?' I said.

Eyes blazing like a beast he raised his hand to strike me so I did the same. Seeing I meant to hit him back he ran to Mother's room shouting, 'George tried to hit me. George tried to hit me.'

I ran after him to find him lifting a chair to throw at me.

'Who,' I sneered, 'is throwing a chair at whom?' And returned to the sitting-room.

Mother followed me while Father went on ranting in her room.

'How could you? How could you?' she kept saying but it sounded hollow.

'He's mad. You saw it. So much for your happy family.'

Later that day Father gave her an ultimatum: either I leave the house or he would. I said I'd go but not without a hundred pounds. Let him call the police. 'Rotten Iraqi millionaire, child torturer boots his war-wounded sailor son out of the house when he can't even stand.' I said it like I was reading headlines in the paper.

That night Mother said Father'd agreed to give me fifty. She would give me fifty of her own.

My hatred for Father at that moment was black and terrible. Again and again I imagined myself killing him. I had to get him. Mother would lie for me, say he was trying to kill her. I'd come in with perhaps a lamp in my hand. It couldn't be an instrument or it would appear premeditated – but Father wouldn't be at home. I knew he went to a bank in the City. I worked out exactly how to do it. I'd be in my car just as he was about to cross in front of me, and I'd simply run him over. I'd say as I was driving, I recognized my father, waved to him, slipped and stepped on the gas. I carefully visualized my car running over his body. In one daydream as he was dying, still pinioned under the wheels, he'd give a last look and with his dying breath he'd say accusingly, '*You*! My own son!'

And I'd reply, my face an inch from his, 'Yes, me. Your son!' a fiendish look of revenge on my face.

The *mise-en-scène* repeated itself over and over. But something always went wrong. A passer-by would witness against me, or he wouldn't die, or he'd remain a cripple, blackmailing me for the rest of my life. I'd even plotted how to get rid of him after he'd been crippled. Before doing him in, I'd bring a man home, two men, and make them humiliate me sexually in front of him. I'd shout: 'Watch it! This is your son and this is my last present to you, to thank you for all your slaps and the jabs with that needle and beating the soles of my feet and watching mother drink her ammonia and swindling your family and fucking mother's cousins.'

But I knew he was stronger and cleverer than I was. I knew I'd never get the better of him.

11

I packed and went to stay with Garith Windsor's French friend, Bertie Gilou, who had stayed with me in our little flat when France fell. After a few days of being in shock I found work as a film-extra sitting on a horse in *Henry the Fifth*. My back couldn't take it and I had to stop. To console myself I adopted a mongrel. We became inseparable. I took him on my next job as an extra but that also came to an end because some man tripped over the little bugger who squealed his head off and I shouted, 'Look what you did to my dog. You didn't bloody say sorry.'

'To the dog?'

'Yes, to the dog.'

The man was from the casting department.

I rang Tony and we arranged to meet in the Park. Who should pass by just before Tony arrived . . . my father. We just looked through each other. When Tony finally arrived he borrowed another pound from me. After an hour or two in the sun, I saw that the dog had now fallen for Tony.

'I learned dog talk at the Berlitz school for dogs,' he explained.

Pym, my mongrel, and I were such buddies, so independent of each other that I never stopped losing him in the Park, in shops, at the railway station. Having him had not limited me because until then I hadn't started working. I would now have to. I got a job as a messenger-boy collecting materials for two colourful ladies, the Krassin sisters, whose father had been Soviet Russia's first ambassador to England, but the job was too strenuous for my back.

Gilou said I should make hats; that the income derived from the capital in the millinery trade was phenomenal. I was in business overnight. I didn't know how to steam or block so I just changed things around adding feathers or flowers or bows. I used velvet mysteriously and got some well-known clients. A woman censor in Whitehall had ordered a marvellous creation from me with birds all over it. When I delivered it she was in a disturbed state.

'Look at this,' she said, handing me a letter from a sailor to his woman. This is what I read (my punctuation):

My darling Elsie,
'Ope this finds you as it leaves me, in the pink . . . 'Ope the kids are alright. I'm alright. Is Mum alright? I don't like abroad. The beer's cold. Remember the day we was sitting on the lawn mower and I says to yer, 'I wanna cuppa tea, Elsie?' and you goes to the kitchen and then I follows yer. You don't 'ear me coming. Then I grabs yer and I says, 'Got yer, I got yer, I've got yer,' and you says, 'Oh, c'mon Alf, I'm making the tea,' and you takes no notice of me and I grabs yer again and ya pushes me and ya says, 'No, Alfie, don't – I'm makin' the tea,' and I says 'Fuck the tea,' and you says, 'I'm thirsty,' and I says 'So is I, but I want sumfink else right now,' and you says 'No, Alfie – no don't.' And I makes yer and yer says 'Oh, Alfie – 'ow could you do such a dreadful thing just when I'm makin' the tea' – well, that's what I feel like doin' right now. Enclosed is a bit of 'air from you know where.

I went to the desk where I'd left the envelope and turned it upside down. A mass of fuzzy hair fell on to the censor's desk.

'Ugh!' she grunted, and with a ruler pushed it on to the floor. 'Throw it into the dustbin!'

'You can't do that,' I said. 'You must put it back.'

'I won't. You put it back. No, don't. I've got another idea.'

Looking diabolical, she ran to a cupboard and pulled out a broom. I thought she was going to sweep the sailor's hair into oblivion. Then she cut off the spike ends from the broom and popped them into his envelope.

'Now you've ruined a marriage,' I said.

Next time I rang home, Mother was weeping hysterically. Father'd walked out and left her. Now I could return home or perhaps Father'd had the row on purpose so that I would be able to go home and he could be free at the Club. I advised her to divorce him.

'I'll soon be making enough for us both,' I said.

What with my new income and the sale of her jewels, she didn't really need him any more. She was listening, thank God.

A few days later I returned home to find my capital valueless. Pym had discovered the joy of destroying feathers! (I felt like those men in New York jumping from skyscrapers during the Wall Street crash.) Ostrich, cock and paradise feathers littered the floor. My career had ended. My depression was without limit. Mother and I spent all day sitting and staring. A telephone call from Tony saved us.

'My poor old Dad died last night. He'll leave whatever he has to me. I'll be taking a flat in London where you can stay.'

'. . . and you can return me my three pounds,' I thought.

Tony took a flat just down the road from Mother's. Now I would have two homes. I learned to cook – made the best powdered eggs, for no eggs were to be found in wartime, and we decided to run a friendly boarding-house where, of course, nobody paid. Pamela came, dragging in with her a series of American officers, which at least meant we were never short of cigarettes or booze. She also brought into the house scabies and the only one of us who didn't catch it was Garith who was sleeping with her.

In the meantime, I was getting to know Tony better. He was constantly getting drunk and lying about everything. Sometimes I thought it was deafness and not deception that made him say 'Yes' to any question one asked him.

In the sitting-room was a large framed picture of a touching gentle creature, his sister who'd died. I used to look at her with compassion, hoping it might bring her comfort to know this stranger was caring about her. One of Tony's friends said he'd known the sister well and it wasn't her picture at all.

Mother, Tony and I were constantly in and out of one another's homes which didn't stop Mother cutting me dead when she saw me shopping, still in my dressing-gown in the early afternoon. That same day she wafted into Tony's flat to find me stark naked trampling on a week's laundry, floating in the tub. Lifting her veil carefully, a look of pain on her face, she moaned, 'To think . . . we sent you to Harrow and Cambridge . . . to end as a "dhobey boy".'

On the floor below us lived a family called Blount. The father was thin and wretched, the mother, thin and wretched, the daughter, thin and wretched, and on top of that, had a face covered in scabs. I wish I could recount the terrible evil tricks I played on them but I couldn't think of anything worse than pouring vinegar on to their window-sill where they kept their milk uncovered as they didn't own a fridge. The

103

war between us came to a head over Pym on the back stairs. The daughter claimed I'd hit her and torn a scab from her face. They took me to court and their lawyer cross-examined me.

'You tore a scab from this young lady's face,' he accused.

'Which scab?'

The magistrate was a nasty son-of-a-bitch called Paul Bennett with a Victoria Cross and he fined me ten pounds. I put a curse on him and next time I saw him he was in a wheel-chair. I didn't know he'd been in one for years. When I did, I put another curse on him and he died peacefully in his sleep – eleven years later.

Blount did, however, get the sack from his job and the man who took his flat was a famous Pakistani lawyer called Sir Zafrullah Khan who was to become Prime Minister. He had burning black eyes and was impressive. He also liked me, and we might have developed a lasting, meaningful relationship had it not been for Pym who became obsessed with Sir Zafrullah's slippers which had two sprigs of corn on the top which quivered as he sat cross-legged shaking his foot. Pym kept trying to jerk off on Sir Zafrullah's foot and coversation came to an end.

I disliked most of Tony's friends. There was Margot Clark, a fat drunk with a bawdy past. She'd been the girl-friend of one of the rajahs who had given her a ruby-and-diamond necklace as a parting present. When she was back in London she took it to Cartier who declared the jewels to be boiled sweets. Furious, she returned to India to berate her rajah, again staying at the palace doing whatever those people did: pig-sticking or polo or fucking.

'It was a cruel joke,' he admitted, 'but it was fun. Now here is the real thing.'

With that he gave her another necklace. Back to London. Cartier declared they were different boiled sweets.

Margot once arrived at Tony's trying to hawk a pair of drawers belonging to Queen Victoria. Mother dashed to get the first crack at buying them, till she discovered they were of rough cotton and too large, even for her.

Pamela couldn't stand her, but her own life was so full of the men she brought home that she ignored Margot. Pamela took sleeping-pills, smoked and burned holes in everything. Only when she went out at night was she perfect. Not a hair out of place, not a speck of dust on her suits. Her heels were ten inches high like those one sees in whore-shops. She had endless love-affairs. On one occasion she accused a lover of stealing her jewellery and in retaliation stole his passport. He called the

104

police. When they asked her what she'd done with his passport she pointed at a saucepan on the stove. In it, bubbling away was a lump of sticky goo.

It was about this time that we learned Father was to be honoured at the investiture at Buckingham Palace for his services to England. Mother was torn between longing to become Lady Hayim and wanting him to be disappointed. It is usual to take one's wife to such a ceremony. Instead, Father took Moya.

'I've had twenty-five years of hell with that man and saved his life again and again. He's only met Moya twice,' she said bitterly.

Perhaps Father said, 'I've had twenty-five years of that woman and enough is enough.'

She pretended she was happy that he failed to get a knighthood and got only a CBE, but it fooled no one. I was far more upset than she, as I'd have loved him to get it.

Before long Dick returned from Burma. Illness had ruined his looks but not his fantasy. He told us endless tales of adventure, embellishing them at every turn. Nothing could stop him talking about 'the Jap'. 'They were all drugged, shouting: "Mashi, Mashi. Hai, hai Banzai," and tearing across the paddy-fields, bayonets ready to strike. Millions of them! I sat there cool and collected, just waiting. Then I let them have it. "Go for the knees," I told the chaps. Padadadadadadad. I gave them a burst. They kept on running.'

'You mean you missed?'

'They went on running on their knees, they were so drugged they didn't know what they were doing.'

'You got close!' I said.

'That was nothing! I killed one with my own hands. It happened at night. There was not a sound, nothing moved. Over the way, I heard a noise. Silently, I crawled towards it. It was a Jap screwing his girl. I knew it would soon be over and they'd fall asleep. Then I'd get 'em. A few minutes later I heard him snore. I crept over like a panther. I could just make out their silhouettes in the light of the moon. They were both asleep, locked as one. Slowly and carefully I put my wire over his neck and then with one jerk . . . I'll show you how it's done George, come here.'

'No.'

'I strangled him. I used a Japanese method to kill a Japanese.'

'And did the girl wake up and say "Pinkerton San! Tellifick"?'

He didn't laugh, but continued: 'I fucked her.'

105

There was an uncomfortable silence so I asked, 'What about all those famous Burma rubies. Did you get any?'

'The Japs took them. All the temples were looted. They'd take the stones and put them in an empty cartridge and then shove the cartridge up their arses to hide them. Our secret service knew. They knew everything. Every time we saw a dead Jap, we'd jump on him and out popped the cartridge with all the rubies.'

'Did you find any?'

'I did about four bellies but one of the other chaps got a cartridge full of stones, on the first jump.'

Eventually, the war ended and Tony met up with some pre-war friends, the Pilchers, now living in the Canary Islands. Pilcher was a tomato exporter and his wife, Betty, a nice drunk. They'd borrowed all the Spanish customs: hugging you after the first meeting; slapping your back saying, 'You are a señor. I am a señor. My friend, your friend. My house, your house.'

We gave them our house and they invited us on a trip to their place in sunny Las Palmas. The cold of winter had set in and I couldn't wait to leave England. I immediately started to learn Spanish.

Next step were the visas. Toe (I now called him that) strode grandly into the Spanish Embassy in Belgravia, poff, poff, poffing away.

'And how's old Jimmy Alba? And Doña Sol, the Duchess Santonia? I haven't seen that lot since we all sailed up the Thames in the Royal barge.' I loved it when he spoke of the Empress Eugenia as 'My Tante Eugenie'. When the ambassador himself received him, Toe dropped a few more names. 'How's the Condesa del Puerto? And Natasha Rambova, Rudolf Valentino's widow, whom her son married?'

I'm sure they finished their interview with, 'You're a señor, I'm a señor, down with the Reds.'

Toe now bought a Packard cabriolet with one of those back seats that pops out of its tail and in which we put the corgis. I then emptied London of nails, bolts, needles, thread, matches, elastic, string, buttons and blades. Mother also gave us the address and number of Monsieur Ton, her furrier, with whom she had left some priceless sables.

I remembered Monsieur Ton well. Mother always used an expression at the dressmakers: 'ton sur ton', 'shade upon shade' and I always imagine old Monsieur Ton lying on top of old Madame Ton. But this time I was nearer crying. They would surely have perished in some horrific gas chamber.

We crossed the Channel on a cold December day. The French

Customs men were poor, proud and dishonest but a couple of needles and a light-bulb fixed that.

In Paris we stayed with a bright young money-changer and his wife in a flat where the walls dripped with damp. Our hosts talked only of food, money and women in that order. Every man seemed to have a mistress and every woman a lover. Our English pounds went far on the black-market so we went to over-heated restaurants and ate game, steaks and *foie gras* while the public queued all day for a potato. I asked our hosts if anyone read books or went to plays and the following night they took us to see *Antigone*. I knew nothing of it except that as it was a Greek tragedy everyone in it would die. When the curtain rose showing a corpse surrounded by men in tails and top hats, I asked our friends if we hadn't come in at the end of the matinée performance.

'Sh-sh,' they replied. 'It's extraordinaire.'

I asked Toe what he thought and he said he was dying of cold. I told him our host would explain the play later. The men in evening-dress then shuffled off with the coffin and the audience clapped. Our friends repeated 'Extraordinaire'. Toe got up to leave, but a man appeared on stage and told us that we were now about to see *Antigone*. We swore never to go to the theatre with those friends again, but the following night we found ourselves with them at another play, *The Eagle Has Two Heads* by Cocteau, about a queen who was an anarchist and an anarchist who was a queen. It all made perfect sense except for an earnest woman who kept on at both queens as she read from a book.

'Why is she carrying that book?' I asked.

'Hush.'

Old Toe hated the woman, hated the book, hated the play and said so. Our French friends said 'Hush' three times more, following it up with a couple of "Extraordinaires' and the curtain fell. When we learned that the woman simply didn't know her lines, Toe was so angry with our French friends that he took back some of the needles and half the razor blades we'd given them. Thinking we might be returning to Paris, I gave them all back again. Toe thought it would be chic to contact the British Embassy. The attaché he asked for turned out to be a yachting man and as Toe's father Heckstall-Smith had written all the rules for yacht racing while in command of the King's yacht, *Britannia*, Toe was immediately *persona grata*. So it was more 'poff, poff, poff,' pink gins, George five times, Edward seven times and old Bend'or Westminster and how Queen Mary loathed yachting and vomited and how Queen Ena of Spain hated bull-fighting and the Duke of Norfolk

107

kept repeating, 'Oh what a wind.'

He got the attaché to write him an official letter asking the French authorities to give him every assistance on his trip through France.

Just before leaving Paris I thought I'd ring old Monsieur Ton, never dreaming he could be alive.

'Monsieur Ton speaking,' answered the voice on the other end of the line.

An hour later Monsieur and Madame Ton, not lying on top of each other but sitting happily together, received us waving Mother's sables. I covered them with string and coffee and tea and needles – everything – and we left for the Spanish border.

We dashed through Spain to get to the Pilchers and the sun of the Canary Islands. Cars hobbled along, reduced to having wooden tyres and everyone helped everyone else on their way. They were all noble and helpful and offered us their homes, their goats, their coats . . .

Toe drove into a cyclist one night and for a moment we both saw ourselves spending ten years in a Spanish jail. But in the end the man came round and insisted it was all his fault and offered us everything he had on him. We bought him a new bike and left with his coat.

On arrival in Madrid we bought a paper to see what was happening in the world. There were headlines about 'Los Restos de Maestro Falla': the dead body of composer La Falla. His remains had been transferred on a liner to the Argentine only to be returned on another liner back to Spain. The body was now returning to the Argentine for the second time on a ship called the *Cabo de Hornos*, and as I'd remembered Darwin's account of the stormy conditions there, I felt terribly sorry for the poor body and got it all confused with the coffin in the production of *Antigone* we had seen in Paris.

In Cadiz we were fêted by a grand family called Gomez who had staggering English furniture. They told us admirals and generals like Nelson and Wellington travelled with their own furniture and had probably left the stuff in Spain during their campaigns.

Three months in the Canaries were enough. We took a boat to Barcelona where we met up with a notorious blonde Spanish beauty whose husband had caught her with a lover and had banned her from attending their daughter's coming wedding unless, of course, she went to Rome to get purified.

'And what happened there,' I asked her.

'They followed me in the street shouting, "Che belle gambe" (What smashing legs!)'

We took a house on the Costa Brava where we lived for a couple of years having friends and family over. We drove Mother all over Spain and showed her all kinds of virgins. In the church in Saragossa, I got off with the sacristan so I told Mother to wait in the car. I wanted to see the Black Virgin there. When I returned, Mother asked what it was like.

'Rather exciting,' I told her.

In Toledo, Mother got diarrhoea and told our guide to take her to the cleanest loo in town. The man sprang to life and took us to the synagogue.

After that Mother shut up her London flat and settled in Paris for some years. The modest life in our tiny seaside village was interrupted by a meeting with Guillermo, a young and dashing bad boy of the village with a Hispanic moustache and a reputation of having had every whore in the region for nothing – I fell for him. He awakened certain things in me that have remained. The friendship was not well received, particularly in summer when the village suddenly filled with holiday-makers from Barcelona who had previously thought of us as mysterious nobles and now thought of us as decadent foreigners.

In the middle of it all Pamela arrived with her long legs and high heels. Our black-market money-changer called 'Boy' fell for her, which upset his wife Lina until Harry Kitson arrived and consoled her.

Boy and Lina came during the weekends so Guillermo consoled Pamela during the week. Unfortunately, Guillermo gave both Pamela and myself the clap. We all had to go to Barcelona and get penicillin every four hours so we installed ourselves in the Ritz Hotel and spent our days together.

Boy insisted I accompany Pamela to a specialist known as 'El Grande' and I was told to wait in the next room while he examined her. She gave a few squeaks and when I asked her if she was in pain she said she was enjoying every second.

In the end everything went wrong. Boy was hounded by the police for changing money. Pamela got pregnant, El Grande and Boy claimed the child but, of course, it was Guillermo's and Pamela lost it anyway.

I was so in love with Guillermo that Tony and I actually came to blows after which I said, 'Toe, as long as I'm in the same country as that man, I'll agonize. Let's leave, leave for ever.'

We left Spain, grateful for a thousand kindnesses, but the time had come to go. I suffered from nostalgia for the country, the people and the flamenco for some time, though today I can't stand any of all that.

We drove across France and landed in Monte Carlo where we took an apartment belonging to a Balkan countess with lots of black pencil round her eyes. She had a live-in maid, Marina, whom she said was included in the rent. Marina later told us she wasn't. She was around seventy with the kind of white skin that comes from never leaving the house. She was suspicious of Toe and me and hated the idea of our dogs until the bitch gave birth to puppies right on Marina's face after which Marina felt herself a totally fulfilling mother and part of our family. So when we left Monte Carlo for Cannes we took Marina with us. There we hired a villa belonging to a Marquise de Crozet who used to sign her letters 'Mise de Crozet' which Toe said was provincial and common.

Marina told us she'd once worked in Cannes' Majestic Hotel so we reserved a table to take her there on New Year's Day. After blueing her hair and painting her face, together, Marina hanging on to my arm, we entered the great glass doors of the hotel, lackeys bowing. After taking four steps, Marina crashed to the ground. She lay there squawking like a run-over hen, my cleaner, my 'mother', my regent, my queen unable to move. No doctor was available. In the end we contacted a healer who carried her into a chair and carried the chair into the car. We couldn't take her up to the healer's place, so we brought the healer home instead. He made her strip, despite her resistance, and covered her with a sheet. A visiting woman friend asked to help but Marina said she hated women and wanted me to help. The healer then asked for a rolling pin which he placed on the floor. He then took Marina by the hands and made me carry her by her feet and slowly laid her on her back on the rolling pin. We then pulled her back and forth, resting on the rolling pin. We hadn't done it three times before she gave out a piercing yell and announced she'd been cured.

That winter Toe and I took a modest mountain hut in Auron. One day, looking for a skiing companion in a hostel, I knocked at a door and was answered by a loud whisper. 'Come in.'

'I hope I'm not disturbing.'

'Of course not. I love humanity. People and books interest me – after God, that is. I'm Michel de Buisseret, by the way.

'Aren't you skiing?'

'Not on Sundays. Sunday is the day of rest. I'll wait till Monday, avoiding the girls' schools and the men from the Post Office. Quite dreadful!'

He took a breath and went on:

'We're all God's children and it's wonderful to be alive in the mountains with all this clean white snow, so near to Heaven! God is everywhere, isn't He? What's that book under your arm? Is it in English or French? Not that I care. I'm completely bisexual . . . Hahahaha . . . you know what I mean. Oh, it's Graham Greene,' he shouted. 'Are you one too? I am! It's far better to have chosen it than to be born a Catholic.'

'What did he mean "Are you one too?"'

'I've had an audience with the Pope. I love Popes. I've kissed at least four toes. I think God's divine – simply divine. I've given up all my vices. Look at this.' He pulled out a gold powder-box. 'This used to contain cocaine. I have since been converted,' he continued, 'but I did give some to the cat in Rome. It's tail went stiff and it jumped straight out of the window and disappeared. It never made my tail go stiff . . . Hahaha.'

I thought this man was mad.

'Don't be alarmed,' he said. 'I've been hyperactive ever since they gave me arsenic injections for syphilis in Bali.'

Saying this he pressed his palms together above his head and fell into a Javanese dance. I asked him how long he would be staying.

'I'm off to St Maximin, a glorious monastery, to do a retreat but they may not accept me permanently. I try my best. I don't think God really minds. He's everywhere. In the trees, in the breeze with the bees . . . in the *cheese*.' He ended in full crescendo and with demoniacal peals of laughter.

We were interrupted by the arrival of a young German skier. 'Heil, Deutscher Freund. Sie sind Catholisch?'

The lad bowed and began, 'Protestan . . . '

'Nay, nay,' said Michel, 'nicht Protestantisch, Heretisch. I forgive dich.'

The boy bowed, clicked his heels and introduced himself, 'Dieter Schranz.'

'Dicker Schwantz,' guffawed Michel, patting Dieter on the head. Michel turned to me, 'Why don't you come to St Maximin with me? The monks are terribly grand, all cunts. Someone made fun of Father Preworski because he scratched his head with his fourth finger. Father Preworski is a Count *and* a very dear friend, so I had to defend him. I said the rest of his hand was paralysed. Later, when returning there, I noticed there was nothing the matter with the Father's fingers, so I said he'd been cured – by a *miracle*.

After that holiday in the mountains Michel came to live with us. Before the war he had lived the life of a glorious chevalier servant to his rich aunt, the steel heiress, Lady Hadfield, who owned a sumptuous villa at Cap Ferrat where the bright young things swam, ate and played tennis all for free.

When war was declared, Lady Hadfield fled to England. Michel joined the Belgian armed forces. Belgium was quickly out of the war and Michel returned to the villa to continue the same life as before. His friends were another flapper couple who did the same as Michel – sun and tennis parties. Lady Hadfield was lonely in England and sent word to Michel to come and join her. An underground group was contacted and Michel was guaranteed a safe passage through the Pyrenees to Spain and then England. The morning he was due to leave the flappers begged him to stay for a tennis party and Michel agreed. Again, Lady Hadfield pressed Michel to join her so he contacted another group of guides who were traitors. He was arrested on the mountains and sent to Buchenwald.

'Poor Michel,' I said in horror.

'The German officers knew I was an aristocrat and that Prince Charles of the Belgians had tried to help me. They were awfully nice to me.'

Now I knew Michel was mad. After the war, Michel became involved with diets, retreats, meditations and Catholic monasteries. His aim was to be accepted by Father Preworski, Head of St Maximin, a beautiful twelfth-century abbey. To retreat or not to retreat – that was the question.

Father Preworski – a playboy and Polish Count – considered Michel unsuitable and suggested an institution instead, a 'prison without walls' run by a Franciscan, Père Aulnes. Michel stayed there, charmed the 'Père' and spoilt the inmates. The Père introduced his new Count to all the local gentry and closed his eyes to Michel's relationship with the prisoners.

On one of Michel's social visits, he came across a penniless British wimp who had just uncovered his family title. He was now Lord Audley – penniless and desperate.

'Become a Catholic and join us – then you can live for nothing.'

Lord Audley moved in with them there and then. Within a week trouble started. Michel had a favourite amongst the prisoners, Audley another, and the Père, a third. When Michel's favourite heard Père

Aulnes swank to the local gentry that the new Lord Audley was far more important than the old Count de Buisseret, he repeated it to Michel.

Joining up with Lord Audley in a moment of self-righteous humbuggery, the two noblemen got into Michel's Peugeot and drove off to see the provincial Father, Père Aulnes' boss, to rat on him.

'He has a carpet in his room. He has a man to massage him. He is vain and social.'

They got him sacked. Not only did Michel tell me the story, but brought Audley to stay with us a few days later. Audley's bleak future had a moment's respite when he hit the news by marrying Churchill's daughter. He again hit the news when he was found drowned in the Port.

Through Michel I met European aristocracy, did the diet of clay, another of Royal Bee honey, had foot baths in some magical bottled water and met Victor Hugo's grandson, who told us, 'The last time I saw Grandpa – he was eighty – he lifted up his nightshirt to show he had a hard on. "Look at this my children and remember, at my age, this is indeed rare." '

Not long after Michel went off his head.

12

Out of the blue Mother rang from Paris. She wanted some sun and was arriving next morning with her maid. We planned things so Mother could relax and enjoy herself. No sooner had the maid unpacked and steamed the dresses in the bathroom than Mother started smacking her lips saying, 'I'm pregnant, I'm pregnant. I can't think of any other explanation.'

'Mother, please.'

'Don't be rude.'

'Then don't be silly.'

'I'm *dying*. Do you hear me? *Dying* for some Italian ice-cream. Let's all go to Italy. I just want a wonderful ice-cream. There's a place in Florence I remember from before the war. If you don't take me I'll go alone.'

'Tony,' I said, 'Mother's pregnant. If we don't take her to Florence, she's going to lose the child.'

Two days later we left at dawn for Florence. It never occurred to us to stop at San Remo or Bordighera and have some ice-cream there. No, we had to go to Florence to Mother's special ice-cream place, which, on the way, she kept shifting from next to the bridge to behind the bridge to Piazza Santa Maria Novella or Piazza Michelangelo. The ice-cream place must be exhausted by now. Mother and Tony then got all worked up about Italy.

'Dear, dear Florence!' sighed Mama, who hadn't mentioned Florence before.

Late that evening, we all rolled out of the car into the Excelsior Hotel, Florence.

'The hall porter will remember me,' said Mama.

'Was it Mario or Luigi?' asked Toe, pronouncing the 'g' hard. He didn't know that 'i' after 'g' makes the 'g' soft in Italian.

After a good night's sleep, we visited a famous jewellers as Toe had little money left and wanted to sell a gold oblong eighteenth-century box he claimed Edward VII had given his father. Its surface was like moiré silk, its edges surrounded with differently coloured embossed gold-leaves and in the middle an oval miniature of a stately lady in a white wig.

'It's the Princess San Faustino,' said Toe.

'No, that was the lady who went up in the lift *alone* at the Royal Danieli in Venice. This is the Princess de Lamballe. It was really she who said, "If they have no bread give them brioche." '

While we were at the jewellers, a large limousine arrived. A chauffeur helped out an old couple who were joined by what appeared to be their son, a fat pork of thirty. They wandered into the jewellers and interrupted us.

'Signora Gertz, I will be with you in a minute,' replied the jeweller.

I stood back and watched Mrs Gertz looking at Mother's diamond. She turned to nudge her husband who in turn nudged the son. The jeweller took the box and disappeared into a back room. Mother called Toe and me to her side, looked disdainfully at the Gertzs and muttered loudly, 'Ashkenazis.'

'Nazis?' said Toe.

The jeweller came back, handed Toe a wad of notes.

'Let's all have a drink,' said Toe beaming.

'Injudicious,' said Mama.

'Chewish Dishes?' Old Gertz butted in. 'My vife iss good cook.'

Mother gave Toe a sharp kick.

'You kicked me,' shouted Toe.

''Tis an ill wind,' said Mother.

'I feel no vind,' replied Gertz.

Mother walked out of the shop. The Gertzs now fell all over Toe. To them he personified the 'English gentleman'. They subsequently filled him with booze and schmooz, vanity, flattery, debt, calmity! The Gertzs learned Toe was really a writer and guessed correctly that he was broke. They offered this stranger a job. In the meantime, Toe's reserves had disappeared into thin air – his mother's annuity, his cottage in the country, the brandy, silver, etc. This was the moment of truth.

'We need someone connected with printing,' they said.

Toe didn't ask printing what, he accepted.

115

I didn't know what would become of me with Toe gone and no money of my own. I slept badly worrying about my future but never once did I think of working. Mother actually had enough for herself and me, but she was fat and lonely and her husband hated her. I could always find my fun in the streets at no cost at all. She never paid for me. She let Old Toe do that though she would have sold her beloved jewellery to save my life.

I woke up early a few days later and went to get the Rome *Daily American*. On the front page were headlines: 'International Swindlers Unmasked'. The Gertz family, after successfully selling shares in South Africa and then skipping the country, had done it again. They'd disappeared. Toe would have to go back to London and find a job. Also Mother wanted to return to London as she'd heard there was now a question of her land in Shanghai getting sold.

We all stayed at Uncle Reggie's and paid him rent. Mother was disgusted that her brother, who had sponged off her for years, should charge her rent.

'Pay and shut up, Mother. It's costing a fifth of the hotel.'

Uncle Reggie had bought a huge house in Hampstead with money from the property he sold in Shanghai. Mother hated Hampstead and said so. She'd never set foot in a subway and the only way she travelled was by taxi. But she hadn't that much money left after paying for her suite in the Royal Monceau.

Reggie gave us a lift one day to an Italian restaurant. As we entered, I noticed on the kerb a large limousine and a chauffeur sitting in it. Hardly were we seated than we were set upon by the Gertz family.

'I thought you'd been arrested,' said Toe.

'Ach nonsense! It was all because of tax. Do you pay taxes? Ha ha! Would we be here with the car in England if Interpol was after us? Do you still want the job with us in Canada?'

Three weeks later the Gertzs left and Toe with them.

'*Inshallah*,' sighed Mama.

'Does that mean, "Thank God, he's gone" or "Whatever will be will be"?'

'Granny always said it,' she replied.

I now returned to Cannes, the villa, Michel and Marina. With paying guests, I was able to manage.

One evening, I was stopped in the Port by a man with a strong Swiss accent speaking bad French and worse English.

'Please will you come with me?' he said.

116

'Where?'

'I mean go with me?'

'Go where?'

'I want to make love with you,' he blurted.

The man looked like Groucho Marx. Now I've always been generous and given myself to almost anyone who wanted me. It's something you can give away and still have. But not this time. 'I'll show you where you can pick someone up,' I said.

Later that evening in the Port we met again. This time he blurted out, 'I gif you five tousand francs' (ten dollars in 1948).

My cock went hard. I was so ashamed that I fled into a sleazy bar round the corner, where a friend producer, Peter Glenville, sat drinking.

'Peter! Groucho Marx offered me five thousand francs to go to bed with him and I went hard. What shall I do?'

'Go to bed with him.'

I left the bar and sat alone in the dark on a bench. Within minutes Groucho was back.

'I gif you seven tousand francs.'

I thought of Mother's diamonds and pearls and of Father and the Rolls, servants and Harrow, but it didn't help. Seven thousand francs! My cock was harder still. Again I returned to Peter in the bar.

'Groucho's offered me seven.'

'You may lie, your prick can't. Take it and shut up.'

Not only did I do it but promised to be there when he returned from Zurich the following month – just for me. And then I thought: I must buy something for Mother with what I've earned – a leather wallet perhaps and when she'd accepted I would say, 'I've prostituted myself to buy you a wallet.'

She would only answer, 'Madame Charlotte makes Hermes wallets for half the price you pay at Hermes.'

Besides I had other things on my mind. Uncle Eddie, Mother's brother, had called from London, wanting to come to stay having also sold his property in Shanghai. God-loving, gentle, boring Eddie ended up saving my life. He had loved Dick and me and even lived in Mother's house with us till he had a row with Father. That night after he arrived, he told me all about their quarrel.

'I used to work in your father's Shanghai office. My brother, Freddie, worked in another broker's office. One day your father ordered me to get rid of some shares. I discovered he had given my brother Freddie a

117

tip . . . to buy them. I confronted your father with this. "Are you working for me or for your brother?" he replied. So I resigned. I used to adore your father. We all believed in him. When my sister, Vera, and her husband left for Canada, they left their affairs in your father's hands. Your father ruined them and then lent them a lot of money to help them out.' It never occurred to any of us that he had done it on purpose. He had, in fact, frequently made people go broke and then generously come to their assistance. He wanted them in his power.

'You, George, are a thorn in his side. He is spending a fortune on helping Dick in his printing business. He would do the same for you, but you won't work. You won't even pretend to work.'

Eddie then wrote to my father in Shanghai.

Dear Ellis,
George lives with impoverished nobility in a broken-down villa. He is little more than a servant. It is painful for me to watch him tire as he trudges down to get the food. He cannot even walk properly! I suggest he comes with me to Canada and you give him an allowance. People are criticizing you. He has had a bad war, you know.

Eddie was out to help me. I amused him, but he didn't amuse me. However I was grateful.

Very soon after, Eddie received one of Father's peculiar telegrams: 'Most grateful for your concern. I am here to protect my flesh and blood. *Shemah Israel*. Ellis.'

A week later a letter followed: Father would give me an allowance of one hundred and fifty dollars a month if I went to join Uncle Eddie in Canada, *but*, he wrote, I must *immigrate*, and he underlined the word.

Marina and I hugged and wept when I left Cannes. Drawing me close, she said, 'It'll be cold there.' Then tugging intimately at my sleeve, 'And what will you do about . . . you know . . . lovers?'

'If I can't find some, I'll have to make some.'

With that I left for Uncle Eddie's in London.

At this time Mother was also in London, living with her old friend, Lady MacLeay, whose grandfather was Sir Robert Peel, after whom London police were nicknamed 'Bobbies'. Mother'd always been impressed by Lady M. Her husband was the first diplomat Mother had

118

ever met. I couldn't stand Mother when she was at MacLeay's. She was different and fabricated and just gossiped about the Royals and meeting dowagers, until – until the arrival of a mysterious trunk.

'I've just received this trunk from America. Is it yours?' accused Lady M.

'Is it addressed to me?' replied Mama.

'No, it's addressed to me. It's full of old clothes,' she said with distaste.

'Perhaps they're for the poor,' said Mama.

'If they're for the poor, I don't know any!' replied MacLeay.

Yet Mother loved living there and eating anything served off antique silver polished daily by the butler. She would also use Lady M's influence to get her George into Canada. I'd filled in the forms and was awaiting an answer. Father's offer of a monthly allowance was on condition I asked for an immigration visa and not a visitor's visa. He didn't want me returning to my wicked, wicked ways in the South of France.

Canada House finally replied. I would never be eligible because I was of Middle Eastern extraction. This law had been passed after Uncle Eddie had immigrated. Best of all was the last sentence in the letter: 'If you have been refused an immigration visa, you will not be allowed a visitor's visa.'

I screamed with joy. Nothing is more cruel than to be told you're not wanted, whether it be by the Club or by the loved one. '*Not wanted*' is hard to swallow. I swallowed it easily. I would get my one hundred and fifty dollars a month and not have to go to Canade. I, Georgie Porgie the gallant sailor, whose medal had been stolen by the chief buffer, was forever forbidden the land of mink and maple syrup, while the sons of General Stuelpnagel, Kesselring or Kuttlefisch, who had shot fifty thousand allies, would be welcomed with open arms. Was there no justice in this world?

Mother then started a campaign to get me into Canada.

'Do you want to go where you're not wanted?' I asked her. 'Wasn't Father blackballed from the club in Shanghai because he was Jewish?'

'They begged him to join a few years later.'

'I'll wait till they beg me to go to Canada a few years later.'

Mother had nothing to gain by my going to Canada and she'd be twice as lonely. She went blazing into MacLeay's.

'My dear, look what these *Eskimos* have done to my son.' And she explained the Canada problem.

119

'I'll ring Lady Willingdon. She was Vicereine of India.'

'Wasn't she the Governor's wife in Australia?'

'What about Beaverbrook? Didn't one of the Dolly Sisters marry a Canadian?'

'George's friend, Harry Kitson is the great-great-grandson of Lord Strathcona. He owned Canada.'

If Mother succeeds, I'll get an axe and chop off her head. But I'd never bought an axe and wouldn't know where to find one. My fantasy was interrupted by a call from Toe: 'These farmers are so dumb. They'll buy anything. I'll explain when I arrive next week.'

I hung up rather worried.

Toe arrived with the Gertzs, who settled into the Savoy Hotel. He took a flat in Mount Street. The plan was to open a firm in London. Toe looked peculiar when I saw him.

'What about this printing business?' I asked.

'We're branching out into a new venture.'

Toe proudly told me the firm was to be in his name.

'They're snobs, and they know about my father's friendship with George V. They can't do without me.'

'Don't you do anything without first ringing Salach,' said Mother.

Toe was in a state of nervous alcoholic euphoria. Eventually we fixed up an appointment with Salach.

'Sign nothing without me,' said Salach, 'and, before you start, you must have ten thousand pounds put in your own name . . . just in case . . .'

'Poff, poff, poff,' grunted Toe.

One more drink, or even no more drink and Toe would sign anything. On that note we parted.

Now in 1947–8, Shanghai was in the middle of an astronomical boom. Father repaid in local currency an immense debt he had incurred, using Mother's land as Mother was now free to sell her land. Eddie and Freddie, like Reggie, had sold their land and bypassed certain tax regulations. They assured Mother they could do the same for her. Obviously, Father was the best person to do the deal and it was in his interest to see Mother rich. He actually telegraphed her to increase the price she'd asked the Standard Oil Company. Yet Mother would not give him her power of attorney.

While the deal was under discussion, Mother found no difficulty in borrowing money to go to New York, buy a wacking great emerald and discuss her 'investments' with the Bank. She telegraphed Dick and

Moya, Tony and myself to join her in Paris on her return from New York to fête her new wealth.

From America she arrived with fur coats, capes for Moya, the money-changer's wife and others, forgetting both Toe and myself. The day she sat grandly in her salon at the Royal Monceau handing out these sumptuous gifts (it was principally an excuse to buy furs which she always loved buying) I asked her what she'd brought back for Tony who had been so kind to her. She stammered a bit and then said she'd ordered something that was not ready.

'And where's my fur coat?' I asked bitchily.

She wracked her brains for a moment and came out with, 'I thought you'd like a nice trunk.'

'What's the difference between a nice and a nasty trunk, Mother dear?'

She got the message, so the next day she asked Toe and me to the Ritz grill for lunch.

'After lunch I want to buy my Georgie a gold watch from Boucheron,' she said.

Lunch was a success. Mother and I would weave about tables looking at old ladies and their diamond solitaires and there were many, often double the size of Mama's.

After lunch we walked to Boucheron's where I chose a watch.

'Give me two. One for each son,' said Mama to the vendor.

I was furious. I looked after her, I took her to Spain, did everything for her. I didn't want to be treated the same way as Dick who never did a thing for her. Eventually, Toe took the watch for himself and I calmed down until the next morning when I caught a delivery man in Boucheron's uniform. He had left a third watch with Mama so I sold mine, returned mother the money and sulked.

What I really wanted was for mother to say: 'You're my real friend. You know all my secrets. You care. You're the one I love best.'

She knew it, but she was excited by Dick's looks and proud of his conquests with women. She didn't see him as I saw him, a vain, swaggering, posturing Walter Mitty with one of those appalling red kerchiefs pulled through a ring and tied round his neck.

Yet he was kind and would drive some old hag to the airport at 5 a.m. and not even mention it. I'd do the same, tell everyone how boring she was and what an angel I'd been.

Only his rapport with his boxer dog endeared him to us although it was annoying that he only spoke to it in French which Moya couldn't understand. The dog was divine but that did not justify Dick claiming it had walked down three flights of stairs, gone to Harrods to get the meat and returned with the change. At least Moya had the wit to add, 'It wasn't Harrods, Dick. It was the grocers round the corner.'

We were all on a high waiting for the money to roll in when, instead, Mao Tse Tung rolled into Shanghai before the land had been sold.

MOTHER HAD LOST HER WHOLE FORTUNE.

She never truly realized her loss. If she had known how rich she'd been, she might have jumped over a cliff.

'Perhaps Dick will make enough for us all with his new printing firm,' she said.

Father had given Dick a huge amount of money to start a printing business. Machinery arrived from Germany and a specialist was called in but Dick was often absent. He'd suspect some mistress was betraying him, abandon his work and try to catch her out, or else he'd give us all generous lunches at a famous steak house in the city 'on expenses'. Neither he nor mother could understand that you have to make money in order to 'put them down to expenses'.

He had soon lunched himself into bankruptcy. That wasn't all. He now abandoned poor Moya for Ginette Hart, the pretty daughter of Mrs Hart, daughter-in-law of Lady Hart of Holland Park.

Moya was broken-hearted. She adored Dick and to lose him to what I considered to be a flinty metallic number like Ginette was terrible. But Ginette had a trump card. She was half French and spoke it – not only with Dick – but also with his dog. When Mother heard the news she had a fit. She'd lived in Grosvenor House for years and seen Ginette sitting alone showing lots of leg, first in one armchair and then another. All of which Mother said was not becoming for the daughter of Grosvenor House's Mrs Hart. Besides, Ginette had always been something of a joke in our family except when she came over to Paris and stayed at the Royal Monceau. Then she became a menace because she 'dared' to bow to Mother in the lift – so Mother told us.

The excitement over selling the land and the disaster it turned out to be was now a thing of the past. Father was in Shanghai, a prisoner of Mao, while we sat in the Royal Monceau waiting for our monthly allowance which always arrived on time.

We should all have been on our knees before Father who got no satisfaction from any of us but went on paying. But we felt it was conscience money and never enough.

I left Michel and Marina in Cannes and spent some time in my maid's

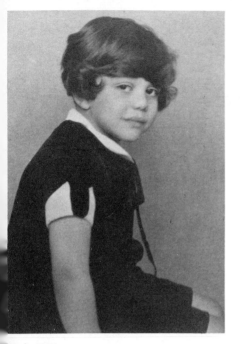

Me in 1924

Mother

ick and me, 1924

Mother, Dick and me, 1929

Mother and a Russian aunt in Monte Carlo

Drawing which I photocopied and sent out to my father's friends, to embarrass him. When five years old, I was pricked in the lips with a pin by my father as a punishment for having said a rude word

Dick and me at Harrow, 1935

Dick, 1943

In the Royal Navy, 1943

Tony Heckstall-Smith, 1947 ('Old Toe')

With Jean Genet

Marina, Michel de Buisseret and me, 1950

Pamela and me

dmond, about whom I wrote *Obsession*, 1965   Me, 1952

rge Marquand, Roger Vadim, Princess Ercolani, David Niven's son, Mrs Niven, Peter Viertel and
fe Deborah Kerr, David Niven and me, Klosters, 1958

Edmond and I using some help, with *femme fatale*, St Tropez, 1968

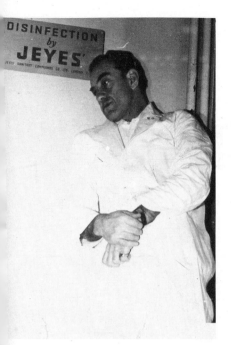

Earls Court Exhibition Centre loos, 1966

th Noël Coward

Mother aged seventy, 1962

Father in Hong Kong, 1966

Me and my dog, 1987

room in the Monceau, looking after Mama.

She woke me early one morning to announce that Marie, her darling Marie, was about to leave Shanghai for Paris to join her. Marie had been so loyal and brave and jaunty under the Japanese that father had once said in one of his dramatic moments, 'We must build a monument to this woman.'

To this Marie had replied, 'I razer 'ave ze cash.'

Marie's arrival made up for the loss of Mother's millions. Marie took over, cancelling clothes Mother had ordered, screaming at Mother saying, 'I don't want to be there when you're crying that you have no money left. And where do you go to wear evening dresses of white silk crêpe with embroidered beads, for God's sake?'

In fact, Marie and I must have saved a lot by stopping Mother spending.

As Mother knew few people and had no social life, was neither an avid reader nor a passionate concert-goer, the only time she ever saw anybody was when we went out to lunch and here I'd have to watch her.

We'd enter some chic place like the Plaza Athenée and be bowed into the dining-room where the wine waiter would appear.

'Un petit apéritif?'

'We'd shake our heads. The *maitre d'* would then appear extolling the magic of pheasant or salmon.

'No fresh water fish and no game.'

'A small plate of oysters?'

'We never eat shell fish.'

'*Foie gras?*'

'Those poor geese with those brutes shoving things down their throats.'

'I'll have *oeufs perigord aux truffes*,' Mother might say.

'When you're better, Mother, you *know* what the doctor said.'

'I *am* better.'

'What about some fresh beans?' the *maitre d'* suggested.

I'd seen them on the menu. They cost almost what Mother was paying for her hotel room.

'Beans, beans!' I cried. 'What did they tell you at the hospital?'

'They said nothing about beans.'

In the end it was an *entrecôte* with salad inclusive and no dessert. Instead I'd slip her a chocolate under the table.

'You don't need those things, Mother. You just want to go out and see people. Go without beans!'

123

'I never thought I'd live to see the day that I couldn't afford a bean!' Mother said, a tear dropping from one eye.

News now reached us in Paris that Toe's enterprise with the Gertzs had collapsed. They had escaped to Brazil, leaving Toe to carry the baby. At his trial Tony heard the judge say, 'You allowed yourself to be used by ruthless swindlers and you turned a blind eye to what was going on.'

Toe was sentenced to eighteen months in jail.

'Beastly Ashkenazis,' said Mama, blaming the Gertzs instead of Toe.

Toe served half his sentence, wrote a book about his case and eventually came out of it as a hero and prison reformer.

13

There was little I wanted to do in Paris so I returned to my Marina and Michel in Cannes. I'd hardly arrived before a call came from Charles Martin, Pamela's husband, who was with her in Italy.

Pamela had tried to commit suicide. The line was bad and I couldn't understand much.

'Could I put them up, till she got better?'

'Of course I could.'

I nursed Pamela slowly back to health while Charles made arrangements to sell a boat he had in Cannes harbour. No sooner was Pamela better than they began to quarrel and decided to split up. For fear of Charles selling the boat and not giving her her half, Pamela went and lived on it, but Charles had already sold the motor or pawned it. I was glad to see her go, not because she was a nuisance, she wasn't – she'd just lie in bed all day reading. I was glad because ever since she'd arrived there'd been a terrible smell in her room and although I washed the place a couple of times the stink had persisted. It was only after she'd settled in her boat that I discovered parcels of doodies wrapped up in newspaper in her cupboard.

I used to visit her on her boat where she'd hold court before groups of sailors from the US Seventh Fleet. The fact that she lay in yet another dirty kimono dabbing herself with yet another old pair of underpants soaked by water from a the leak in the ceiling, didn't stop her gathering crowds. When some sailor started getting fresh, Pamela would recite him a poem or something of Dostoevsky's and say, 'Compassion is all,' and return to what she was reading or the eye she was dabbing.

Because the boat had no engine, Pamela had no light or hot water so she read by candle-light, knocking the candle over, falling down and bruising herself in the dark..

There were periods when she dressed up, and once got a job in a bar called the 'Trois Cloches' where she was the big attraction with her wild red hair, long legs, high heels, her class and her madness.

After the bar closed she might be seen chasing some black sailors and when they got fresh she'd stand on ceremony and say, 'You make me nostalgic for Tanganyika, our house in the hills, the pink flamingos on the lake, my German stepmother who tried to kill me, the beautiful servant who used to kiss my feet.'

It might end in a fight or the boys offering money and Pamela furiously refusing it and then begging for a packet of cigarettes instead. She resembled Blanche Dubois in *A Streetcar Named Desire*, but she was better educated.

At one point I hadn't seen or heard from her for a week so I called. There were a few homeless kids sleeping on the boat. They told me Pamela had been found unconscious in the street, her passport said she had been born in Brighton and the British Consul had had her sent there. Later a letter came from her in the home where she had been placed. With the letter was a beautiful painting of flowers which she had done with blood, ink, lipstick and anything else lying around.

'Mise', the Marquise du Crozet, now returned to live in her villa in Cannes so we had to leave. Marina took the one remaining dog with her. Michel was already in a home and I went to London to find a cure for my worms.

On a bus there, I found myself sitting next to someone who tapped me on the shoulder, 'Hello George.'

I had no idea who it was and didn't want to repeat what happened once before when I replied, 'Can't remember your name. Have we been to bed together?' 'No, I'm your postman,' had been the reply.

Maurice Doss was not the postman. He was an ex-lover from Cairo who had reproached me for being a 'oncer'.

'It's Holy Year and I'm on my way to Rome,' he said.

Rome! Italy, where Enrica came from. I longed to go. He interrupted my reveries, 'I have an extra ticket. Will you be my guest?'

Of course I'd be his guest. He'd booked at the Boston Hotel off the Via Veneto and, as soon as we arrived, Maurice got undressed and lay on the bed. I took a shower, put on new nylon underpants and started to shave. Suddenly, 'Yoorr bortom it like a bahloon,' said Maurice in that terrible accent of his.

126

That was the end of the affair. I returned the fare and found a *pension* behind Via Veneto.

Rome was a revelation. The stones and the people. Beautiful women in strapless diaphanous gowns wafted down the Via Veneto, handsome studs, sporting older women on one arm and winking at others, ambled along all evening. Famous film people, Maseratis, Ferraris and Lamborghinis filled the area and ravishing adventures were there for the seeker. This is where I would live. But now for Capri, before summer was over.

I lived there in a room without light or water in the middle of an orchard down by the port – which didn't stop me making vast social progress. I met them all, the Viscontis Arrivabenes, Noël Coward, the Bismarcks, everyone! The most amusing was a Hungarian beautician called 'Eve of Rome' who catered to the smart set on the island. In a moment of indiscretion I told her about an adventure in London that she immediately repeated and which gave me the notoriety I always seek.

I'd picked up in Hyde Park a strong silent bikey – long before Marlon Brando had made them famous. A friend had lent me a ground-floor garden-flat and I invited him home. My right leg was in a splint after an operation and I couldn't bend it. When I was seated on the bike we were unable to turn right because of the angle that would have bent my stiff leg so we had to make a huge entire left circle to get round to the right. At last we got home.

'I'm bringing the bike off the street,' he said, pushing it in through the garden gate. Then he said, 'I'm bringing it right into the flat.' That was forcible penetration. Nor did he do it discreetly. 'Vroom, vroom, vroom,' went the great machine in the garden, in the house and into my head.

Bikey how pinioned me down on the floor, all his leather gear still on. He buried his head in my neck repeating, threateningly, 'The motor bike, the motor bike, the motor bike.'

I got away only to have him lock my head in his arm and continue to mutter, 'The motor bike, the motor bike, the motor bike.'

As I was coming off, Mr Harley Davidson revved up his motor bike, motor bike, motor bike, to two hundred miles an hour and I shot my bolt.

For the next few weeks in Capri, groups of people would say, 'Vroom, vroom, vroom,' as I passed by.

I returned to Rome and would have stayed there for ever had Mother not bribed me back to Paris by selling some ear-rings and buying a car. When I went skiing in Klosters that year, I had an accident dislocating my right shoulder when I stuck a ski-pole into the ground, and on the drive home to Paris, I leaned over to wind up the far window and dislocated my left shoulder as well. When I arrived in Paris I blamed Mother and reproached her for not having breathed on me when I was born.

'Horses breathe on their foals and everything comes together. You forgot, and look at me now.'

Mother asked Father to pay for the operation.

'Do whatever is necessary for George,' he answered.

Mother woke me up ecstatic, 'This is your chance. You can have everything done, Daddy will pay.'

I was due in hospital the following morning for the operation that was taking place in the evening. Hardly had I woken up than there was a knock on the door: Mother had sent the maid with a note telling me she was waiting for an apology, after her violent behaviour during a nasty quarrel.

I ignored it and left for the hospital. That afternoon they gave me a sedative and before I fell asleep another note arrived from Mother demanding my signature for the sale of the car.

That evening, after the operation, I was lying in my bed unable to open my eyes. I thought I heard Mother's voice. I forced my eyes open and saw blurred in the far corner of the room a nurse and Mother.

'Get that bloody Mother of mine out of here.' I picked up a glass and hurled it at her.

To think this woman I had protected, fought Father over, driven around, washed, dressed and loved, should turn on me and do me out of the joy of a car!

Later I did sign. I also refused to see her, left Paris and had no contact with her for over a year.

Then one October afternoon, I saw her. The sun was shining thinly and Mother was ambling up towards the Monceau. She looked old, bent and sad. It would not be enough to ignore her. I ran round the block so that I would be able to walk straight into her and say something cruel as I passed. She was now but fifty yards away, walking slowly and watching her steps. I almost walked into her.

'George,' she exclaimed, joy and fear in her voice.

'You have no George, spiteful bitch. I don't want to see you again.'

128

Eventually, an old lady who knew us both and had lost her son in the war spoke with me.

'You can still have your mother and she her son. Mine is dead.'

She arranged a meeting between us. For an hour over dinner. I crucified her. I knew how lonely she had been but I wanted her to realize she had behaved rottenly.

'Do you understand?' I said at one point. 'Do you?'

She nodded listlessly. Nothing had sunk in.

Mother had always dreamed Marie would stay with her for ever. They had a game going, teasing each other, particularly about Marie not finding a husband, although she had a pretty face in an old-fashioned way and had often said to Mother, 'Madame, I'm going to get married.'

'Get married,' Mother laughed. 'Who would marry you with your crumpled lips?'

Yet Mother would love to have been responsible for getting Marie married. There had been various concierges in luxury hotels earning as much as Father sent Mother who might have married her.

'One was very in love with me,' Marie used to say and Mother answered what she always answered. 'Yes, but that one was married.'

The discussions would always end with, 'Anyway, you can't marry anyone else – you're married to me.'

That spring in Paris, Marie told Mother she wanted to have a serious talk with her.

'Only, Madame must lie down.'

'Why should I lie down?'

'Because Madame will fall down when I tell her.'

No sooner was Mother lying down than Marie announced, 'I'm getting married.'

'Shut up and don't waste my time,' shouted Mother, getting up angrily.

Marie rushed up and forced her back into her chair. 'I'm getting married,' she repeated.

'No one, repeat, no one will marry you, and if you can name one, name him.'

'Phillip Sopher! He wants to marry me.'

'He's ten years younger than you are and he's Jewish. And he's still in Shanghai.'

'He doesn't care. I am eleven years older and you have made me more Jewish than Phillip.'

Phillip Sopher was a boring lump who went scarlet before speaking and despite being perfectly intelligent was still a lump.

'Phillip is arriving from Shanghai in a few months. I will stay with you until then,' said Marie finally.

The fact that her lady's maid was about to marry Phillip who had two childless millionaire uncles and would one day be far richer than Mother didn't worry her at all. She went on shouting at Marie and Marie went on shouting back, and nothing changed except that Mother chose Marie's engagement ring. Our excitement was interrupted when I found I would have to have an operation, this time on my rectum.

The laboratory employee who had taken tests said with bated breath, 'Your surgeon sees the most elegant rectum in Paris,' all without a trace of a smile.

The evening before the operation as I was walking home I picked up a man and took him home. Half way through our evening the man said, 'I shall take great care of you tomorrow.'

I told him I'd be in hospital having an operation.

'I know,' he replied. 'I'm operating on you.'

After the operation, for what seemed like days and days, I lay on Mother's couch sweating and unable to move, a solid stool stuck in my anus. I sweated and had my legs up in the air, a towel like a tent covering me. Mother sitting at her dressing-table painting her face suddenly let out a yell and began banging a foot on the floor.

'Darling! Marie! Where's Marie, George? Come at once!'

She hobbled over to where I was lying.

'Sit up. Massage my foot. It's gone to sleep.'

At that moment Marie walked in. 'Marie, what can one do with mothers?'

'Love them,' she replied with a shrug.

Next time Mother had trouble with her foot, it was to be more serious. She'd noticed a growth on her little toe causing her to limp. Soon she was only able to wear three of a hundred pairs of shoes.

'I can't ask Father to buy another hundred pairs of shoes. An operation would cost half and Father'd pay.'

France Dimanche, the terrible weekly paper that told us what school of eroticism had taught the Duchess of Windsor to seduce the Duke, had an article about a Dr Valais who'd just operated on the Queen of Italy's toe. In a way Mother felt that through Dr Valais she could somehow become connected to the Queen of Italy. So she arranged it. Her conversation over the next weeks was only Umberto and Marie José and the House of Savoy. She was angry when I told her Umberto liked men.

'Nonsense. He's the son of King Victor Emmanuel. I was in Rome at the Church of the Jesu, when . . .' Mother was in heaven.

They operated on Mother's toe early one morning and she was brought home on a stretcher the same evening. Time passed. She started to hobble about but something was wrong. She couldn't walk. Valais came to see her.

'I cut under the little toe, and it retreated. Now the big toe is pressing against your shoe. It's only a tiny job. Leave it to me.'

Back went Mama. Big toe retreated and she returned home two weeks later. She still couldn't walk.

Back came Valais.

'Ah,' he said. 'Now the middle toes are pressing. It's only a tiny job.'

By the time she'd gone back and forth again and again, her foot had been deboned like a Peking duck and she still couldn't walk. It took a considerable time and further treatment before she could walk again.

In Zermatt the following year, I was skiing with a Parisian whose wife was having trouble with her toes.

'Hope you didn't consult Dr Valais,' I joked.

'We did just that. I took my wife to see him. As I opened the door the secretary said, "C'est pour une intervention ou une re-intervention?" [For an operation or a *re*operation?] I left.'

From Hong Kong Uncle Ronnie now wrote he wanted Mother to take Yvonne Sou Pig for a trip to Spain and the South of France. Mother brought Ronnie up as a child and Ronnie was always spoiling her with presents. Mother was loving and kind to Yvonne, which speaks well for Mother because Yvonne was neither rich, aristocratic nor titled, but she had taken her over as her child.

Only once did they quarrel. It was when Yvonne needed a pair of glasses. Mother took her to fashionable Myrovitz who tested her eyes and told her to return for her glasses on the following day. When Yvonne put on the new glasses she said she couldn't see.

'They make mistake,' she said.

'They never make mistakes,' Mother snapped.

131

'I can't see,' insisted Yvonne.

'Of course you can.'

'Mimi,' said Yvonne, walking defiantly up to Mother. 'Are you my sister-in-law or Myrovitz's?'

The glasses belonged to another client.

We drove with Yvonne to the South of France and showed her the sights. At Eze Village, Mother pointed out the ruins of a castle on the hill.

'Hong Kong better, every year paint white,' replied Yvonne.

We drove down to Malaga and stayed a week at Marbella's newly opened Club Hotel owned by the Hohenlohes. It cost a pound a day, all meals included, and there wasn't a soul on the beach.

We drove in and out of Portugal, rested for a week at the Hotel Real in Santander where it cost us two pounds a night inclusive of all meals. Mother ate and ate and ate and ate.

'Have you gone mad, Mother?'

'It's paid for,' she replied.

By the time we left she weighed a ton and could hardly get through the door.

Eventually, Yvonne went back to Hong Kong and I drove Mother down to Florence. I made her visit the galleries and palaces and read books on the Medicis. I knew more about art than Mama but we were both fooled when we admired a painting labelled 'Catal'.

'I've never seen his work,' said Mama.

'Nor have I, Mother.'

It was an abbreviation for the word 'Catalogue'.

We landed up at the Excelsior in Rome, where the staff all fell for her. Italy and Spain were about the last countries where women still had personal ladies' maids who travelled with them, whereas in Switzerland or Sweden women, far richer than Mama, could be seen hacking away at blocks of ice on their front-door steps. In England, the rich shivered without central heating in their multi-million-pound estates and drank a ghastly syrup called Camp Coffee.

The Excelsior and Rome were to transform Mama's life. Every night there were crowds of colourful people outside in the Via Veneto that walked past the cafés, and inside the smart set would hang about the Excelsior bar. The public loved Mother and they'd stop her in the streets saying, ' Che bella signora' or 'Che bel capello'.

She had her special seat in the lounge of the hotel next to the Contessa 'this' and the Marchesa 'that' and she was absolutely happy.

132

I took her to the opera to see the audience rather than *Renata Tebaldi* but when friends introduced us to Mario del Monaco, we returned. I spoilt one of Mother's operatic evenings when in the middle of the foyer I lifted my trousers saying, 'Look no socks.'

'Must you shame me?' wailed Mama. 'Here in the smartest place in Rome?'

'You hadn't even noticed,' I told her.

'I have now and you've spoilt my evening.'

She must have simmered over it all night because the next day she exploded while sitting at Café Doney's with me. I'd been trying with my right hand to extricate the lump of sugar from its wrapping . . . throwing sugar paper and all into the coffee. Mother shot out of her chair, shouting at me,

'One hand. One hand. Always one hand.'

My life was that of a mad bohemian at that period. In Paris I'd stay at the grand Royal Monceau. In Klosters, skiing, it would be in some wretched underground hole. In Rome, with Mother preening away at the Excelsior, I'd be slumming in any down-and-out back room, but nothing prevented me being social. In Klosters I'd met an aristocrat called the Princess Palavicini Rospigliosi who lived in the finest inhabited palace in Rome after the Colonna Palace. On my return from the mountains, I rang her and she immediately invited me to lunch. I walked through salon after salon of marble tables, Boticellis and Donatellos, eventually arriving at her private quarters. There were several guests and every one was discussing Nini Palavicini's coming-out ball for her daughter, to which she now invited me. It was rather a nasty lunch because the Princess was making fun of the poverty of many of her noble friends, wondering how they would pay their fare from Austria and Germany and hire a tailcoat as well.

She then pulled out a letter which she read aloud.

'Noble lady,
My beautiful daughter is of the same age as yours. Don't you think having her next to your lovely girl would add a tone to your ball?'

When I got home, I wrote her a thank-you letter for having invited me and added that I had a stunning chauffeur. Might I bring him to add even more tone to her ball?

I never got the invitation. Mother was heart-broken and only came to life again when she heard half the guests had been disinvited. Her architect had told her the floors of her palace would have collapsed if all the people she'd asked had stood in the ballroom together.

14

Ever since the heaven-sent refusal by the Canadians to allow me in, I'd become an independent young man with a hundred and fifty dollars a month to spend. I decided to visit Venice. I had no idea what hotels cost, but I'd heard so much about the Danieli that I automatically took a boat straight from the station to this famous hotel. I *had* to see the ghost of Jane San Faustino going up in that lift alone.

Tourist travel after the war hadn't got underway, the summer sun had gone and Venice was empty. I got a room at the Danieli for fifteen hundred lira a night without bath (two and a half dollars). I couldn't believe I was really there, nor could I believe that the first woman I saw entering the hotel as I walked into the Piazza was Maria Callas.

At the end of the Piazza were two men, one tall and elegant, the other short and stocky with long curly hair all over his head – all very Renaissance. I sauntered up to them and in my best Italian said, 'May I talk to you? I am alone.'

They were surprised. The young tough looked at me provocatively. The older one replied, 'I speak English. Where are you from?'

I said I had been born in Shanghai, which immediately interested him. A moment later he said, 'Come with me. We will leave this young gigolo.'

I looked hard at this tall and exquisitely dressed man in his white-silk suit. Was he perhaps another kind of gigolo, a penniless prince looking for a Babara Hutton and would the evening end by my lending him a pound or two?

He was so fascinated with my Chinese background and my mention of Chinese food that he insisted on accompanying me back to the hotel, so I gave in and went to bed with him but he had no bite and I couldn't

135

get it up. So we gave it up. He was informative about Venice and it was not a boring evening. Just as he was about to leave he said, 'Please order me a motor-boat and lend me some money. He promised to return me my ten dollars but failed to turn up at our meeting on the Bridge of Sighs the next day.

The following evening there was a knock on my door. A sinister looking man appeared with a parcel.

'From Signor Wild,' he said.

I tore it open. No ten dollars. Instead I found a robe of heavy woven, white silk. I threw off my clothes, draped it around me and pirouetted round the room, ending before the mirror.

'Mirror, mirror tell me true
Am I not a lovely Jew?'

Before mirror replied, phone rang.

'I'm Renato Wild. Please forgive me and dine with me tonight at Harry's Bar, eight o'clock.'

I accepted. I wanted my ten bucks. I sat alone in a corner waiting for him at Harry's Bar.

Wonderful food was being waltzed round the room, hot fried shrimp sandwiches, multi-coloured ice-creams. I was starving and occupying a table and it was already half-past nine. I got up to leave and as I did so there was a hush in the bar. It was Renato coming into Harry's. He must have been six foot five. Following him was the man who'd brought me my robe.

'I am late,' he said.

'I am hungry,' I replied.

He took no more notice of me, just held out a hand to the man following him who now handed him a crocodile box. Out of it he drew a gold cigarette box with black stripes.

'This is a cigarette case. I stick strips of black paper along the parts when the box folds. As you will see it folds in ten places. As you bend it a cigarette drops out.'

'Even if you don't put one in?'

He didn't laugh, but said, 'I'm Swiss.' He continued, 'Germans can't say the word "finger". They pronounce it like "swinger". Pause. 'And this,' he turned to the sinister man, 'is Sabbatino.'

'How do you do Saturdino.'

'Sabbatino.'

136

'The train leaves in an hour,' said Sabbatino.

'I terribly hungry.'

'We are going to my villa in Como. I have reserved you a wagon-lit.'

'I'll run home and get some clothes.'

'Don't. We'll buy what you need.'

We ate a hearty dinner after which Renato told Sabbatino he was ready to leave for the train.

'The train left an hour and a half ago.'

'So? We'll go tomorrow night.'

We caught the train the following evening. I didn't really like Renato or Sabbatino or the crocodile case but when we got to Milan and the chauffeur ushered us into the Bentley, I thought, 'I'll get back my ten bucks.'

We didn't go straight to his villa. We went to an antique dealer's, where, for four hours, I was made to sit through a pageant of Persian gowns, Sassanian bowls, Coromandel screens, and lastly, a mangy feather-coat from Pago Pago Island, where, Renato explained, feathers were used as local currency.

At last we left, sped down the Autostrada and arrived at Como. From there we drove on a narrow winding road above the lake with hooting buses and hairpin bends. At last we came to an imposing gate where the chauffeur hooted and the gates opened.

We continued downhill for a mile under an umbrella of thick foliage, on a white pebble path, arriving at a clearing at the level of the lake. There lay a vast nineteenth-century mansion in all its gloomy splendour. On the entrance steps stood seven servants, looking like a group of lunatics who might one day up and kill their Lord and Master.

At eight sharp, the gong went for dinner. Nobody appeared. Sabbatino paced up and down, smouldering.

Meanwhile, snooping around the house, I counted five pianos, eleven Florentine marble tables, countless Greek heads, Chinese carpets and a strange object, like a fragment of an old chariot.

Sabbatino explained it was a Roman bed, which I found hard to believe, the bed having neither spring nor mattress. I then returned to my room till ten when the gong sounded again.

We were seven at dinner, Renato's boy-friend, his girl-friend, his doctor, the doctor's wife (who wrote letters nightly to Renato complaining about her husband's frigidity), and the doctor's daughter, 'Din din', short for Geraldine, a precocious child who told me everyone at the table was on Renato's payroll and that they were a bunch of

'Putane' whores. The servants were worse, and she hoped they'd kill Renato, whom she loathed.

After dinner, we retired to the study where Renato awaited us, dressed in a brocade tent. He made us look through his latest acquisition, an X-ray machine that measured the density of diamonds, rubies, sapphires, emeralds. By the time we reached amethysts, citrines and tourmalines, the room was empty and I'd fallen asleep!

In the early hours of the morning, Renato walked into my room.

'I've swallowed my tooth,' he announced.

'Mashed potatoes,' I mumbled.

He rang for Sabbatino who woke the cook to prepare him a potato purée.

'Should I take a laxative and shit through a sieve?' he asked.

'Essential,' I replied.

At eight a.m. a weary Renato woke me, saying in a deep voice that the tooth wasn't in the sieve.

At nine a.m. he telephoned his dentist in Switzerland.

At eleven, he came to my room holding the tooth in his hand.

'It was on the mantelpiece,' he said without a smile.

Eventually, we returned to Venice, where Renato retired to his hotel room, telling me I could use his cabana at the Lido and put my lunches on his account.

The cabana was impossible to miss for it was entirely draped in Bokhara shawls. As I approached, Leonor Fini was lying on the bed like a sphinx. I mumbled some words of introduction. She didn't reply. Suddenly, taking my chin in her hand, she turned my head this way and that, and said, 'Have your nose fixed,' and fell back on her bed. I asked her what she thought the operation might cost.

'Renato will pay,' she replied.

Gathering up her things, she left, only to return a second later and stuff into her beach-bag one of Renato's Bokhara shawls.

The following year I asked Renato if I could bring Mama and her maid plus Rex Harrisons's wife, Collette, who was a star in Klosters where I ski'd. Mother was jealous of Collette and furious when I slept the night in her room . . . purely to save money ('I improve your reputation and your Mother complains,' snapped Collette).

Renato was charmed with Mama and before she'd even washed he'd dragged her to his special machine and put her jewels into it. I couldn't understand how a man with so many millions could be impressed by Mother's diamond. It was famous in our circle, but unless you have a thirty-carat, perfect, blue-white stone, you may be able to name-drop, but not diamond-drop. So she name-dropped. 'Aly Khan! Randolph Churchill! Rubirosa! Lord Fitzwilliam!' Collette watched with disdain. When she couldn't stand it any longer, she whispered to me, 'Those fools can't stop talking about people they've never met. I've been to bed with all of them.'

On another occasion Genet was living there until such time as he could succeed in engineering the escape of one of his lovers from a military prison in Algeria. Genet looked like a misshapen embryo but his piercing, accusatory blue eyes and his passion, often full of humour, blotted out the rest. He was happy to find someone other than Wild to talk French to and we became thick as thieves. He offered to do a Rorschach test on me. I spent a long time thinking about the designs before me. I gave him some answers thinking he might have discovered in me a very extraordinary creature but all he said was, 'You get tired very easily.'

I didn't, however, disappoint him when I told him about an adventure I had some nights later. I'd made love with a workman in the town of Como. At a certain moment after we'd both come, I wanted him to do something unusual. He couldn't though he tried and tried. I had to be in the mood for it and he had to be able. It can happen. It does happen but it's rare and often more due to circumstances than prowess or virility. It's also shocking.

'Non posso. Non posso,' he replied. 'I can't, I can't.'

At which point we both fell asleep. I don't know how long we were asleep but I was awakened by my mate who was suddenly able to do what I'd wanted him to do.

'Posso,' he said with a long sigh.

From that moment on Genet called me 'Posso'.

15

Uncle Reggie now suggested Mother and I come and stay in his huge house in Hampstead. We always paid, which annoyed Mother who had done so much for him over the years. I was on Reggie's side, not because he was right, but because it was costing Mother a fifth of her hotel in Paris.

'Of course it's cheaper. It would be cheaper still in the Congo but I don't want to be here in the first place,' she said, although she loved arguing with Reggie.

Just before the war he had married Betty, a beautiful, tall Jewish girl from a modest family. He took her out to Shanghai to show her off. When they returned, Reggie brought back a Chinese servant. 'Boy' was to run the house, cook and do the shopping. Poor Betty used to have to borrow the odd shilling or two from 'Boy' to buy herself cigarettes. As time went on, Betty found herself doing more and more housework while Boy was let out to different houses to save Reggie paying his wages. Betty tried to escape from the dullness of her life through music, painting and literature, but Reggie's friends made fun of her.

'I've given her everything. A fine house, two fine children, servants. I've been a good father and a good husband,' said Reggie.

'There are other things in life, Reggie.'

'Don't you worry about that. I'm a good bang, if that's what you mean.'

'He's a good bang all right,' Betty agreed, 'but I don't want his bang. I'd like some love.'

I felt sorry for Betty and helped her where I could. First of all I implored her to speak more naturally. She had adopted a ridiculous ladidah accent that made people laugh.

'I'm doing my best. You hardly want me to speak the way my family does.'

One summer Reggie took the whole family to Toe's villa in Cannes. Everything went wrong, ending with the daughter getting her hand stung by a Portuguese man-of-war.

Reggie took her pain with much stoicism and promised to let her off potting and planting when they all got home.

'And Hebrew lessons?' bargained the child.

In Cannes, Betty had started flirting around. She neither cared nor asked whether Reggie had noticed.

'You see,' she told me, 'I can only stand Reggie if I have someone else in my life.' Then she continued mischievously, 'But he has been a good husband and a good father. Anyway, don't be sorry for him, he's having it off with Mrs Britt, a sharp-nosed twig of a woman who lives round the corner with her dogs.' She took my hand and dragged me to her bedroom window. 'See the greenhouse. In there, amongst the orchids!'

'What does she look like?'

'A stalagmite. Have you ever made love with a stalagmite?'

One day Betty met a tall dark Chilean. He had no money but he was musical, artistic and beautiful. She left the 'security' of Reggie's vast house and went to live with her lover.

'How could Betty do such a thing – leaving me with this house and the children on my hands? How could she betray me?'

'You also betrayed her, Reggie.'

'I never, I never . . .'

'What about the twig you've been screwing in the greenhouse?'

Caught red-handed, he remained silent. Then blurted out, 'We're getting married.'

He thought it would make his screw more kosher.

'I hear she isn't a beauty but her dogs don't care what she looks like.'

Mother was consulted. She preferred Reggie marry the other woman who wanted Reggie – a huge monolithic block with a very pretty face and Jewish. Mrs Britt was Scottish and rich and lived only fifty yards away so Mrs Britt won and married him.

They drove to Capri for their honeymoon and returned without having argued once until . . . It was pouring with rain and when Reggie dropped Mrs Britt at her front door her dogs leapt all over them both, following them into the house and covering everything with mud. Reggie now had second thoughts about the marriage. He went to the loo and when he grabbed the roll of paper he had third thoughts. Mrs

Britt used a paper called 'Bronco', transparent stuff you had to rub against itself with both hands to make it soft.

They quarrelled. Neither of them visited the other's house again and to her great joy they got divorced and he married the monolith.

I suggested Reggie change the house round a little for the new wife and called in Ricki, the talented beautiful wife of John Huston. Reggie received her sweetly and offered to show her his orchid collection, finishing the tour of the greenhouse with, 'Please choose one for yourself.'

Ricki pointed at a flower.

'I can't give you that one,' apologized Reggie.

'What about this one?

'I'm afraid I can't let you have that one either.'

'Well, why don't you choose the one you'd like me to have.'

Reggie leaned over and chose an orchid with a nasty black stain on it.

'You're not giving my friend that orchid, Reggie. It's been fucked.'

The flower had in fact been pollinated, resulting in the stain. After that Ricki spent a while advising us about the house.

'Discard that rug. Take off those lace protectors from the arm-chairs. Paint the walls elephant-grey. Dye the curtains moss green so the old coral upholstery doesn't look shabby . . .'

At each suggestion, Reggie replied that one of his previous wives or girl-friends had wanted it that way.

'And they all abandoned you, didn't they, Reggie?' I reminded him.

I chose a day when he was stuck in the office. I tore down the curtains, sent them off to be dyed and began painting the walls grey. Reggie and the monolith arrived home late that afternoon and threw a fit.

'You shouldn't give your Uncle aggwavation,' she lisped.

'When you're that size you either pronounce things right or not talk at all. Aggwavation,' I continued, 'is the worsening of a situation. Nothing could be worse than this house and your wubbish.'

She burst into tears and told Weggie I'd been wude to her.

'I can't stand her, Weggie, and nor can anyone else.'

'It's not twoo,' he replied, now muddled and imitating me imitating her.

'All our fwiends like her.'

'Name one,' I replied.

Father was due in London any day now. I hadn't seen him for thirteen years and I was apprehensive. Nevertheless things might have changed. Perhaps the dark days were over. He'd never stopped my allowance. He'd paid for my operations and had now offered me a new wardrobe. I sat at home pulling out old letters and reading them. Amongst them I found one from him.

' . . . you boys had everything money could buy. The best schools, hotels, teachers, expensive holidays, Rolls-Royces, the best country houses. People would wonder, "who are these princes?".'

I threw down the letter in disgust. Perhaps I shouldn't see him at all. I did hate him and didn't forgive him anything. I also justified my idleness by saying it was aimed at him to make him pay for his sins. At other moments I longed for him to put his arms round me and say, 'Forgive me. I've been cruel, I want your love.'

I'd go waffling along conjuring up scene after scene, each of which would end more happily than the last, and then I'd be jerked back into reality.

Father arrived and took a room in Grosvenor House. I was at Uncle Reggie's. It was a warm May morning when I took the bus to the hotel. As I entered his room he jumped up theatrically and embraced me, repeating, 'My son, my son!'

His room was just like all his rooms anywhere. Already there seemed to be a smell of Eau de Cologne 4711 which I abhorred, and also some other indefinable musty odour giving one the impression he had been there weeks. Father now took my head in his hands and carefully rubbed something away from my eyelid. I'm sure there was nothing there to rub off, but it made me uncomfortable. It was one of his usual ploys to make people feel ill at ease. I dearly wanted to make a success of this meeting but in my heart I knew nothing had changed or ever would change. How could anything change for a man who had never said he was sorry or wrong?

'Father,' I said, 'it's been thirteen long years. That's half my life. Let's go for a walk in the park and chatter.'

'If you have anything to say, you can say it now,' he replied flatly. Sensing I was outraged – I was going to walk out of the door – he gave me one of his crocodile smiles, adding, 'What a good idea, but I can't walk far with my back.'

Father was not interested in anything I started to say but he himself was interesting, telling me about life in Shanghai and especially dealing with money matters. He'd loaned some Spanish priests a huge sum of

143

money in 1947, against some land they owned. After Mao walked in they claimed they no longer could return the money. When Father threatened to go to the law, they inferred it would embarrass him if the papers printed that he had charged the Spanish Fathers six per cent per month. Luckily Father was able to prove that those same Fathers had lent that money to another lot of priests at seven per cent per month. At the end of that period Father was lending his secretary money at ten per cent per day, and they both made money on it.

Father had a meeting with Cardinal Spellman in the States resulting in an agreement in which the Catholic Church agreed to restore the money to Father minus interest.

After explaining the story, Father seemed tired and wanted to go back to the hotel. Nothing had been settled between us but we were on speaking terms. A few days later he asked me to lunch, the other guests being a dull woman and her child. I was particularly careful not to take over the conversation, but at one point the woman asked me for some information which I gave her. No sooner had I started than Father cut in sharply, 'That's enough now. You're doing all the talking as usual.'

It was meant to sound quite friendly, but I felt the jealousy and anger of Ellis Hayim.

'I am Ellis. I am God. I am One.'

'If you don't wish me to open my mouth, why have me to lunch?' I replied.

'Of course, of course. Please go on, son, what were you saying?'

'It is not important enough to say twice. Excuse me I must go now.'

I ran out of Grosvenor House and to my shame started to weep. What was the matter with me? How could I go through war and pain and operations like a man, and yet fall apart after ten minutes with my father? Tears of shame and anger poured out. Here I was at an age when most young people were fully independent and I was weeping in Park Lane over my nasty father.

16

The years 1956 to 1962 mostly followed a pattern: Rome in summer and skiing in winter, a trip or two to London and Paris. However rich and princely Italians are, they all long for Paris. On one of these trips Mother's young maid was in a crash and had to leave. Mother took a fading beauty queen of forty, a moving, poignant Russian, who had spent the last twelve years of her life in a convent. She'd only been with us three weeks when mother's sister was taken ill in Canada and begged Mother to come and take care of her. The Russian, hearing Mother might leave Paris, became desperate. Mother felt so sorry for her that she arranged for her to stay on in a maid's room like mine at the Monceau, after the woman asked for a loan.

'I have to buy some books on the Kabala,' she said.

When she left, Mother whispered to me, 'Isn't it Jewish?'

'It's got to do with numbers, that's all I know.'

After she had bought the books, she seemed quieter. Next she asked Mother if she could borrow a gold chain. Mother, whom I have often seen insensitive, was particularly kind to her, treating her more as a daughter, perhaps wanting to believe she was even a Russian princess.

On this particular day Mother and I had been out to lunch. When we got back, Mother put her room key into her door: the lock opened but the door remained bolted from the inside.

'Something's happened,' Mother said, worried. Then, after a minute she added 'The chain! The chain I lent her! She put it back on my dressing-table. I noticed it before lunch.'

'Sit there, Mother!' I pushed her on to the settee at the end of the corridor. 'I'm going down to reception.'

When I got there I said off the top of my head, 'My mother's maid's

145

killed herself in the bath. She locked the door and we can't get in.'

'What makes you think precisely that?' the man behind the desk asked amused.

I realized I was being hysterical, yet I had an image in my mind of the woman, face downwards and fully dressed, in the second bathroom. He accompanied me back to the suite, twiddled about with the master-key and finally called the police.

Shortly, four burly firemen in light-blue trousers and leather jackets carrying axes appeared. Then they started breaking down the door.

'Ça y est! That's it!' cried one after a great whack at the door with his axe.

They all ran in. I ran straight to the bathroom. The poor girl lay there exactly as I had seen it. They fished her out of the tub and laid her on her back on the carpet.

'Belle fille,' one said.

'Beaux yeux,' said the other.

Mother was shattered.

'What should I have done for her?' she asked.

'I've never known you sweeter to anyone than to that poor creature. Don't take any blame now.'

Shortly afterwards, I learned that Bertie Gilou, who had stayed with me in London in 1940 in my little flat, had had an altercation with a man in a car. The man had jumped out, punched Bertie, who fell splitting his head on the pavement and died. We were glad to get back to Rome.

It was October, and the sun still shone warmly on the beach at Ostia where I went to spend an afternoon. I heard some one cry out my name.

'Giorgio. Giorgio. Where have you been?'

It was the Countess Tripcovic with the Princess Ruspoli.

'I've been in Paris.'

'Che meraviglia. Che bello,' they hummed back in unison.

'Not this time,' I said and told them what had happened.

'Si vede, che Dio ha abandonato la gente per bene,' said the Ruspoli. (Evidently God dropped the upper classes.)

'Ma non cara,' replied the Tripkovic, 'siamo noi chi abbiamo abandonnato lui.' (We dropped *him*.)

I was back skiing in Klosters, it was February, cold, dry and sunny. I'd

just got home when the phone rang. It was Dick calling from London.
'Georgie,' he said.

I always felt guilty when he called me 'Georgie', it showed affection on his part but I'd stopped loving him, so it embarrassed me.

'Moya's sick,' he said. 'very sick. Can you look after her there in the mountains and give her some fresh air and sun and some of your lovely cooking?'

'What has she got?'

'Hodgkin's disease, it's a lymph disorder. It's serious.'

'Send her,' I said.

I was in what I called my dungeon – a large room with the boiler underneath the house. I had no bathroom so I bought a plastic tub and washed myself far better than if I'd had a bath. Of course, I'd find a room for Moya somewhere. I'd become quite a star mixing with film directors, millionaires and best-selling authors.

Eventually, I reserved a room with a woman who let rooms. I wondered what Moya looked like as I hadn't seen her for ages. When Dick had left her for Ginette, she'd married a young man with aristocratic connections. Moya'd always been pretty and courageous though I'd never particularly liked her, but how little all that mattered now. At this point, she had to get well – I'd get her well.

Nevertheless, since I'd learned the name of the disease, people had been despondent about her case.

The drive down to Zurich airport finally came to an end. I had been extra careful, imagining some accident and Moya arriving to find no one there to meet her. I ran up to the first floor of the airport terminal to watch the passengers come through Customs and I spotted her. She hadn't got fat or gone grey. She looked taller, slimmer; her face seemed tiny, her eyes enormous. We fell into each other's arms. She smiled wonderfully, so much hope in that smile! Her hair seemed thinner, but soft and velvety and she told me she had lost a lot of it because of the cobalt treatment.

'I have a lymph cancer. At times I think it's going to get me. Right now I think I can beat it.' She pointed to her underarm. 'There's the lymph and its affecting my throat. It seizes up and I can't eat. I want to vomit and can't swallow, as if I'm being choked. Right now I'm hungry. All I want to do is to get into bed and have a cup of warm soup.

'Dick has been marvellously kind. He has done everything for me. Unfortunately, that red-haired cow is always with him. There are times I'd just like to sit quiet, holding his hand, the two of us, alone.'

147

She showed me an envelope addressed to a Professor at the Cantonspittal in Zurich.

'He's the man we have to see if anything goes wrong.'

'What can go wrong, Moya?'

'You never know, but I would look silly if I was in trouble and didn't know whom to visit.'

We got out of town and started the long drive back up the mountains.

'I know nothing of your life over the last few years. I rarely see Dick and I can't stand *her*.'

She paused, debating whether to tell me all then and there, or even to tell me at all.

'I'll make it short,' she said. 'It was bad enough to have to go through it, I don't want to relive it all again. Besides I can't talk much, it tires my throat, but I'll put you in the picture. Dick and I broke up after five years of constant worries over money and his affairs with other women. He'd return home at any hour, if at all, and then be nasty. Between these love-affairs he could be caring and loving, swearing never to leave me. Temporarily it would soothe me and later made me even more anxious. Why should he keep telling me he'd never leave me if it wasn't already in the air? He was really in love with a woman called Doe. She was married and wasn't going to break it up for Dick. He still loves her, I think. Then he started up with this Frenchy bit, Ginette. You do know her, don't you? She's terribly pretty and has a great figure. We have a nickname for her 'Mademoiselle O-la-la'. I see her selling biscuits to the Brits in Verdun in the war. Yet she comes from a good bourgeois family. Whatever she is, she took Dick from me. Maybe it was because she was French. You know how Dick loves to show off and talk French at the top of his voice.' She stopped for a moment.

'After he left, I met Nicky Paget, a nice-looking boy related to the Anglesey family. We got married. His mother, Lady Victor Paget, wasn't too pleased. I was penniless, Catholic and divorced. We were happy for a few months, then his behaviour became erratic. He would fly into rages and insult me and argue. Just about the same time I began to be sick. I had no energy and this pain in my throat started, so I went to hospital. I learned I had Hodgkin's disease. I told Nicky I might even die of it.

' "If you're ill, then stay in hospital," he replied.

'I looked at this once kind man and burst into tears. Instead of putting his arms round me, he took my jewel-box and left the house. I didn't see him for a few days and when he returned he was as sweet as he had been at the beginning and explained he simply had to have some cash and swore he would return my miserable jewels.

'I started having cobalt treatment. I was weak and run-down. To start with Nicky was sympathetic but that soon changed. Once when I literally collapsed to the floor, he glared at me and said, "If you're going on being that ill, why don't you bloody well die?"

'I thought I would that minute. He again left the house and when he returned he threw a mass of banknotes over the bed, gave me back my bits of jewellery, and was loving and solicitous. He said he wanted to get us a house now that he had inherited money. I no longer knew where I stood. Subsequently, I found out he had, in fact, inherited money and had gone round London putting down deposits on various properties. He never had enough to buy any of them, but he had blocked the sale of four or five. When the time was up he lost all his deposits and here we were, still living in our little flat. One day he picked some futile quarrel and left for good. He took no clothes, just disappeared. Eventually, his mother rang me to tell me Nicky was in a nursing-home with some mental disease. It was the end of my marriage.'

The drive was coming to an end now. The sun had gone down and it was suddenly cold. I stopped the car opposite my dungeon, took out Moya's small suitcase and walked her to the front door of the house where I'd taken her a room.

'All I want is my cup of soup and bed,' she said.

When I rang the front-door bell, the landlady opened unsmiling and silent. Something had gone wrong.

'Frau Dettlinger, what has happened?'

'I can't let you have the room.'

'But it's arranged. I paid you.

'Here's your money,' she replied handing me my deposit.

'You know my sister-in-law is sick. You can't do this to her just as she arriving.'

'I've let it as a double room. I can't afford to let one person stay in a double room. I lose on it.'

'Haven't you another you can give us?'

'If your sister-in-law is not well, I can't have people gossiping. It's bad for the guest-house. You must leave.'

She didn't apologize. She shut the door in our faces and that was that. Moya and I looked at each other in disbelief.

'It's my fate. I'm surrounded by mad people. I'll have to sleep in your bed. I'll have been to bed with both brothers,' she said, eyes twinkling. I took her to my dungeon, sat her down on a bean bag and gave her soup. I then climbed up on to the main house and spoke to the owners. They were considered bohemians by the locals in Klosters. They were Catholics in a Protestant village and were not approved of in the community, the general opinion being that Catholics were dirty and unconventional. I found most mountain people hard and horrible and preferred the unconventional Catholics to the regular Protestants. My landlord was a sweet man, always willing to be responsible for deliquents and drunks in their moments of hardship. The wife loved to lie about and read. Mountain folk did not read, they learnt trades. Well, this man's wife read. She was sympathetic when I told her how the shrew opposite had cancelled the room but not surprised.

'What can we do now?' I asked.

'Wir kommen durch,' she replied. A lovely expression meaning, 'We'll pull through somehow.'

She emptied out a room on the landing, used as a cupboard but big enough to take a small bed. It was all we needed. Her linen was clean and fresh and within an hour Moya was all tucked up in bed.

'I have a feeling you're going to save my life.'

'I know I will, sleep tight.'

Next morning the sun shone bright and warm. Moya woke up ecstatic.

'I'm hungry and I'm happy. I never want to leave.'

'Then don't,' I said.

Why, in fact, should she leave? She was costing me nothing. It was a matter of pride to me to get her well and defy fate. I gave her fresh bread with home-made jam and honey, a thick creamy yogurt and tea.

'Let's go for a walk. I'm longing to see the place but I don't want to meet people,' she said apologetically, knowing I was a social chatterbox. 'My throat can't take it.'

I planned to give Moya four or five meals a day instead of three. I thought up delicate, tasty dishes served on a large plate, making the helpings appear small. It worked and she blossomed.

'What a shame we didn't all love each other then like we do now,' she said out of the blue.

'We were young. We had other things. But it's happened now. You don't know how important you make me feel getting you well. I feel like Christ, and I'm just about the same age. I probably look like him. You don't think he was a bearded, blue-eyed Celt do you? He was a wog.

150

You've made me into Christ for this short holiday so, "Carry thy bed and ski." '

Moya's improvement was astounding. The bony hips started to fill out. The face became fuller. She was always hungry. I felt I was making up for my life of laziness and pleasure. If I needed to give and get love, here was my chance.

It came as a shock some days later when Moya said she didn't want breakfast. Why wasn't she hungry? Perhaps it was something to do with menstruation. It certainly wasn't her condition playing up. How could it be when I'd cured her? I had planned her triumphant return to London, a husband with money, and a job. She'd tell the world how I'd saved her life. This set-back was just a mistake. She'd be hungry at lunch and all would be well! She ate lunch. Not as avidly as usual, but enough to allay my fears. The following morning she ate normally.

'There you are,' I said, 'I knew it was nothing.'

But the next evening she refused dinner and complained of her throat.

'All right, don't eat. Have a good sleep and breakfast tomorrow morning. You've done so well. It's ten steps forward and only a few back. You'll be OK.'

She was no better next morning. Her face was strained.

'Would you like to see the Professor in Zurich?'

'If it gets worse,' she replied.

She ate nothing all that day. The next morning I rang Zurich. I told Moya I was sure it would pass. Actually, all had gone so wonderfully well, that I couldn't believe it could go wrong. But it was wiser to take her to Zurich. I made an appointment for the following day.

The atmosphere had changed. We were no longer bubbling with excitement. We were alarmed.

'I tell you Moya, it's ten steps forward and nine steps back. Look how much weight you've put on. Even if the thing comes back it will go, just like the last time. Ten steps and nine steps, you know . . .

Hospitals are depressing. We were shown into the Professor's waiting-room and hardly had we sat down than the man appeared, short, unattractive, no light in his face, no expression, no humour: a face like a walnut. He had an Italian name, so to break the ice I spoke to him in Italian.

'I am not Italian,' he said. 'I'm from the Engadine, our language is Rhaeto-Romanic, an Italianate language.'

Moya handed him the report from her London specialist which he

151

studied. He didn't speak much English but as he was familiar with the subject he didn't have to. He did not seem involved in what he was reading, for he showed neither concern nor sense of urgency. He walked slowly, stopping in front of her.

'What is the matter?' he asked.

What was the matter! What was the matter with him? He knew what the matter was. That's why Moya was there. Perhaps he wanted her to be more specific.

'My throat is blocked. I can't eat, I can't swallow.'

She spoke slowly, clearly, like one does to a foreigner.

'So you cannot eat now. You must have the cobalt.'

'I can't, I can't,' she shouted. 'Not till May.'

Taking the report from the Professor's hands, she put her finger on the date when she had had her last treatment.

'You see I can't have it for another two months . . . or I'll die . . . I'll die.'

'So,' he said, adding a moment later, 'you've had it.'

Moya let out a wail. She ran over to where I was standing and clutched my arm. She was crying.

'He says I'm going to die. That terrible, awful man! He's not fit to be a doctor at all. How could he stand there coldly and tell me to my face, "You've had it"? What a world. What a horrible, heartless, senseless, awful, bloody world.'

I put my arm round her. I wanted time to invent something to soften the terrible blow.

'Moya, he doesn't speak English. You can see he doesn't. He's standing there saying, "You've had it," but he means, "You've had the cobalt," that's all. How would he even know such an expression? It didn't exist when he learnt his English. Do you really think a doctor would look you in the eye and say "You've had it"? Now go outside and I'll see if I can get some sense out of him.'

I left her in the waiting-room and returned to the Professor. In German I asked him to explain what he meant.

'She has had the cobalt treatment and she cannot have it again.'

'I know all that, that's why we're here. What do we do now?'

'She must return to her doctor in London.'

Go back to London! I would have to explain somehow on the journey back to Klosters. I returned to an anxious Moya.

'What he's saying is that there would be no point in your being treated here when you could be back with your own doctor. We have to

152

go back to London. You're stronger now. Even if you don't eat for a few days, at least you've got some reserve fat on you.' Moya just hung her head.

'Maybe I have "had it".' She tried to clear her throat but the voice still came out rough. 'I've been going through this for some time now. Each time I think it's all over. They give me the cobalt and I get better, then I get worse, and again they give me the cobalt. It goes on round and round: better and worse, better and worse. Sometimes I wish it were all over. I don't mind dying. Yes, I do mind dying but I wouldn't mind suddenly being dead. Can you understand?'

I had to find some hopeful phrase. Something to make her feel better before leaving.

'Moya, what would you do if the doctor told you you had seven years to live?'

'That would be good news.'

'Look at your watch, follow the second hand round the face for five whole minutes and when they're over let me know.'

She did as I told her. The five minutes took forever.

'Doesn't she read slowly?' I thought. I started to laugh. 'Didn't that seem a long five minutes?'

She nodded.

'Now think how many five minutes there are in seven years.'

She seemed to believe she did have seven years, so my ploy had worked. After a few moments she said, 'Seven years is quite a long time. Seven months are shorter and seven days shorter still. Perhaps I will last seven days – seven days!'

I stuck my elbow playfully into her ribs and she smiled. As I helped her out of the car I said, 'You truly have beautiful eyes.'

The following day I drove her back to Zurich airport. Dick would meet her in London. As she was going she fell into my arms and wept, 'If I get worse, will you come?'

'I shall be going to London anyway,' I said.

Dick phoned me the following day.,

'Happiest holiday of her life. She's seeing the doctor now.'

I couldn't get Moya out of my mind. I had lost all interest in Klosters. Five days later I was in London.

When I got to her ward I saw her before she noticed me. She was propped up in bed, fiddling around with something. Her tiny face lit up as I walked in and she lifted up her arms for a hug.

'Careful,' she whispered, 'I'm frail.'

153

Small pieces of jewellery were spread out on the bed: a gold chain, ear-rings, a brooch, a bracelet, a pearl necklace . . .

'For my friends,' she said. 'The butcher, the grocer, the milkman. They have been kind. Who else have I got?'

I tried not to weep. It was unbearable that this girl should have had five years' misery with that hopeless brother of mine, then lose him to that red-haired thing with her stinking scent and flinty presence. Just then there was a flurry at the door and there stood the 'thing', dressed in black, pulled-in waist, high-heeled shoes, covered in baubles and talking French at the top of her voice to Dick as she hung on his arm. Dick bent down and kissed Moya while Ginette babbled away.

'I wanted to bring you my new toy poodle. I've never seen anything so sweet.'

'I don't think they let dogs in,' Moya replied.

Ginette sat on the edge of Moya's bed, bored and posturing, while Dick discussed Moya with the nurses. A few minutes later they left.

'Is that the first time Ginette's come?' I asked.

'No, she always comes with Dick. That stinking "Jolie Madame". I can't bear it.'

I stayed on in London another fortnight. I phoned Mother in Rome and she wept. Moya had always liked Mother and Mother had begun to love Moya after Dick married Ginette. I visited Moya on several occasions. Each visit showed her markedly weaker. She couldn't last long now. The nurses agreed it was pointless feeding her intravenously, but it had to be done. At the end of my stay she was too weak to recognize anyone. Moya died two days later. She had no parents, no brothers and sisters, no relations. She died alone.

17

By now I had Rome 'under control': my life, Mother's life, food, sex and shopping. However, no one's ever totally content. The car was tired and shabby and I'd just seen a picture of the new Mark 10 Jaguar in a magazine.

'Now that's the sort of car you should be in, Mrs Hayim,' someone told Mama.

I agreed but I wasn't going to ask Mother to sell yet another bit of jewellery. I'd try Father first.

'Father,' I wrote, coming straight to the point, 'some years ago Mother sold some ear-rings to buy a car. Today, it's about to be buried. We need a car. One stroke of your pen and we have one.

'I know I've been a disappointment to you, but you can't kick someone down the stairs when they're a kid, and then complain for the rest of their life that they limp. You are now making up for the past by looking after us both. What difference can a thousand or two make to you at this late stage in life? Make my mother's last years happier. Be nice – give her a car.'

I didn't expect the following letter by return.

Dear George,

How extraordinary! You must have been reading my thoughts. I'm a director of Fiat out here. Contact Fiat in Rome. You can drive it away tomorrow.

Mother handed me the letter. 'You must have a diamond comb or a Chinese pot or something. I know what – that diamond thing to shorten

155

your pearls. Sell it, add the money to the Fiat and we'll buy a Jaguar. Can't have my mother sitting in a Fiat, can I?'

A month later, Mother and I embarked on a trip to Greece, driving down through Brindisi in the new Jaguar, with Mama's maid – an old duck from France – plus fifteen trunks on the roof.

We got out of Rome on to the Autostrada and I put my foot flat down. We cruised at 190 kilometres an hour, hitting 200 whenever possible. What the hell were we doing at that speed with no boat to catch and no rendezvous? Then an Alfa Due Mila passed us. Mother and I blazed with rage. We raced for 30 km till he stopped for gas. I had to do likewise. My oil gauge was jumping up and down so I asked them to look at that. As the mechanic appeared, I saw the Alfa shoot past. I slammed the door and gave chase. On the left was the monastery of Monte Cassino, before us a dead straight, flat road. I'd catch that rotten Alfa and show it what a British Mark 10 Jag could do. A minute later – my foot flat down – there was a thump. I knew, just knew, this was the end. Oil leaked for hundreds of yards back and was still spilling out of the car when we came to a halt. A man came up smiling.

'Everyone goes full out on this stretch – happens every day.' Then, 'You've shot a piston through the motor.'

I didn't even ask how long repairs would take. Three tired, old travellers finally returned, dragged backwards all the way to Rome at ten miles an hour.

Jaguar agreed to give us a new engine under guarantee. The maid unpacked the trunks. The Excelsior welcomed Mother back and I bought seats for *Samson and Delilah* at the opera. Mother looked a dream. I told her everything was for the best and after the opera I drove her home singing 'Softly Awakes My Heart'.

Rome had gone to Mother's head. All she wanted now was to be in the swim. It was no use telling her that she was sixty-nine, had nothing but her monthly allowance, wasn't particularly tactful or witty, and that the only people she'd really ever met had been through me.

'Lots of people like me,' she defended herself.

'I also like you, Mother. You have endearing, faithful ways and you're a dish, but socially you are no one.'

She alternated between telling people how short her husband kept her and how rich she was. She looked disapprovingly at my friends,

156

afraid they might be mere waiters. Her friendship with Galanti, the plastic surgeon, and his wife, Mara, gave me more liberty and took her off my hands. But even that friendship was based on wrong foundations. They were impressed by Mimi and Mimi wanted to impress – or perhaps those were the right foundations for such a friendship.

When Mother asked me to drive her to Paris to buy hats I reminded her I'd tried on the last lot when I was in Paris myself, and sent them all to her in Rome. She wanted to show the Italians that she actually lived in Paris – not in provincial Rome.

That summer we had been in a traffic jam in Rome. Opposite me, her elbow outside her car window, was the most beautiful creature I had ever seen. The tilt of her head, her shoulders, the transparency of her hair, her huge almond china-blue eyes, she looked like a magical mythical golden horse.

'Look at that, Mother!'

'Must be a princess or diplomat's daughter,' she replied.

Just then the man sitting next to her began gesticulating. The sun was in my eyes and I thought he was telling me to stop staring but soon recognized him as a friend of mine from Klosters, a handsome Swiss-Brazilian. I got out of the car and ran to him.

'And what, may I ask, is that glorious Pegasus? I've never seen anything like it.'

The woman smiled slowly. She had longish teeth, but they suited her face. Her eyes seemed to be set in the wrong place and when she smiled she showed just a little gum. She should not have been that beautiful, but she was.

'My wife, Sandra,' said Alex.

I fell in love! For three days I showed them around Rome and when they invited me to Rio I said I'd do everything I could to come.

The night before leaving Rome to drive Mother to Paris, I went out cruising and picked up two brutes who attacked me in the car. When one put his hand over my mouth, I bit it with all my might, so he wrenched his hand away, including in it a front tooth of mine. When Mother asked if I'd been in a fight I invented an idiotic story. It led to our worst quarrel ever. I couldn't wait to get rid of her and leave for Brazil. A previous Paris trip had left her penniless. She and the maid were now obliged to sleep in the same room at the Galantis' until her allowance arrived and she could return to the Excelsior.

One evening, one of my street friends had recognized the Jag outside the Galantis' late one night and shouted, 'Giorgio, Giorgio.'

157

It had upset her deeply. Did she think that I was ruining her socially or endangering my own life? Whatever the reason, she became impossible. I left her on bad terms.

I drove back to Paris, left the car in a garage and took the train to Antwerp where I boarded a Belgian ship for Rio. With me I took Hugo's *Portuguese in Three Months*. There was not a soul I could stand on board. On the last day of the journey laughing dolphins leaped out of the sea on both sides of the ship's bow welcoming us into Rio de Janeiro where the beautiful Sandra and her husband, Alex, stood waiting on the quayside.

I wanted to be there for the Carnival, so I first set off on a tour. The bus to Belo Horizonte left the lush surroundings of Rio and drove through the night. I liked the stops. There were surprises and sexual adventures around every corner. If the bus stopped for more than half an hour, one would find an adventure, even in the desolate surrounds of a station miles away from anywhere.

After a few days of touring, and before returning to Rio, I went to the city of Salvador de Bahia. On the bus a woman read my palm with a pendulum. She told me I would escape with my life very soon and that I would be shocked by something far away.

Salvador de Bahia is artistic, colourful and lazy. It is also hot, and rains all through January, but it's got magic, though I could never stand its smell as everything is cooked in palm oil. Salvador was in a state of excitement for its festival day, the Festa de Bonfim. I'd wander about at nights and watch people burst into song and dance. Women rubbed up against men, men against men. It was decadent, erotic and dangerous.

One night I met two huge mulattos on the port and suggested we spend the evening together. They promised to return with a rowing boat. The market was on one side of the road; on the other was the port where I waited. Rats, as big as dogs, dragged hunks of meat from the market across the road and into the boats over the still bodies of naked, sleeping families. I had a one-thousand-cruzeiro note on me and thought that the mulattos might rob me, so I slipped it into the turn-up of my trousers. They rowed me to an island ten minutes' strong rowing away. There was a wooden pontoon and little else. I wandered inland and saw what appeared to be wells with flames burning at the bottom, like volcanic craters. The mulattos called when I was fifty yards away and I joined them. They put their arms round me, frisking me at the same time. They appeared uneasy and waiting for something.

The something soon appeared – another boat. Out of it climbed two

158

men. One without a shirt and wearing a hat, a cross hanging from his neck. They hardly looked at me as they approached and each carried an identical knife. They walked straight up to me and each casually put his knife to my stomach.

'Dinero, dinero.'

So that is what they wanted, but not what I wanted.

'I have no dinero. I'm a student from Paris.'

I told them all this in my month-old Portuguese. I turned to my original mulattos for help but it was clear they were all in it together. They ordered me to take off my shoes.

'My shoes! My shoes! I have trouble with my feet. My right foot is longer than my left.'

Later I made a movement as if I'd found a stone in my shoe. I put out one hand to steady myself on the shoulder of one of my mulattos; with the other I took off my right shoe, which I hit against the earth repeatedly. When this was over, I went through it all with the other shoe. I didn't want to take my shoes off on their command, but I also wanted to show them I had nothing hidden in them.

The excitement was over, and the knives were put away. I had risked my life for that one-thousand-cruzeiro note – exactly 75 cents.

The two mulattos made love with me on the boat going back and as I said goodbye, one asked, 'Where do you live?'

'In Paris,' I replied.

'I know a man in Paris,' he said, giving me a name. Incredibly, I knew him.

Once back in Rio I passed a man selling fish from a street stall so I bought one. Mouth watering. I ran up Alex and Sandra's stairs, fish in hand. Sandra opened the door, took the fish to the kitchen and gave me a letter that had just arrived from Rome.

It was from Enrica, Mother's Shanghai maid, who had returned, aged seventy, to look after her.

'Dear Giorgio,' she wrote. 'Whatever you do, keep out of Rome. The police are after you. There has been a scandal over the baker's sixteen-year-old son. The police have been at your flat. Don't dare come back to Rome or you will be arrested.'

What son? What baker? What was I supposed to have done? Who'd complained? I don't know how long I stood there reading and re-reading the letter. Something was wrong. I didn't know what, but it stank. Rome is a funny place. Gossip becomes scandal, scandals burst and a foreigner can get kicked out of the place without explanation.

159

They give you a 'Foglio di Via'. No discussion, no lawyers – out you go.

More letters came from Rome and one from Mara Galanti. She said young people had been apprehended at my entrance door. It was better I didn't return to Italy. Her husband, Tonino, wrote offering to buy up my furniture. He said Mother insisted I sell the Jaguar. Dick wrote that he'd gone to see Mother in Rome, and at the frontier they had stopped him until they realized he was Dick and not George Hayim. 'You are staining the family name. Father must be told.'

I was in despair. I could recall nothing of this story. I don't like young boys. If the boy in question was that young, he must have been a giant. If he was a giant, he wasn't a young boy. Barred from Italy! Italy was my home! My furniture. Friends. Books. Everything I possessed! I wrote to my lawyer in Rome.

'What have I been accused of? Who has denounced me? Answer immediately.'

A letter came back: 'I was surprised to get your desperate letter. I hurried to the police department and asked what accusations had been made against you.' In capital letters he had written: 'NON C'E NIENTE AL SUO CARICO.' I didn't know the expression. It means: 'There is no charge against you.'

Mara now wrote. The cleaning-lady had been bullied by the police when they had visited my flat. Dick again wrote: 'I'm afraid we can't have this, old boy. You're letting the family down.'

The rotten, pretentious, self-righteous sod! I made photocopies of the lawyer's letter and wrote at once to Father:

Father,

This is a sad and hard letter to write. I have just received letters from Enrica, in Rome, and one from Dick in London, telling me the police were after me and that I must never return to Rome, that I'd assaulted a sixteen-year-old boy and dishonoured the Hayim family.

Father, my life is my own, even though it's a bohemian life. I would expect solidarity and help from my family if I were in real trouble, even though . . . you and I . . . are unhappy strangers to one another.

Instead of loyalty I have received the enclosed letters. Mother has ended my lease and sold the contents of my flat. Dick flew out to be with her. Her friends, Doctor Galanti and his wife, have advised me to stay out of Italy. Mother didn't even write. Dick wants to be the first to tell you. He considers he is upholding the honour of the family.

160

As a result of this 'plot' I find myself alone. You have kept me for all my life, but you have never been a friend. I have fought you to help Mother over the years, incurring your enmity. This I did because I loved her and not because I thought she was right. You are wiser, stronger and richer than Mother. She has no weapons and she will always be in love with you, unwelcome and expensive though this love may be. I have now repudiated her. As for Dick, he is as stupid as Mother. He might really have believed Mother's story, but he never verified it. I would expect you to stand by me, just as I would stand by you even though I often hated you.

As you can see in the enclosed letter, nothing happened. Nothing at all.

George

Two weeks later I received a reply:

Dear George,

I have never listened to gossip. I have arranged with Pan Am in Rio to fly you home when you wish. Contact them.

18

With my name cleared and my mother out of the way, I settled into my seventh-floor maid's room at the Royal Monceau Hotel which was still 'home' for all of us. Due to my antics and extravagant behaviour in Klosters among the jet set, I found I now was invited to parties and balls in Paris, all of which delighted me to start with but brought no real satisfaction. Furthermore if you go to dinners and parties, there's no time for sex because my fellows are not to be found in drawing-rooms. I like rough men, their muscles, their voices and their smell.

First, I'd have to find a partner. Homosexuals were automatically excluded. Ideally he would be some strong, healthy layabout, a bit bored and new to such a scenario. Whom with some coaching I could talk into creating a mood, that of a powerful rapist about to satisfy his vice.

The best place to find these partners was a bar called La Nuit in Montmartre, frequented by young yobbos looking for anything to fill up their day. Eventually, I met a stunning youth called Gil, a gigolo who thought that as I had a Jaguar I might be a good client, but who gave up all thought of money once he saw the hot-plate in the corner of my tiny bedroom in the hotel. All I had to do was to wait until Gil called and I'd be content for three or four days. But when he didn't call for two weeks I became nervous and drove to La Nuit to get news of him. One man told me he thought that Gil had had a heart-attack and I wouldn't be seeing him again. I continued trying to get news and finally I knocked into another mate of his.

'I'm sorry to hear about poor Gil's heart-attack,' I said.

'Heart-attack!' He laughed. 'Armed attack! He's in for three years.'

With Gil no longer available, I looked for something else, turning my attention to amyl nitrate, that stinking, foul substance that people inhale to stimulate their hearts. It gives one an extra fillip just as one is about to come. The smell is so revolting it stinks the house out and knocks you out to such an extent that it still shows on your face twenty-four hours later. Unlike most people who break a capsule and then sniff it, I only got turned on when it was imposed on me against my will. That's one of the reasons I hate porn films. They're always showing couples happy to be doing it together. I have to be made to do things unwillingly. The amyl nitrate business has to be done right – even taken by surprise. Ideally, I would have to be overpowered and bound, even blindfolded. Once helpless, my partner would take his time. My mouth would then be taped, all the while my captor continuing his talk while placing strip after strip of tape over my lips. My great moment comes when the phial is broken and shoved up my nostril but here again the game can go wrong. One nostril should be blocked so that the other is the only source of inhaling. In his excitement the partner would often pinch the whole nose making me unable to breathe at all.

When the thing was perfectly done, I went over the top. As if one phial wasn't enough the captor might then break another, another, and another until I was helplessly groggy.

Even so, it didn't substitute what was missing in my life. What I really needed was to be totally involved in some powerful, terrible love; one that gives you the strength to carry a house. So from that moment on every young man I met became a potential object of my consuming need to love. I believe I would have fallen in love with almost anyone who gave me their time. I looked about me like a talent scout hunting for the face that was about to rocket into stardom.

One morning my friend Mirella Ricciardi phoned to tell me she would be shooting some stills in the Champs-Elysées. Could we have a coffee together in the sun? Mirella is the finest photographer of mood shots I know, be it of a lion in Africa, a child in Brazil or a lake in Guatemala. While she worked, I concentrated on the crowd. The French have a great word for looking unashamedly and out-rageously at people. They call it 'devisager' ('to unface'). Standing next to me was a hard-faced, tough-jawed youth: six foot, eyes like a panther, good body, straight hard nose with a cruel curve to the nostrils.

'This is it,' I thought and began talking to him.

He appeared annoyed that I was interrupting him watching shooting. When Mirella stopped for a break I button-holed him. We were

163

standing close, closer than was necessary. He looked arrogantly into my eyes.

'Vous devisagez souvent les gens comme ça?' ('Do you often "unface" people that way?')

'Come and join us. I'm having a drink with the woman whose taking pictures,' I replied.

After our coffee together, Mirella got up to leave. I told the boy to wait, I had something to ask him.

'What do you think of him, Mirella? Isn't he terrific?'

'Just a good-looking young man. He's nothing.'

I was disappointed but put it down to her preoccupation with work. I succeeded in getting the boy home, gave him a bath, a wonderful dinner I'd cooked on my hot-plate, lots to drink. Then as he lay panting, warm, relaxed and a little drunk in my armchair I sat on the floor at his feet.

'I want . . . I want someone . . . someone who will walk into my life, take me over, fill my heart, my mind. I want somebody strong and young to care for, even if he hurts me.'

As I said this I had his hand in mine. I then placed it on the tendon from my neck to my shoulder and was getting him to knead it harder and harder till it hurt. I went on talking and creating a mood when suddenly he punched me on the chin. My mouth filled with blood; I was stunned, but excited. He hurled a peach which exploded against the wall, then glared at me.

'Ça y est, that is it,' I whispered, 'I love you.'

He flopped back into the armchair, slowly stretched out a hand towards me, drew my head towards him and unzipped his pants and forced my head down on him. That's how it began. Subsequently, I bought Edmond to London. Girls threw themselves at him. He was young, handsome, strong and 'ze French lover'.

Robin Middleton – my best friend – was renovating his house in London; there were gaps between walls and holes in the ceiling. We went to stay with him. I spied on Edmond through bathroom holes, keyholes, ceiling holes. I used to loathe the silly girls he brought home, but I'd love them if they appreciated him. After a while Edmond left to go and share with friends. I told him an inspector had been round. He had heard Edmond was working without a permit. He had to drop his job, return home. I could no longer conceive of life without him. I felt trapped and helpless. One night I told him, 'I'm a butterfly that you have taken and pierced with a pin through my back.'

I got him actually to stick one into my back.

I then took a tiny flat for us both. One day I returned home to feel something was different. Edmond's suitcase, which normally stood in a corner, was no longer there. On the kitchen table was a note: 'I have left. I will contact you.'

I stared at the empty space where the suitcase had been and then my knees gave way. I fell with a sob to the floor. That evening, in despair, I went out to look for someone and brought home a giant I couldn't handle. He was out to rip me off. I talked away, finally interesting him in some imaginary woman I was waiting for: why didn't he wait, I'd ring her to come. I rang Edmond at the bar where he worked and told him in French that he must come at once.

'She's coming now,' I told the giant.

Miraculously I heard the dit, dit, dit of high heels. The door opened. In walked a girl with long, beautiful legs, followed by Edmond. I was saved. Later when the girl was out of earshot, Edmond said, 'She's a hooker. Only eighteen. She took one look at me in the bar where we met and said she was in love with me.'

Edmond went with her to her place that first night and never returned to me again. I got to know the girl later. She was honest and nice but undoubtedly was responsible for Edmond suddenly having trouble with his eyes. I interfered in their lives by actually dragging him to a venereologist where I learned he was going blind from gonorrhoea. Edmond showed no gratitude to me for having saved his eyes. I begged him to visit me daily but he didn't.

Depressed, I wrote to Immigration and denounced him for working in England. He was about to be sent out of the country when the girl came to see me and begged for my help. I again wrote to the authorities, saying the boy had undertaken not to work again. I left for Paris. I had lost him.

During the following weeks I started my book on Edmond. I would call Edmond's prostitute occasionally and say a few words to Edmond. On one occasion the girl told me he had gone. I was like a madman. I rang the bar but they must have been warned about my calling.

'He's gone,' they said.

James Fox, the actor, had invited me to stay in Hollywood while he made *The Chase* with Jane Fonda and Brando.

'You will die of chagrin if you don't get away from Edmond and all that.'

I had some weeks to kill. I'd get my visa in London, stay at Robin Middleton's and visit Toe. I could continue the work on my book about Edmond from London. Robin was patient, but anything I did in the house went wrong. They'd ask me to polish the floor. I'd put the tin of polish on the gas to warm it: it caught fire, my eyelashes caught fire. I broke things. I lost things. I forgot things. I left the door open or locked it so that no one could get in. I simply had to get away from everything.

Old Toe was now living modestly in Brighton. I'd spend a few days with him there.

Fully rested I returned to London to stay with Robin again. One morning just as I was entering the sitting-room to join him for breakfast, he stood before me blocking my way.

'There are two policemen here. They want to speak to you.'

'What about?'

'Whatever it is, just tell them the truth.'

He led me into the room and left me with the two large men in uniform. They started with the words you always hear in movies.

'Anything you say may be held against you. It's about a murder.'

'A murder?!' I was relieved.

'Did you . . . go by train lately to Brighton?'

'Yes.'

'And you stayed at this telephone number?'

'Yes.'

'You're living here and your name's George Hayim?'

'Yes.'

'Did you talk to anyone on the train on the way down to Brighton?'

'Of course, I talk to everyone, everywhere.'

'What sort of strangers do you talk to?'

'Athletic men mostly.'

'We have a statement from a man you picked up on the train to Brighton.' He began to read it out. ' "A peculiar man started up a conversation with me. He asked me what sports I did. Then he said, 'I'm sure you could hold somebody down, make them helpless. I bet you'd know how to strangle them. You're powerful. Please ring me.' "

'Do you remember talking to this man?'

'Gentlemen, I don't remember which man on which train, but that's how I talk to anyone I want to pick up.'

The policeman continued, 'A murder has been committed. A young

166

man has been strangled, his body found in a trunk. It's in all the papers. Does that mean anything to you?'

Suddenly I caught hold of the unwilling arm of one of the policemen and put myself in a stranglehold. They were getting all worked up. The other policeman's pen and notebook were shaking.

'Go on, go on.'

'I love being overpowered. I feel myself fainting, going, going . . . with my last strength I tap the man's arm in despair. He will then, please God, let go.'

It was an awful anticlimax. They thought they'd solved a murder.

'Would you mind making a formal statement for me to this effect?' one asked as they left. 'We'll come back and get it tomorrow.'

They came the next day. I had written:

Sir,

This is to certify that I like men. I get kicks by being overpowered by heterosexual athletes. I talk to everyone in buses, trams, trains and planes all over the world.

They read the statement.

'By the way, I'm off to America next month. They won't let me into the States if you show them this.'

They sat me down then and composed another letter for me to sign:

Sir,

I do not live in England, I therefore don't know anyone. Being shy and lonely. I talk to strangers.

I signed the document and probably kissed them both. As I went to close the front door one of them beckoned to me.

'If ever you hear of "anything" – you know, like about this murder, just ring up Scotland Yard and ask for the Murder Room, OK?'

Fox was expecting me in Los Angeles. First, however, I stopped in New York to visit a lovely American. I'd met her in France and found her gorgeous but at the same time I was afraid of the interest such a beauty should show in me. We became friends and she invited me to stay at her apartment in New York.

I found her tender and protective. At night she'd stand naked in the bathroom and take off her face, then take pills and fall into a deep sleep in the bed we shared.

After a couple of nights I found the courage to explore. She was knocked out cold so I caressed and kissed her. It's stealing to kiss someone fast asleep. You wonder whether they'd let you do it if they were awake. Next evening she went to the bathroom as usual, took off her face and picked up the pills.

'Don't,' I said, 'you don't need them.'

Then I went through everything I'd done the night before when she'd been asleep, finally going down on her. I'd never been down on a girl before and when you've never been anywhere, you usually don't know where you are or what to do, but if you're sensual you just know: this way it fits, that way it doesn't. I was doing fine. Fine? I was sensational. She thrashed and groaned and cried and I went on and on and on until she screamed,

'Do it, do it!'

Do it? I had nothing to do it with. So I didn't do it.

Fox met me at Los Angeles airport and drove me to his beach-house in Malibu. He had really saved my sanity by inviting me . . . pretty damn sweet when he was starting on a new career and I was so scandalous. Here in new surroundings I felt free of England, France and Edmond. I was myself again, not the remains of what Edmond had mindlessly ravaged. Fox insisted I write ten pages of my book every day and thanks to his bullying I finished it. With the three hundred pages under my arm. I returned to London. As soon as I arrived I rang Edmond's girl.

'He's here,' she said. 'We can come and see you.'

At least the agony of not knowing where he was, was over. I returned to settle down in Paris.

19

That winter was bad. Everything seemed to go wrong for me. The Jag's
power steering gave up. I had to find money to fix it. There was an
occasional stiff exchange of letters with Mother. When the person you
love most in the world has turned out to be a traitor, something snaps.
Also, for the first time in my life, I'd asked my Father for five hundred
dollars and he'd refused. I was hurt and dejected. Then an English
woman-friend rang me.

'George, I'm off to London. My Russian uncle is dying. You must
take over and look after him.'

For the next week I looked after the dying uncle. I drove him to
hospital, cared for him, listened to him and amused him. I forgot my
troubles.

Now that the old man no longer needed me, I returned to Robin's in
London.

'You'll have to do what a million people do every day – *work*. You
might enjoy it.'

He handed me the *Evening Standard* and I looked down the job
offers: 'Lavatory attendant at Earls Court Exhibition.'

There's a job I could do and let my Father know his son is a lavatory
attendant. He'd have to give me money. How can a rich man laugh off a
son working in a public loo in Earls Court, or even Mayfair! What if
they didn't take me? Perhaps I could write to my Father saying that I
was in such bad physical condition that they wouldn't accept me in a
public loo?

I rang Earls Court. They were polite and called me 'Mister'. I should
come and report to their Traffic Officer. Traffic Officer? Was there that
much traffic in that lavatory? Why had the man been so nice on the

telephone? Had he guessed I was not the usual type of attendant?

Working hours were nine to five. How would I cope with my laundry? How do the working millions manage? Had life caught up with me? I was *not* going to be just any old lavatory attendant. Miserable, angry and devious though my intentions were, some good would come of it. I'd charm the clients, bring combs, an electric razor, sticking plaster, aspirin, a hot-plate! I could see the headlines:

MILLIONAIRE'S SON FRIES PANCAKES IN PUBLIC LAVATORY.
ORIENTAL POTENTATE'S PROBLEM CHILD RESORTS TO . . .

Problem child? At forty?

It takes ten minutes to Earls Court station from where I was living. I got up two hours before I was due. It was, after all, my first regular job. I asked for Mr Tyndall, the Traffic Officer. He hadn't turned up yet. He grew, as I sat there thinking about him, till he became a huge gruff man with a bunch of heavy keys, pushing us attendants into lavatories as we muttered, 'Bastards, those bosses!'

I'd read Koestler's book, where a political prisoner in Spain gradually comes to believe the stupid jailer really is his superior. Tyndall was superior already. A small man with white hair approached us.

'Gentlemen, this way please – I'm Mr Tyndall. Come to my office for a briefing.'

Briefing? Was I on my way to space in a steel ball? Tyndall asked me for the name of my next of kin. Might I be swallowed up or down a water-closet? On my tombstone would be written:

'Died defending himself against an irresistible current.'

I gave Tyndall Father's name and title – his CBE! I must now choose a background of Jeyes fluid, mops, buckets and lavatory seats and have pictures sent to Father, his friends, the Queen, the bank manager in Hong Kong. Tyndall took us across the hall. Workmen were bustling round, painting and hammering. Lights were flickering, plastic containers littered the floor. Large letters in all colours advertised what was on sale: 'Switch gear, Busbar chamber', 'Cartridge fuse links', 'Hydraulic high press tools', 'Moulded case circuit-breakers', 'Earth leakage circuit-breakers' – I'd never heard of any of this.

I was sent to the Labour Exchange in Kensington High Street to get my card. When I returned Tyndall took me to see Taylor, the other attendant. I decided to say nothing of who I was. Anyway, who was I? It

170

seemed unnecessary to explain one wasn't a real lavatory attendant. Maybe he wasn't either. Taylor told me not to go down for tea without leaving the towel rollers out. On my return, I should hide them.

'Give customers fresh towels. That's how you make the tips.'

Taylor reminded me that I wasn't wearing my white coat. I pulled a new one from the clean laundry pile. I couldn't get into it. It had been so starched that I, a grown man, was unable to prize the sleeves apart! Finally, I made it. I usually got tuppence as a tip – and I spent most of my free time telephoning from a call box outside the lavatory. When I saw a client approach, I'd ring off and rush in to get my tip, realizing too late that a telephone call cost fourpence and I was losing tuppence on the deal. In addition to which, I always rang back to finish the conversation. Eightpence spent to earn two. I was not cut out for business.

Edmond never came to see me at work. Dick came. He was upset to see me there. He wired the family to add fuel to the blaze I'd started. The next day I brought my typewriter and a camera. I settled down to prepare the photographs that were to outrage the family. I used up a whole roll, posing on my knees between two lavatories, a bucket and a mop beside me. That would shake them!

I then went to the hospital to see if I had TB. Why should I have TB? Oversexed people do often have TB; or is it that people with TB are oversexed? I would send the pictures, the work certificate and the TB diagnosis home. Then I'd refuse to be cured and I'd tell the world I was the abandoned, tubercular, second son of famous Hong Kong Tai Pan, Ellis Hayim CBE.

The job in the lavatory forced me to get up early. I felt marvellous. I even had time to work on my memoirs. Father had *not* sent telegrams ordering me to give up my job, nor had he sent me the thousands of pounds I expected. Had it all been a waste of time? Half my life was over and here I was working in a public lavatory. There had to be a confrontation. We couldn't go on this way. Then my old friend Harry Kitson slipped two hundred pounds into my hand and told me to go to Hong Kong. A week later I was on the plane.

Mother was due to meet me at Rome airport, where my plane stopped over for twenty minutes. I hadn't seen her for three years. I'd refused to see her or make friends and it was only after three or four abject letters

171

of apology that I agreed to start seeing her again.

I hung about the gate, nervous and depressed, but no sign of her. Just before I had to re-board she appeared. She wore a huge blue straw hat, off her face, her grey curls bunched up against it, a long open woollen spring coat with a lighter-blue dress inside.

'Ton sur Ton,' I thought, and ran to her holding my arms wide open.

'I'm sorry, I'm sorry, I'm late. It wasn't my fault,' she said.

She looked so beautiful, so rich and warm.

'I'm worried darling, be careful.'

It was our first kiss in three years. I ran back to the plane. I still loved the silly creature.

On the flight I wondered how Hong Kong would be now. How would Father act when he heard I was in his town? What could he do? Could he have me deported? Would he smooth it over and ask me out to dinner with Y. Y. Chow or P. P. Wu and buy me another gold Rolex? Or would he not see me at all?

He might say, 'Why should I give you anything at all?'

I could answer biblically, 'As thou soweth, so shalt thou reapeth.'

'He could reply, "Buzzeth offeth." '

I chose a cheap hotel in Nathan Road, and strolled round town. As I walked upstairs to my room. I sensed a shadow behind me. It was the night porter.

'Masta wanty woman?'

Had he said, 'Masta wanty Wuntun soupee?' I might have accepted.

He returned later,

'Masta wanty girl?' Pause. 'Small girl?' Another pause.

Instead of perhaps a schoolgirl I thought he meant a dwarf and I shuddered (which I had no right to do because I've had a dwarf and quite liked it).

Exasperated, he continued, 'Watting masta likey?'

'Masta likey big, husky bloke.'

'Velly solly Hong Kong no got.'

Girlless, soupless, and blokeless, I went to bed for thirty-six hours.

Later I drove in a bus past my Father's house. It not only had '41' written up, but also in large black threatening letter on a white background, 'Ellis Hayim'. I saw Repulse Bay and Aberdeen with junks and sampans, then on to Wanchai where I got out opposite the Suzy Wong Bar and I wandered round trying eels, crabs and French beans by the yard. I also tried a fortune-teller, sitting in the road on a stool. He

172

lifted his glass-shielded candle to my eyes, saying, 'One dollar for news. Two for good news.'

I paid two.

Next day, still delaying facing Father, I visited a Chinese doctor to cure worms I'd been cursed with over the last twenty years. I'd had every treatment, swallowed pills of every colour, with corresponding red, violet and turquoise stools. I'd sat on garlic, next to a gypsy with bad breath playing an abominable violin to charm them out of me. Maybe Chinese medicine could cure me. Mother'd tried it for her allergies. She'd been given birds' feet and dried flies to boil over a coal fire in an earthenware pot with iron scissors on top. It had cured her.

When I found enough courage I rang Father's office.

'I am his son,' I said when asked who I was.

'There's some mistake,' the voice replied. 'My Hayim will be back tomorrow. He has two sons and they both work in England.'

'Work?' I asked. (Dick blowing us all up with his gadgets and me writing memoirs in a public lavatory.) 'I must be the third son,' I said, 'because I'm *not* working. This is the name of my hotel.'

That night I dreamed the family had sent a huge car to take me home. But the car wasn't big enough for the small girl, the dwarf and the bloke I wanted and that Hong Kong 'no had'.

Next morning when I awoke, a large car was there. Father had sent it to bring me to the Repulse Bay Hotel where he'd reserved me a suite.

I went to the family house and walked into the sitting-room where my ninety-six-year-old grandmother sat, transforming her chair into a throne. I bent down to kiss her.

'Granny, I am George.'

She turned her sharp black eyes to me, then pulled me to her, peering closely.

'George? My George?' Pause. 'Your nose too big.'

Next, I was driven to Father's office. Though I had found just enough courage to face him, nothing had changed the effect his presence had on me; he, his handwriting, even the scent of his eau de cologne. Although apprehensive, this time I felt on sure ground. I was on his doorstep and I knew he was embarrassed by me. The car drew up in front of a skyscraper. A lift shot me up to a high floor, where I was ushered into an office. Through an open door I could see an elderly man smiling and bowing, thoroughly uncomfortable, mumbling as he withdrew.

'Yes, Uncle. No, Uncle.'

173

Later I was to learn many of his Chinese employees were encouraged to call him 'Uncle' like 'Godfather'.

'Hello, son,' said Father with fabricated charm and his crocodile smile. 'You *are* looking drawn.'

As always he had to make some personal remark to upset me. Oh well! Things couldn't be worse, they could only get better. I'd already fallen in love with my grandmother. I would stay awhile. I intended to see a minimum of the family and much of Hong Kong. But after trying to find some affinity with the British and the Americans there, I found I was happier at home. Even so, there were worrying moments such as when Aunt Maisie said, 'You don't drink or smoke and you're with us all day. Have you no vices?'

Or when Uncle Ruby, reading at random from the Talmud in English, suddenly quoted a bit about a man going with another man 'shall be stoned to death'.

One night on a tour of the town I found myself in a queue outside a tattoo shop. Inside, the parlour was hot and fetid with naked men. On a table, on his stomach, lay a naked sailor; a needle-happy Chinese was tattooing a huge blue eye on either buttock and between them the letters ICU. I told Aunt Maisie and Granny, who both shook with laughter. Later, Granny told Uncle Albert who didn't laugh at all. In her excitement, she'd told him in Arabic.

I used to spend hours sitting with Granny getting her to tell me about Baghdad in her youth.

'Girls didn't go to school. I was the very first one. I learned English and French, as well as Arabic. Hebrew we learned at home.' She paused – her eyes dreaming. Then suddenly, 'I don't like England now. See where the Queen wears her skirts!' and she pointed at her knees.

'You're only saying that because your legs are prettier, Granny.'

'They are pretty . . . come, I kiss you.'

She told me how they prepared manna, that Jews dressed differently from Arabs, but that there was no trouble between them. But she kept slipping back into Arabic.

In Father's home everything appeared asymmetrical: the walls, the windows, the steps.

'In a Chinese house,' explained Uncle Albert, 'there is a superstition that by building things out of line one can beat and escape the devil. When you're in the streets of Hong Kong, look at the steps into the houses, even the Mandarin Hotel. The bottom steps are always off-centre.

174

They loved me at home. I was taken to the doctor, the dentist, the tailor, to eat this, avoid that, told to sit here not there. I never minded: there was always a reason.

My family had the wisdom of old age without its senility. But I'd come to talk to Father and we still hadn't talked.

'Just what do you want from your father?' Aunt Maisie asked me.

'I want to *know* him, hold his hand, laugh, chat, tell him stories. I want him to . . . to . . . talk to me.'

'Talk to you? He can't talk to anyone. Do you think we can talk to him? Nobody can. Accept him the way he is. He supports families, floats companies, starts charities. You can't change him and he can't change you. Your Father is this way to everyone. *You* haven't been singled out to be hurt. He is not the father you wanted. You are not the son he wanted.'

Every time I came upon Father in the office or at home I'd be welcomed like a long lost child, which indeed, I was.

'Hello there, my son!' or 'Sonny boy' or 'Georgie boy' and 'Tell me . . .'

Then he would talk non-stop and if I began to tell him anything, he'd raise a hand in alarm, gasp for breath, and tell me to go. A few months earlier I'd sent him a dark purple cashmere dressing-gown from London. He kept referring to it but I never saw it. One day I was summoned. Amah stood on one side, Father on the other, both hovering over a hideous, strident, crimson satin robe covered in fiery dragons. Pa smiled inscrutably at Amah, who smiled back inscrutably.

'Clever Amah. You found Masta Georgie's present.'

One afternoon, I decided I'd drive back home with Father from his office. It was a sunny day and I sat by the waterfront with his chauffeur waiting for Father. At a quarter to four, he appeared, limping painfully towards the car, hugging the wall and protecting himself from the crowd with his stick. He wasn't expecting me and didn't notice me holding the car door open for him. Just as he was getting in he saw my face and gave a start.

'Oh, my son,' he cried, bent his head and kissed my hand on the car door.

Later that evening I felt I had to go to give him a hug. I knocked at his door and opened it. He was sitting against the light of the setting sun. Tingling with affection I said, 'I thought I'd just pop in!'

His face went black. 'Nobody "pops in" to see me,' he said with fury.

The following evening Uncle Eddie's widow Marty came to the house

175

to see Father. She stayed for a long time with him in his study. Granny sat in the sitting-room fuming. Eventually, she called for the servants to help her get up. Then she shuffled over to Father's study and banged on the door.

'Enough, enough,' she cried till the door finally opened. Glaring at Marty she said, 'Ellis tired. You go.'

May in Hong Kong is always wet and sticky. You need an umbrella, a raincoat. You lose them, you get frozen in cafés and hotel lobbies if you don't carry a pullover. It's just nasty. Only the knowledge of the gentle beauty of what Hong Kong used to be fifty years before could make May in Hong Kong bearable.

Also I was nervous. For the moment Father and I were friendly. Nothing had been discussed and although I knew I would leave financially better off one way or another, all this was disturbing for me. But I did realize one thing. Father was as nervous of me as I of him. He knew I was scandalous. He knew that I could dishonour them all and of course he thought he was so important and so famous that everyone would be interested. My trump card was his vanity and respectability.

I lay in bed thinking about all this when there was a knock at the door, the bell boy with a telegram.

'Mamma rotta femore Anna Cameriera.'

I didn't totally understand the words. 'Mother broken femur Anna Maid.'

I hadn't seen Mother in three years except for those three minutes at Rome airport. I guessed her current maid was called Anna. The wire had come from Abano, a town near Venice renowned for mud-baths and a couple of hours from Bologna where there was a famous orthopaedic centre. I was not unduly worried. I asked a local doctor what a broken femur might entail.

'Three things are important,' he replied. 'That the patient not be fat; that the patient not have heart trouble; and the position of the break.'

Mother had a bad heart and was notoriously fat. It didn't look good.

I left Hong Kong better off. Something had been achieved – if only temporarily. Father had to face the fact that my health was shaky and that I was always turning pale. What he didn't realize was that it was he who was causing it. Now my health is remarkably good.

I arrived in Rome at dawn and the Galantis drove me to the clinic

176

where they had put Mother, a quiet small place easy to reach. She looked lovely in one of her thousand lace nightdresses, her face perfectly made up for the occasion. She was uncomfortable but not in great pain. She'd insisted on being transported from Abano down to Rome just to be near Tonino and Mara. A twelve-hour drive in summer heat for a fat seventy-three-year old woman is insane. But now seeing me was all that mattered.

In three years of not seeing each other we had exchanged only a few letters. Hers had been stupid; mine precise, pitiless and unforgiving. Looking at her in bed I was again reminded of how pretty she was. Those huge brown eyes, her hair, grey and springy. The corners of her lips went up whereas at that age mouths droop. She wore two large pearls in her ears that I hadn't seen before.

'What're those?'

She took them off and put them in my hand.

'They're not absolutely round. That's how I got them cheap, but what a colour! Crème rosée!'

I told her all about my time in Hong Kong. Tears filled her eyes whenever I mentioned Father.

'I used blackmail, Mother. You should have done the same. You had rights as a respectable wronged wife. I was just a bum. You could have created a scandal. He'd have given in.'

Lunch was served. She couldn't sit up to eat in comfort, crumbs kept dropping all over the bed. I looked after her tenderly. I'm an impossible patient and therefore a fabulous nurse. Only when one is sensitive to every single crumb or noise as I am can one know what the patient is going through. She told me how the accident had happened.

'I was tired after my mud-bath and had just returned to my room. Anna, my maid, had her day off. I was looking at myself in the mirror when I fell – like a stone! I don't know if the femur broke on its own, or if I fell and broke the femur. I lay on the ground groaning. I couldn't move. I tried to shout. I could get little or no sound out. In the end after I banged on the floor the people below came up. I was taken on a stretcher to the hospital. It took five of them to carry me. I felt so alone, so helpless. All I wanted was to be with friends. Anna doesn't speak English. I was dying to be with somebody I knew so I told them to take me to Rome.'

'But Mother, Bologna has the best orthopaedic reputation in Italy.'

'I was alone, I was alone. I didn't know what to do. I don't speak Italian and who was going to change my cheques and wash my things? It

177

is bad enough in your own country with your own people.' She changed to a calmer tone. 'I'll be all right and I'll go back to the Excelsior when I can walk.'

The break, I learned, was in the best possible position. Much later I learned all it would have needed was a surgical pin and Mother would have been walking within the week.

I spent a couple of nights with a friend in Rome. He was more concerned over Mother than I was.

'It's the bed that gets them in the end,' he said. 'Pneumonia.'

I didn't quite understand what pneumonia had to do with a broken femur. In any case, I realized Mother would be an invalid for some time. I'd fly to London and bring back the car.

'Don't leave,' she begged.

'I'll be back in three days and I need the car.'

I must have been mad to leave her in that condition to get a car. I was planning to leave after she had been given the anaesthetic to have her hip set. She would wake up, and feel me near. Alas! The operation was delayed. I couldn't miss the plane and literally left her just as she was going into the operating theatre. I cannot bear to think of my stupidity.

On the plane I came across a letter the maid had given me in hospital and which I hadn't opened at the time. It was in Mother's hand:

My darling Dick and George,

In case anything should happen to me, remain friends. I have left instructions about the sale of my jewels. I hope I have not disappointed you.

I burst into tears. I wondered where or when or why she'd written the letter.

I telephoned the clinic in Rome as soon as I arrived in London. I expected Anna to pick up the phone – someone took the telephone off the hook and I heard voices, then a short scream. Then Mother came on herself, her voice normal, almost gay. I could hardly believe she'd been in an operating theatre so recently.

'I'm fine. Come back quickly,' she said. 'I haven't seen Mara yet.'

Although I didn't believe Mother was in any real danger, it was the sort of moment that brings a family together. Dick begged me to spend the evening with them. Hating Ginette as I did, I would have preferred not to, but Dick really loved me and Ginette didn't hate me in the way I

178

hated her. They were living behind Harrods where Ginette shopped daily for anything and everything. I hated her for having a dining-room with a table for twenty people, a sitting-room as large as a football field and a whole room for her clothes, but nowhere for a guest. I also hated Femme de Rochas because she wore it. I hated everything about her. On this occasion she came up to me, her beautiful heavy-lidded eyes looking rather tender – theatrically tender rather than really tender – and she said, 'I wish you would be my friend, I have no family left. I know you don't like me but we should be friends. You know all about furs and you live in Paris . . .'

She trailed off. She couldn't think of any other reason we should be friends. I left at dawn, avoiding having to say 'Goodbye'.

20

I drove back to Rome telephoning Mother every few hours *en route*.
There was nothing to make me anxious. I was too nervous to drive
down non-stop and so I slept the night near Milan. The following day I
was in pain. It was hard to breathe and my chest and back ached. I
needed someone to put their arms round me and squeeze until
something clicked back into place. I stopped at an intersection where a
big policeman was standing idle, no cars in sight. I walked up to him.

'Mr Policeman, please help me. I need you to put your arms round
me, squeeze and lift me off my feet. It'll help me breathe.'

Italians are usually so conventional, they'll never do anything as
daring as that, but this one was helpful. He lifted me off my feet. We
heard a few cracks and something fell into place. I could breathe again.
I arrived in Rome that evening and went straight to the clinic. Mother
looked the same. She was now in a cast and in traction which made her
even more uncomfortable.

'I must be careful not to get bed sores,' she said. 'Rub my back every
time you come.'

The plaster cast was hurting her. I had to push and pull and lift her
and change the position of the pillows constantly to make her more
comfortable. She complained about her heels, which had began to hurt.
Although there were nurses everywhere, there never seemed to be one
when needed. I had to stay with her all day. She wanted me there and I
wanted to be there, although she also kept telling me to go back home. I
enjoyed nursing Mother. She'd say, 'I can't bear for you to help me with
the bedpan, to see me naked.'

To me it seemed almost ordained that after her terrible treachery, we
should be together now, closer than we had ever been. She was

180

constantly worrying about paying the hospital bills and I would repeatedly show her letters from Father where he wrote: 'Send me all the bills.'

Dick offered to come but she said she didn't need him then. She spoke a lot about the past, 'You know Father did love me at one time. He really did. I have letters from him, beautiful letters. "Bring up the children in your lovely ways". That's what he wrote.'

There were tears in her eyes. Two minutes later she was weeping again, this time with rage.

'Why should I have this misery? Damn his eyes! I was the only decent woman in his life and I've had years and years of hurt and now when I'm lying in bed in agony, I have to be worried about the bills as well.'

I managed to calm her until she fell asleep.

Mother liked my being near, so I stayed most of the day. I could press here, lift there, put the pillow behind the knee, above the neck, whatever. I made the tea her way: she liked it burning hot. Nurses didn't do that. How can they have the time? Sometimes I'd look at her and wonder if she'd ever get out of the place. Time was passing and nothing was happening. Why was I apathetic about the doctors' treatment of her? I lapsed into a mindless state. What was this new clinic? Why didn't Mother's bed wind up and down and have all the amenities an orthopaedic hospital should have? Because it wasn't one. It was where her friend the doctor did his plastic noses. Why didn't I get a first-class orthopaedic surgeon and have her removed to the best hospital in Rome? What had gone wrong with me? Why was I taking all this without reacting? I should have sought another opinion. One afternoon Mother needed a change of position. While four or five of us were lifting her, she slipped and fell back into her bed. She screamed. There's something wrong with a hospital where you need five people to lift a patient.

Over the following days, new signs of weakness appeared. Mother'd doze off more often, her appetite failed, she no longer asked for the mirror to see how I'd made her up. She even began refusing to be made up at all. One day, while talking about the past, we mentioned those three years when we hadn't spoken. Originally she had left Dick and me a half-share each of her jewels. Father'd given Dick a fortune for the printing business. I had asked her to leave me her emerald. Ashamed, she had offered me her diamond worth double. I hadn't wanted to screw Dick up over money, I merely wanted recognition from Mother.

So we called Salach who arranged it there and then. When we

181

quarrelled after Brazil and I refused to sell the car, I wrote: 'I want no part of you or your treachery ever again. Keep your emerald and stay away from me for the rest of your miserable life.'

'What has become of that letter, Mother?'

It was cruel even to mention it to the poor woman, helpless and dependent as she was on me, but I was worried she might have changed her will in her rage.

'I sent it to Salach,' she said. 'You said you didn't want it.'

She could see I was upset.

'If you want, I'll ring him now.'

I still didn't reply.

'You'll only eat my heart out until I do, and then curse me in my grave.'

With that she picked up her phone and confirmed to Salach personally that I was to have the emerald.

Next morning a visitor arrived, a stately and very old American – Anna Casati – who had become a buddy of Mother's. The last time I'd been with the two women was at a reception in Rome, when Mother told her: 'I sold some ear-rings to buy my son a car.'

And Anna had replied, 'I sold my necklace to buy mine a horse.'

She must have been eighty-five but she walked tall and straight into Mother's room.

'It's Anna.'

Mother didn't open her eyes. She hardly reacted, just held out her hand. Then Anna knelt on the floor, held Mimi's hand to her lips and kissed it. I thought of those paintings of *The Visitation*: two women comforting each other. Tears welled up in my eyes. Anna found Mimi's condition bad and said so.

Anna left and nursing nuns wandered in and out of Mother's room. They looked clean and holy, hurrying along the corridors in pairs, dressed in their long white robes. When Mother was fast asleep, I left the hospital to have the car washed and in the boot found the shoes with the cork wedge the doctor had told me to order. I knew they would never be used . . . Letters began flying back and forth to friends, to Marie in America, to the family in Hong Kong.

I supposed if Mother were to die, it would be a relief to Father. He didn't love her, had a guilty conscience over her and probably justified his behaviour by adding up what he had spent on her over the years. He couldn't stand her. He found her stupid, boastful, egocentric: alas she was all those things. She had also saved his life: once by getting him out of prison in Shanghai and twice by getting him through illnesses. As Mother's friend Tess had said, 'Whatever defects Mimi has, if you look long enough you'll find she's saved your life at some stage.'

She'd even saved mine once in Paris. Just looked at me and said, 'I'm taking you to have tests.'

I was dying of a virus.

Life for Father, living with a tactless woman like Mother, must have been impossible. But why was I recalling all her bad qualities now? When Uncle Reggie had arrived at Bryanston Court with a young bride-to-be, almost thirty years ago, Mother'd been condescending and overbearing and never stopped telling Reggie, 'You're thirteen years old than she is.'

'Stop it. Stop it. Stop condemning your dying Mother,' I told myself. What if she died? I couldn't conceive it and yet I'd have money – no more worries! Yet I'd loved her so much for so many years, I wanted to sit at her feet and cuddle her till she was an old, old lady. Of course, I didn't want her to die. So why was I wondering what it would be like if she did?

I would sit in silence watching the poor pathetic figure in that wretched bed in front of me and recall thing after thing that had happened over the years.

Once she'd had an operation in Paris. I'd stayed at her side, even gone into the street and found out whose dog was barking and disturbing her, and got its owner to take it indoors. Dick had arrived from London to see her. She'd been awakened by the smell of Dick's smoking. He'd leaned over to kiss her and she, too weak to talk, had taken a swipe at him.

'Get out. Stinks,' she whispered. I was the one she wanted.

I remember also one day when we'd returned from the beach at Ostia. It had begun to rain and I stopped at a garage where I'd been having a thing with a young man. He was coughing badly.

'Take him to hospital,' said Mama, 'he's got consumption.'

I loved the way she still used the word 'consumption' when the rest of the world called it TB. I told his mother I was taking him to hospital immediately.

'Tomorrow, tomorrow, I'll take him myself,' his mother argued.

Peasant women in Italy, and probably elsewhere, have always hidden TB in the family. It was considered a family dishonour.

Mother said, 'She won't take him. The laundry is on the line and it's

183

raining. She'd rather he died than arrive without clean pyjamas. We'll take him this second.'

When we got there, X-rays showed that his chest was riddled with holes. Mother'd saved another life.

I told Mother I would stay and sleep next to her at nights, but they hired a night nurse.

'She sleeps all through the night,' Mother complained.

I made no plans while she was in hospital. She might need me at any moment. In the evenings, I wandered about Rome. Sometimes I stopped in at the Excelsior to tell them how Mother was getting on. Everyone in Italy is always interested in 'La Mamma'. I wrote to Hong Kong daily, but I knew they had no real interest in her. She was no longer one of them; she was an expense and a reminder of Father's sins. They also blamed her for having spoiled Dick and me. She was a stranger to the 'Holy Family'. I was a Hayim, Mother was not. They did their duty over money and no more. Nevertheless I hoped that Father would write something kind to her, just some nice words, even if they weren't sincere. There are times it helps to tell a lie. I would have been grateful to be able to run to Mother and show her a letter from him wishing her well and promising to buy her lovely things if he made more money.

But Father didn't write.

Mother was not getting better. She was getting worse. Things don't remain static when one is lying in bed. Eventually, we did have a consultation but it was between doctors of our clinic, and that trendy, new, pretty clinic seemed to me to be run by amateurs. One doctor suggested putting wire through her femur but it never came about. Also, each time she was given an anaesthetic it was an additional risk.

As I left the room I passed one of the older doctors sitting in the hall and stopped to ask him what he thought.

As long as she had that plaster 'non ce la fa' (she won't make it) he said shaking his head.

It was early afternoon. The sun shone into her room right on to her face. She was grimacing when I returned to her side but simply hadn't the energy to complain. Why hadn't her nurse drawn the blind? I looked at Mother carefully. She looked worse. There were heavy rings round her eyes and she had no pep. For the hundredth time it struck me she might die. But an hour later she revived and asked me to do her make-up as she was expecting one of her favourite doctors. I again asked if she'd like Dick to fly out.

'Later,' she replied.

I came round the following morning to see her.

'I'm better,' she said, 'much better. But I'm having new problems. My feet.' I brought round things like lifebelts you put under the feet so the heels don't touch the sheet. 'And I've got bedsores after all. Turn me over on to my stomach. It's a beautiful day. We could get the bed to the window and let the sun and air on me. It's the only way to cure bedsores. People die of them. I don't want that to happen to me.'

I ran round the clinic trying to get someone to help. There didn't seem to be any men around. What kind of a place was this? Why was she here and not in a proper hospital?

None of the men I finally found to help turn Mother on to her stomach knew what he was doing. I tried to distract her while we struggled with her. 'Mother, do you remember the story about erecting the obelisk in St Peter's Square and Leonardo or Michelangelo thought the rope was going to snap and cried: "Wet the ropes. Wet them or they'll snap"? That's how I felt getting you over on to your tummy.'

She took no notice – then slowly, 'I can feel the sun. I'll be all right.'

A man delivered a telegram while she lay there.

'Open it,' she said.

I knew what she hoped for: a word from Ellis. It was from her Marie in America. Marie, her loyal friend and companion.

'How I miss her,' Mother sighed and after a minute added, 'Ellis could also have sent me a wire. He was so sweet in the old days, so thoughtful, said such lovely things to me. I taught him how to live. He only started washing himself every time he went to the bathroom after I made him do it. He was so proud of me. It was only after his fall from that horse in 1927 that he became different. You've no idea how tender he was before, how he used to come back from the office and lift you boys up and hug you and kiss you. He was a wonderful, loving man.'

'Mother, the year he married you he dragged your cousin into bed in your own house. The next year he tried to get into a railway sleeper with the cousin's sister. In 1925 he stuck the famous pin into my mouth. The year after, you swallowed ammonia and all he could say was: "I'm sorry for you." When did he become different? Different from what? But enough. We mustn't spend our lives wanting from people things they

185

cannot give. He can give money. Let's concentrate on that. We've never done a day's work, any of us. By the way dear, write me out a cheque.'

'Why now?'

'Because we might suddenly need ready cash.'

'You talk as if I might suddenly die.'

'I can also walk out of this clinic and crash. Come on.'

She signed. Why did I ask her for that cheque if it wasn't that I thought she might well die?

'And just for the record, where are your jewels?'

'I gave them to Marie Adda but when she went to Switzerland she gave them to Jackie, her daughter, to put in her safe instead.'

'Also, Mother, Mara hasn't been around . . . seems rather thoughtless.'

'She's involved with that rich young man she's mad about. They're dreadful people, but the boy is nice, not like his parents who asked Mara whether they should buy dinner-jackets to come and have a drink with me at the Excelsior. You know Mara . . . she loves exciting people with my apparent wealth but it's paid off. One day they came to buy some jewels from me. They thought anything I had was holy, so I borrowed a sapphire necklace from a jeweller friend of Mara's and sat like a clown hidden in the corner of the Excelsior lounge at six in the evening, wearing this priceless necklace. When they asked me why I was selling it, I told them Cartier had rung me to remind me I had it. I'd forgotten. They bought it.'

Mother seemed to have come to life telling me the story but next day she was down again. A deterioration had begun. She became apathetic and seemed to have no fight left. I felt a wave of tenderness for her. I remembered the million times I'd thrilled to see her wafting into a room with her glorious robes, her shiny straw hats, I used to think she was the world's most beautiful cream-puff. And now she was going to die. Perhaps her death would unify Father and Dick and me. But what nonsense! Yet despite this moment of great tenderness, I also felt the very existence of both Mother and Father was stifling me, stopping me breathing and feeling the sun on my head. I watched her carefully during the next two days. First, she got a discoloration on her neck, then one afternoon her face went thin, thin, thin and she started to gasp for breath.

'I can't breathe. I can't breathe!' she gasped.

I put the oxygen mask on her. She let it stay there for a moment, then started to battle against it, threw it down and again gasped for air. I had

186

the duty physician there in a second. He jabbed her with a needle over and over again trying to find her tiny veins. She'd always been so proud of her delicate white arms showing no veins at all. He couldn't seem to find one. But in the end he must have succeeded because she suddenly became calm.

'Riprende, riprende,' said the doctor. 'She's coming to.'

The scene was repeated the following day. Again the desperate efforts to breathe, the doctor looking for a vein, the oxygen mask on and off and on again. She was twisting and turning, tearing at the needles and tubes in various parts of her body. Something awful was happening. She'd become gaunt, thin and grey in minutes. I couldn't let her go. She mustn't die! We'd only just made up after three years of anger. The telegram from Father! It hadn't come yet! She wasn't ready to die! Give her a chance. Let her get better. She can't die this time. Next time, not now, not now! Her head was thrown back, her chin up in the air. She looked like that agonized horse in Picasso's *Guernica*. She panted and struggled. Now she was crying out loud.

'Mamma, Mamma, Mamma. Help Mamma, Mamma. Help me, Mamma.'

Then with one great heave she lifted herself up and fell back, still. My Mother was dead . . . Those soft, brown eyes staring helplessly up to the ceiling. The doctor stuck a needle into her heart. Then pressed down on her chest. Up, down, up, down, up, down. It was no use. Anna, standing in a far corner, burst into tears.

'E morta. E morta,' she kept saying.

I can't remember what happened next.

I lay on her, hugging the poor thing, rubbing my face against her, stroking her hair.

'Come back. Come back,' I repeated. 'I'll look after you.'

The door opened and two nuns came in, dressed in black from head to foot. They'd always been in white. Now they wore black. Death had come.

Tonino ran in breathless. 'She was my mother too. I loved Mimi,' he said, tears pouring down his face. 'I used to sit and talk to her every evening. She'd cry and tell me about your Father and I'd tell her about Mara. I never understood how close we were, considering she couldn't speak Italian and I couldn't speak English.'

I left the room and rang London.

'No! No! No!' Dick shouted into the phone.

Reggie couldn't even speak. He was closer to Mother than any other

187

of her brothers. They'd bickered for thirty years but were inseparable.

I phoned the British Consul and rang the cemetery where I wanted her buried. It's a small, beautiful place surrounded by cypress trees, next to a white pyramid built by the Romans. They accepted all faiths there. Keats was buried there. I'd get a rabbi over to say something and I'd lay her to rest in this beautiful corner of Rome. The rabbi refused. There had been a new ruling. She could only be buried in the Jewish cemetery. Then there was a question of fees. The man I spoke to was so revolting that I told him to go fuck himself.

He rang back. 'We are from the Jewish community and we want to help,' he said.

'To help yourselves,' I replied and hung up.

Just then I heard the searing noise of an electric saw. I ran to Mother's room. I thought they were cutting her leg off but they were only removing her plaster. Mother now looked herself again: they'd washed her body and the blackness over her face had gone. I prepared her face, arranged her hair, put some colour on her lips and pencil on her eyebrows.

I rang Jackie, Mrs Adda's daughter, to tell them Mimi was dead. I also asked Jackie to return to me the jewellery Mother had given her mother for safe-keeping. She said she'd tell her husband Roger, who put it in the safe when her parents left Rome for the summer. Shortly after, Roger rang the hospital.

'I can't return the jewels to you till I've seen the will.'

'It's not for you to decide what to do with the jewels. They were *not* given to *you* in the first place.'

'How do I know she hasn't left them to your brother?'

'I'll come with my brother and the will.'

'Maybe your father wants his share.'

The Addas all knew the situation between Mother and Father. What right had this absurd self-important creature to interfere?

'I don't want any responsibility,' he said.

'Then don't make yourself responsible. You don't even appear in this story.'

'If there is any trouble I shall give them to the British Consul,' he replied.

I phoned Marie Adda in Switzerland. We would see what would happen when Dick arrived. He and Reggie arrived on the same plane. Dick had made a scene on the flight with Reggie and told me he didn't want him at the funeral. Dick never did know how to behave. I took him

188

to the morgue and left him there. When I returned he was sitting outside on the back of a bench.

'Dickie,' I said affectionately.

'Don't talk to me,' he shouted, gesticulating theatrically.

Reggie was deeply affected while Dick seemed to be just a series of postures and noises. He was already irritating me.

I returned to the cold room several times during the day. I wanted to be near Mother, to look at her carefully for the purpose of remembering her perfectly. I couldn't totally believe she was dead. It might just have been a dream. Then she moved her lips. She moved them. They moved again.

'Mother, Mother,' I whispered loudly.

She was still. Gases had caused all that. How many people had been taken to morgues only to go on living another five years? I was dreaming now.

That night Dick and I slept in a big double bed where I was living. I had not prepared it on purpose, but in the morning we found we'd been lying on one of mother's nightdresses. For one second, just then, I loved Dick again. The next day we went to Jackie's together to get the jewellery. Neither the will, nor our combined presence would make her husband, Roger Cohen, return Mother's things. We'd have to get a lawyer.

We had the funeral two days later. Ginette flew out from England and was due to go straight to the cemetery from the plane. It was a beautiful summer morning, there was a gentle breeze. All Mother's and my friends came. There was no religious service. I took over completely, Dick knew none of Mimi's friends. I gave a short speech:

'My Mother was a simple woman. She was lonely and unhappy but she was always smiling. We will miss her, if only because she looked so lovely. I won't have any greedy rabbi here and I can't say a Jewish prayer.'

Eventually, through friends and lawyers and general pressure, that pretentious prick Roger Cohen returned the box of jewels. At the bottom of it, I found a letter in her handwriting.

To whom it may concern. It is my wish and order that the name Hayim should never appear on my grave. This name has brought me nothing but sadness and now that I am dead I want to escape from it forever.

I wept like a fool.

Mother wanted to be buried in Paris. In Rome she'd been happy. I would leave her here. There was no one left in Paris to visit her grave.

We returned from the cemetery to the Excelsior. Ginette was in the lobby dressed up in widow's weeds, strings of plastic pearls round her neck, like a star of *The Merry Widow*. She had arrived in time but had gone to the Jewish cemetery, missing the funeral. I was grateful for that. No sooner was she settled in than she started shopping. Her behaviour was brash and brittle. I couldn't sit in the same room.

Shortly before her death, Mother had bought twenty of the finest sables on the market. The furrier at Dior's said he had rarely seen better. I told Ginette Mother had left some sables.

'Some moth-eaten old things she no longer used I suppose.'

I wished I'd never told her. Dick was ready to leave after a couple of days. But Ginette hadn't finished her shopping so she delayed their departure. She persuaded Rome's famous jewellers, Bulgari, who knew Mother, to let her take a gold powder-box. It has never been paid for. On the day they left, I drove them to the airport. Dick wanted to stop at the cemetery *en route* and say one last 'goodbye' to Mimi, but Ginette was late.

'I want to go to Ostia to get my bathing-suit. I left it at the beach,' she said, pouting.

'Our mother's dead, Ginette.'

'But I'm not.'

We started to quarrel and Dick shouted to us to shut up.

'Don't you talk to Ginette and to me in the same tone Dick, or I'll kick you both out of the car.'

In the end there was time neither for her bathing-suit nor the cemetery.

After Mother's death I was alternately calm and miserable. I could talk about it and not embarrass people with my distress . . . then bang, my eyes filled with tears and I'd weep. I went through her luggage and found things to give to everyone who had been kind to her. I went way back in time, marking down the name of every single soul that Mother had said was her friend. The one I most wanted to track down was impossible to find. It was Irene Gherardi, a Russian from Shanghai, to whom Mother had given her jewels for safe-keeping during the

190

Japanese occupation. I hoped Mother had done the nice thing by her. If not, I would do it now.

Sixteen years after Mother's death I was given the address in Spain of Irene's sister-in-law. I wrote a loving letter, told her that Mother had left her a present and asked her to contact me. I got a sad letter in reply:

Dear George,

With tears in my eyes, I must tell you Irene, my sister-in-law, died last year. You fear that your mother might have failed to do something for her. This is not the case. I only wish we had found each other earlier. Would you like to help me with my charity in Irene's name?
Tita de Gherardi.

Also, before Mother died, she told me she possessed two diamond drop ear-rings that I hadn't seen, seven carats each and perfect. I discussed it with Mara, who had been closer to Mother of late than I had. Mara told me that they were fabulous, that Mother had taken a whole lot of jewellery into America, passing it off as her own. As a reward, she had received these ear-rings. It was the only story I could believe. Mother had never had an extra thousand dollars during those years.

I first saw the ear-rings on a sunny morning and indeed they were dazzling. The shimmering, watery quality thrilled but also disturbed me. I took them to four of Rome's leading jewellers. They did not take the stones out of their settings, but all gave me a quick evaluation – except one who said he was puzzled. I then took them to Rome's main pawnshop, the Monte di Pieta, next to the beautiful Palazzo Farnese, to test them on a special machine kept there, but it was temporarily out of order. The Monte di Pieta is in a street off the Campo dei Fiore, famous for thieves. Some of the streets there are narrow enough to jump from a window one side to a window on the other.

I stood looking helpless, when a man standing behind a wooden table, cleaning and polishing metals, asked me what I wanted.

'I'm looking for some competent person to give me advice about some diamonds.'

'Io sono competente,' he cut in, patting himself on the chest. 'Where are the stones?'

Normally this story can only end one way. The tourist takes out the ear-rings, a motor-cycle appears and whisks the diamonds away. I gave them to him.

191

'Fabul, fabul,' he muttered, but I didn't catch it.

Did he mean fabulous? Taking an ordinary emery-board nail-file he lightly filed a corner away.

'Americano,' he said, 'very expensive – worth four hundred dollars.'

When I got home there was a call from Mara. Those same *nouveau riche* friends of hers had offered me a huge price for Mother's jewels, but they wanted a package deal: the emerald, the diamond, the pearls and the diamond drop ear-rings, which they had seen her wear. We had to call the whole thing off.

I asked Father to arrange for perpetual care for Mother's grave. He paid it without a murmur. I returned there once that year and once the following year; after that, never again. When I wouldn't put the name Hayim on the stone, Uncle Albert suggested:

MIMI, MOTHER OF DICK AND GEORGE HAYIM

But the authorities wouldn't accept it. I'd actually bought a fine piece of shiny black-and-blue granite but the cemetery authorities wouldn't accept that either. It had to be 'white'. In the end, no tombstone was ever put up.

There was no point in my leaving Rome right away if I could stay on in a friend's flat with its terraces. I was glad to be near Mother. So many thoughts run through one's mind after losing a loved one. You feel you have to go to the cemetery or they will be hurt; that you have to think of them or they'll go cold. Despite all that, I avoided going there.

Eventually, I took Mother's jewels to London to see Christie's about selling them. Unavoidably I spent an evening at the horrible Ginette's, at the end of which she came up to me and said, 'You know you missed your vocation. You should have been a tart.'

'You haven't missed yours,' I snapped back.

Uncle Reggie's son, Richard, now an insurance broker, told me she had telephoned one morning, hysterical. She had dropped a glass butter-dish and wanted the insurance to pay up. The sum involved was three pounds. She did not, however, demand payment for the poodle she'd left on the mantlepiece and which had fallen off and died.

Soon after that Ginette's father died. She did the only thing she knew. She rang Harrods. They handle everything for their clients – take the

192

body, bury it, get the stone. Later Harrods rang to ask if he was Catholic or Protestant.

'Jewish,' replied Ginette.

'We don't handle Jewish deaths,' they told her.

When all the sadness was over I returned to Paris to settle down and correct my book. The manuscript was nowhere to be found. When I was in Italy, and realized I didn't have it with me, I was sure I'd left it in Paris. Now I tried London. It had disappeared forever.

My friends were sympathetic. Carlyle lent his manuscript to J. S. Mill whose maid used it to light the fire. Lawrence of Arabia left his *Seven Pillars of Wisdom* at Reading station. I was in good company.

'How can you remember it all?' my friends asked.

'It's written, beaten and kicked into my heart.'

I sat down and wrote it again. Every treachery, every tear, every moment of happiness and despair. Every place I'd shared with Edmond had been hammered into my heart. I wrote most of it sitting on a bench in the sun on Avenue Hoche, outside my hotel.

21

That summer Granny died and Father sent me a ticket to Hong Kong. He wanted to normalize our relationship. I went. It would take my mind off Edmond. The holiday passed amiably enough but I was uncomfortable. It also worried me bringing people home to that hotel where he was well known. I wondered if the Chinese Mafia told him what I was up to. Father went to the office during the day and at night I would see him for three minutes at home. He walked with a stick and had to be helped upstairs. Father rarely mentioned Mama and never asked about her jewels. Occasionaly I'd drive into town with him and Uncle Albert. Nobody spoke. Father was a real invalid and used his condition with maximum effect. I watched him as he entered lifts or restaurants, a showman to the end. Occasionally, employees of people who deferred to him were ordered to take me out to lunch. I was ordered to accept. It was always formal and tiresome to start with, but I'd quickly put people at ease. I'd say, 'I must tell you I have nothing in common with my Father. I don't work and we don't get on, we don't even like each other and I like men. Now let's sit down and talk.'

He himself was ashamed of me, but also pleased and surprised that all his friends took such a strong liking to me.

During the years that followed, each year I would be sent a round-trip ticket and we'd go through the charade of being friends. These visits gave him an insight into my own curious state of health. For reasons I didn't know I'd sometimes have a couple of days when I was pale and unable to stand. Whether he had thought my sickness was real or psychosomatic, he had the evidence of his eyes.

On my next visit to Hong Kong I met up with a very young and beautiful dancer and her four-year-old daughter, who were staying in a hotel. Her partner, whom I had not met and with whom she had temporarily quarrelled, lived elsewhere. I fell in love with the child. Subsequently, I met the girl's dancing-partner lover, a man with a remarkable body. I asked him to stay in my double room and save some money. We became friends and exchanged endless stories: he about his women, I about my men. At one point, I mentioned how the taste of sperm varied from person to person adding, 'I wonder what mine tastes like?'

'I know how mine tastes,' he replied.

'You mean you were making love to a siren in Singapore, came in her mouth and then kissed her?'

'No, I can suck myself off,' he replied. 'You have to have your cock in the right place, it has to be the right size and you have to be pliable.'

With that he sat on the floor, facing and close to the wall and gradually forced his ass up the wall, while his legs fell over his head.

My love affair with the child continued. I even thought I'd take the baby to Bali and write the story of a forty-year-old man and a girl of four. I couldn't get it out of my head. When we had become closer, I asked the dancer if she'd let me take her child. When I finally got her to agree, I ran to Maisie and announced my plan.

'What if she gets bitten by a snake?' replied Maisie.

I left for Bali alone.

The trip back to Paris that year promised to be luxurious. There was no one on the Pan Am plane, but at Tel Aviv we were *stormed* with Jews. El Al had gone on strike. No more stretching out over three seats, there wasn't a place free. Next to me was a tall, strong, Yugoslav-Israeli man I tried to charm. Across the aisle a pretty, drunken blonde, creating a turmoil for a bearded rabbi. I learned my Yugoslav had a girl-friend in London but I still offered to do something for him.

'There's nothing you can do,' he said, 'I've got all I want. What could you do for me anyway – here?!'

He didn't know what Capricorns can do! If I'd told him I'd get a pretty blonde to put her head on his cock, he wouldn't have believed me. With no design other than to stop the rabbi and the blonde arguing, I leaned over to the blonde and asked her if she'd change places – I needed to talk to the rabbi.

'Besides, there's a handsome guy sitting next to me.' She got up and joined the Yugoslav.

'Terrible woman,' muttered the rabbi, 'thank heaven she's gone. Now tell me about yourself. Are you a Jewish boy?'

It was fun to be asked if I was any kind of boy, even a 'so' boy, when I was already forty. I said I wasn't Jewish, but he insisted until I admitted it.

'Where do you work?' he asked.

'I don't work.'

'You're a Jewish boy and you don't work? All Jewish boys work! Why don't you work? What does your wife say?'

'I have no wife.'

'You're a Jewish boy and you have no wife! I'll find you a wife.'

'Rabbi, you're going to get me a job and find me a wife? I don't want a job and I don't want a wife. I don't like girls.'

'That's because you haven't met the right girl. I'll find you a wife in no time and a job.'

'Rabbi, I don't like women and I won't work.'

'When you meet the right woman you'll change.'

'I like men.'

He started to splutter. 'Impossible ... forbidden in our religion, such men get stoned.'

'Too late, Rabbi, I'm already stoned.'

It ended with his saying a prayer for Mother and giving me a hug. (I've never had a rabbi yet but it was a thought!) As the plane neared Paris, across the aisle I could see the girl lying, her head bang on the Yugoslav's cock.

Mirella's husband was due to arrive in Paris from London. He had phoned to say he would be at the Hotel Lutetia that evening.

I was in the hall when Lorenzo walked in accompanied by a man with a thick beard, whom I didn't recognize. It was Edmond. They'd met by chance on a cross-channel trip. He no longer looked handsome but confused, as if he had suddenly found God or lost him. He called the following day for breakfast, told me he'd got a pilot's licence in LA and was going out to Australia. His conversation was: 'What's love? What's truth? What's right or wrong? Right for whom?'

After months of actual physical pain due to my anguish over Edmond, I saw him as he was. I was cured.

'Ladies and gentlemen, we are about to land at Lod Airport, Tel Aviv. Please fasten your seat-belts.'

Tel Aviv! My forefathers! It would delight my family and, who knows, maybe one day I would end up here. As soon as my feet touched the ground, I knelt and kissed that earth.

An empty bus whisked me to the Dan Hotel where I slept till woken by a warm, bright sun. Sleepily I picked up the phone.

'Hot coffee and toast, please.' I wanted to add 'friend'.

'Friend' replied, 'Today's Shabbath. There's no toast. What's your room number?'

'I don't know, I've just arrived.'

'Then get out of bed and look.'

'How dare . . .'

Shut up George and look at your number. I dressed and ran down to the promenade, delighted that Tel Aviv was on the sea. I stretched out lounging at an empty café in the sun. A man was preparing something inside while a scruffy woman in a scruffy coat hovered by me.

'Shalom,' I said.

'Shalom,' she replied.

'Where are you from?'

'Algeria,' she sighed.

'My poor sister!'

'I lost my brother in the war. My mother on the way here. May I sit down with you?'

'Anything, my dear.'

'Can I have a drink?'

'A drink for the lady, waiter!'

'Cocktail,' she ordered. Cocktail! But that went out in the thirties. Maybe here it meant something different, like in Spain where *embarrassada* means pregnant and *constipado* a cold. He returned with a bubbling golden thing that she raised to her lips.

'*What* are you drinking?' I said.

'Mumble, bumble . . . cocktail.'

'What mumble, bumble, whisper cocktail?'

'Champagne cocktail,' she replied, smiling.

'How much does that cost?'

'Twelve pounds.' Same smile.

'Get out! Get out! Gachbazoona!' I screamed, remembering Granny's Baghdad Arabic word for prostitute. The woman didn't react. With time, words are losing their meaning. It probably means pussycat today. I left in a rage.

'Stick to boys,' a voice, my own, told me.

I located Ezra and Masha, distant cousins, and arranged to meet

197

them. I even rang Mrs Dayan, since her daughter, Yael, had been a friend. She agreed to come to my hotel which was good for my ego. From Earls Court lavatory to Mrs Dayan. Then things began to move. I found an idiot who became my lover. Now I might learn some Hebrew and say something to Mrs Dayan in her own language. I'd tell her she had a light in her eyes. It was hard to get my idiot lover to teach me to say it, but I was patient. I pointed to his eyes. Then my eyes. Dragging him into the bathroom, I touched the light above the basin. We toiled for an hour. At last I got the phrase. The day the porter announced Madame Dayan was downstairs, I came down, my speech ready. At the right moment, out popped the phrase. She stared.

'What are you talking about?'

I repeated the phrase I'd learned.

'You said I've got a glass eye!'

The following day, as I was telling the story to Ezra and Masha, I looked down at the promenade of the Dan Hotel and noticed my lover walking down below.

'There he is, the fool.'

Both cousins got up. Then, glancing at each other, Ezra exclaimed: 'He's an Arab!'

'How do you know? You can't even see him.'

'His walk! You can tell them anywhere.'

He obviously had to be replaced at once with one of my own kind. It happened on the same promenade. There were two soldiers whom I invited back to the Dan. As we entered the hotel a porter ran to the lift saying, 'No, no!'

I went to the head porter's desk.

'Who do you think I am? Hardly a risk when Madame Dayan called for me yester—'

He waved impatiently.

'You don't have to name drop to me. All right, all right, so Ruth came. Go upstairs.'

I could have killed the cheeky head porter. I'd change my will. Israel would not get my millions, not without a humble apology. Two apologies, one for each soldier. Once I got the boys up in the room I realized one of them was a loss. I concentrated on the paratrooper. I asked him to return the next afternoon. In the morning I went out and bought a gold parachute with a chain to match, which I like to think I paid for with my hard-earned Earls Court loo money.

When the boy arrived, I placed the chain round his neck, and put an

198

affectionate arm about his shoulder. He didn't react. Gingerly, I explored. Still no reaction. So what do I do now? Either I do it or I don't. I closed the blinds and got busy. I was greeted by something out of the *Guinness Book of Records*. When something like that appears, it's no good pretending one's seen it all before. One hasn't.

'You've got the biggest prick in Israel!' I exclaimed.

'Not as big as Dov Gur's,' he replied.

I forgot Edmond, my family, I forgot everything. My life was about to change. I'd make my home here, keep a haven where soldiers could drop in and eat. I'd order millions and millions of chickens to make soup for all Israel's paratroopers.

After a few days, without news of my soldier, despair set in. I was ready to walk barefoot into the desert like Marlene in *The Garden of Allah* to bring him home. But look! There he was! Walking down Dizengoff Street, a yard away from where I was sitting in a café with my cousins.

'There!' I pointed.

While they looked on approvingly, this time I ran to the boy and threw my arms around him.

'Did you forget my name? Why didn't you ring?'

'I came, I tried. I like girls better. See you.'

Father had asked me to contact another distant cousin, one Jacob Benjamin, who proved to be a great bore until, after talking for some time about Father, I suddenly blurted out all my rage and anger against him, ending with the story of his sticking a pin in my lips.

'This! Baghdad punishment!' he said unmoved and went on to something else.

I did not know whether to be sorry or glad I'd mentioned it. I had always thought of Father as a Jekyll and Hyde monster who'd thought up this evil to use on a helpless baby and here Jacob Benjamin was telling me this was a usual punishment. There had always been the vague possibility that it had never happened, that it was a nightmare, a fantasy of mine. Now I learned that sticking pins into children's mouths was a Baghdadian practice. Father was just being Baghdadian. But Father'd left Baghdad at the age of one. He'd never even seen his own father. He must have heard about what was done in Baghdad in those days and decided, as he was a natural tyrant-dictator, to carry on the practice. Still this knowledge would come in handy . . . one day. Capricorns are a spiteful lot.

199

The next day, as I sat on the plane taking me to Hong Kong, I thought of all that chicken soup I'd intended to devote my life to, and dropped a bitter tear.

I also thought more about what Israel had meant to me. I really did contemplate living there. I'd always loathed the religious side of my heritage but now I cared about Israel. There were shops full of English books, dentists and doctors were first class. Why not give it a try? When I arrived in Hong Kong, Father and I discussed it.

'Any shares you buy there, any money spent there, is nothing but a present to Israel. You will never get your money back,' he said.

Father was a supporter of Israel, but believed it could not survive. The family was pleased I'd driven round the country with my cousins, that I'd photographed a plaque in a synagogue with Granny's name on it. Father was now in favour of son George. Yet even then, if ever there was an occasion to belittle me, interrupt me or upset me, he would do so. He thrived on making people uncomfortable.

Father always created an intimidating aura of distance and fear with family or visitors to the office, although once I heard Marden, who owned Wheelock Marden, say, 'Come on Ellis, you silly ass.'

I couldn't conceive anyone else daring to talk back to him.

One time, Father had told Uncle Albert to take me down to see a woman director in the office below his.

'She will have gone,' replied Albert, looking at his watch. 'It's already five o'clock.'

Father blew up. 'Take him I said.'

He was throwing a fit. Uncle Albert ushered me out of the room.

'He's King Canute,' Uncle said, 'telling the tide to stay put.'

This was now my third trip to Hong Kong. It had lost a lot of its charm for me and when I returned the following year I could no longer stand the tension. Father was histrionic, silent, steely and suspicious, like Nero. One morning before breakfast, as I lay in bed at the hotel turning it all over in my mind, I felt my heart start to play up. I was scared. I held on to my pulse. It had gone haywire. I'd never had a heart-attack, but this felt like one. I rang cousin Ezekiel, who made an immediate appointment with my Father's doctor, a sensible woman. Before she began her examination, I said, 'Dr Evans, I'm under stress being in the same town as my Father.'

She did a cardiogram which shook us both.

'You have serious fibrillations, entirely produced by emotional disturbances. Leave Hong Kong as soon as possible.'

I told Father that his own doctor had advised me to leave. I think he was glad his presence could still affect me that badly.

Before leaving for Europe, everyone insisted that I visit Macao. After Uncle Eddie's death his wife Marty had moved there. She was living in poverty, but refused to sell her jewels, which she said were for her daughter. She had always been in love with my friend Harry Kitson and since he hadn't married her, she'd accepted Uncle Eddie. I'd never particularly liked her but after she had lost Uncle Eddie and gone through the usual humiliations that go with poverty, I had grown to be fond of her.

Of course, she and Father had had some kind of relationship. Hadn't Granny herself shuffled along to his study to shoo her out the first year I'd visited Hong Kong? But if this was the case, why the hell wasn't Father helping her? He knew she was living in reduced circumstances in a third-rate *pension* in Macao, even though Macao is a beautiful, quiet, turn-of-the-century, sad and romantic island where everything is dirt cheap.

Marty, however, had resigned herself to her life and in the evening found comfort in drinking.

I left Macao with deep resentment against Father. Hadn't he bought Mrs MacBain and Mrs Lidell and Mrs Morris and all those Taipans' wives bracelets and furs? Why not this poor thing who was the widow of Eddie, once Father's best friend and admirer? I couldn't get Mother on Marty's side because someone had told her that Marty had accompanied Ellis to a dinner-party at the Mandarin Hotel and had pulled his cock out with her chopsticks. I had tried to reassure Mother by showing her it was impossible. 'It's nonsense,' I said. 'You're good with chopsticks. Try to pull out mine. Go on!'

After I'd returned to Europe I got a call from Marty's daughter, Clare, to say that her mother had taken her own life. Harry Kitson called me the following morning. He had received a letter from Marty in which she'd written: 'I married Eddie because you wouldn't have me and you're the only one I ever loved. By the time you get this, I shall be dead.'

'She's dead Harry,' I told him. 'She killed herself.'

22

The following year I was invited to stay in LA. Edmond had left Australia after failing to earn a living as a pilot and had returned to the States to a girl he'd left pregnant there. I rang him in San Diego, from LA. He told me he was now happily married with a six-month-old boy.

'Shall I fly down for the day?'

'That would be nice,' he said.

After so much love and hate and waiting and hoping, we were at last going to be friends.

I'd hardly settled into my seat on the plane than we'd arrived. Edmond was waiting, handsome as ever. He drove me straight home to a small, light, clean apartment. I chatted with his wife, a cool girl, while Edmond took a bath with his baby. I loved seeing him lying in a bath with another little Edmond on his knees. I took them shopping. Olive oil, French vinegar, mustard and green pepper corns. They weren't interested. They were on a macrobiotic diet. As I left their house, I felt the story had ended well.

When Edmond dropped me back at the airport I said, 'Thank you for a wonderful day. Don't get out . . . and to think I've had all this happiness for a sixteen-dollar plane ticket!'

I turned to hug him but he pulled away as if I'd hit him.

'You translate everything into money and now you want a hug.'

I climbed out of the car without looking back. He rang me the following two days. I refused to talk to him. When I got back to Paris, a telegram awaited me: 'Everything I am is what you made me. I am lost without you. Don't disappear from my life.'

Then silence. I'd angrily thrown away his number but remembered his wife's family name. The prostitute in London finally traced him to a hospital where he had been placed after being caught peddling drugs. I wrote offering to send him French books and papers. He replied, 'I don't want anything. Newspapers don't interest me.'

The doctors diagnosed schizophrenia. I never believed it.

Six months later in Paris, I had a phone call.

'C'est moi.' It was Edmond. 'I want to see you. I'm coming to Paris.'

'Where are you?'

'In the South of France.'

'If you're passing through anyway, I'd be delighted, but if you're coming specially to see me, don't. I'm going down to the country.'

'I'll be there on Saturday morning.'

'I'll have left. Go to my friend Monique's house in Paris. She'll put you on the train and we'll meet you at the station. OK?'

I heard what happened only later. Hirsute and filthy, Edmond had arrived and rung the doorbell. Monique's maid had opened the door.

'Monique is waiting to see me,' he declared.

'Who are you?'

Silence.

'If you can't tell me who you are, I can't let you in.'

Seeing his act was taking him nowhere, he said, 'I'm Edmond.'

The maid then let him in. He had a bath, then sat waiting for Monique to come in. Her daughter found him in the drawing-room, staring at some paintings.

'He didn't even blink,' she told me. 'And during lunch he sat mumbling to himself. We kids died laughing.'

Jenny went to meet the train he was expected on. He was not to be seen on the platform. Eventually, she found him in the waiting-room, alone and all hunched up in a corner. They arrived at the cottage, which was warm and cosy, dinner was cooking, a dog jumped up to welcome him, children played. Edmond flopped into a chair, crossed his legs, scowled and talked to no one and this was his behaviour from then on.

After ten days of it, I'd had enough. He was a fraud but then I remembered what Garith had once said: 'People who pretend to be ill are as ill as people who really are ill.'

Occasionally Edmond spoke of San Diego though rarely of his child. Sometimes he'd burst out with, 'I want two poached eggs and some hot chocolate.'

The day we'd arranged to leave, as if he knew he'd better do something to improve his image, he shaved off his beard.

'God he's handsome,' said Jenny.

When we got back to Paris, I left him sitting in Jenny's car in front of the hotel and went to my room, after saying a curt but correct 'Goodbye'.

There was a letter waiting from his mother: 'Edmond has disappeared. He left the centre where he was being treated and didn't say anything to anyone. If you hear anything, please let me know.'

I ran down in the hope of catching him. Luckily, he was still sitting in the car. I took him up to my room and shook him. In the end, I said, 'I'm sick of you. What do you want to do now?'

'Go to London. I want to see my old girl-friend there.'

Later I heard he'd stayed at her flat and gone into wintry London streets barefoot. The girl couldn't put up with it either. She got him on a train back to France while I kept in touch with his mother. After some months, he left her, refused to give her his address. She died without seeing him again.

I had stopped going to Hong Kong. Klosters also no longer interested me. I was living mostly in Paris. One day I showed my book on Edmond to Alain Bernheim, a film agent. Margie, his wife, was impressed. At a party they introduced me to Gore Vidal who offered to read it.

'It must be published,' he said after reading it. 'Leave it to me.'

In the end, thanks to Gore, my book came out. Irwin Shaw, James Jones, they all sent me congratulatory telegrams and I suddenly felt I actually existed.

Usually in summer I'd take a flat in Rome. That year Harry Kitson came to stay. He had already gone through his third fortune and was down to his last dollars. His future was bleak. My circle was limited to casual acquaintances and vegetable-sellers in the markets of Rome. Everyone was out of the city, when out of the blue came a call from an American cousin of Mother's, who wanted to visit her grave in Rome. They asked me out to dinner and I brought Harry along. With them was a blonde woman in her sixties, the widow of Zeppo, the least-known of the Marx brothers. She fell for Harry and six months later Harry joined her in LA.

Eventually, I grew tired of beautiful silly Rome and took a flat in St Tropez. Dick was staying at Antibes with friends and asked if he could come over and spend the day with me.

'Not with Ginette,' I replied.

204

He arrived with a forty-year-old woman who had beautiful white skin and eyes black as jet.

'This is Natalie, Countess Potocka,' Dick said.

A few days later I got a long letter from her: 'I have loved Dick for years and always wanted to know you too. Now that we've spent a day together, I already feel close to you too. Dickie is presently having trouble with Ginette and is living with me. Stay with us if ever you come to London.'

An extraordinary letter to receive after a single day together. When I did return to London, Natalie arranged a mattress of cushions in the tiny sitting-room of her two-roomed apartment. Ginette had gone to Paris for the weekend and Dick hired a truck and, in good old commando fashion, emptied Ginette's whole flat. The following day we read in the papers: 'Company director steals back household furniture including fridge with wife's dinner.'

'Who is the company director?'

'Company director,' explained Natalie, 'is what they call someone they don't know how to place.'

On that visit Natalie and I began a friendship that became a deep love and remained till the end. She told me, 'I love Dickie. I'm obsessed with him, but he bores me. I'd rather be with you.'

Natalie exchanged her flat for one with an extra room on another floor of the building and I became a regular guest. When I quarralled with Dick, Natalie would take to her bed and weep till we made up.

The next time I came to England. Dick met me at the airport with his boxer dog, Hennessy. From outside the Customs shed, I heard barking and recognized Dick's voice.

'Down Hennessy, down! Heel, heel, heel.'

As I approached, Hennessy jumped up at me and a Customs man tapped Dick on the chest.

'Behind this line, sir, if you don't mind.'

Hennessy growled, spat, sneezed.

'Bite him, son, bite him,' said Dick, 'but don't eat him – we don't eat the lower orders, do we Hennessy?'

'Anything to declare?' the man asked, knowing by now that I was Hennessy's uncle.

'I declare – my brother *insane* and my nephew Hennessy a menace.'

'Go on through.' He smiled.

'We're staying the night with a friend,' Dick said. 'Natalie's away and the flat's being painted.' Now whispering: 'I have a faded beauty in the car: a blonda from yonda,' pulling some yellow hairs off his lapels.

We walked to the car park.

'Come, thou wench,' he said, dragging the woman out of the car. 'Meet my brother.'

The woman gave me a confused smile. Dick pushed us both on to our seats and belted back to London. Every time we got a red light he'd pull a mesh of her hair over, catch it in between his nose and upper lip like a moustache and guffaw. He looked like a mounted Mameluke charging into Napoleon's army. If anyone dared to speak from the car next door he'd raise his right hand and yell, 'See this hand, I've killed a man with this.'

I was vaguely upset. Would Natalie suffer from Dick's adventure with 'Blonda from Yonda'? Yet they talked of Natalie as if she knew all about it. Hennessey chased Blonda's poodle half the night.

I was glad when Natalie's new flat was ready. For the first time in twenty years, Dick and I were getting on. He said he was doing frightfully well with a gun he had invented. It shot out dye and pepper together. The idea being to get the deliquent sneezing helplessly while his clothes got covered with dye that made him recognizable.

'Your idea is good,' Father wrote, 'but you have an offensive weapon.'

'Dick has two,' said Natalie.

Dick swore he had made eighty thousand dollars on the weapon.

'Yes, but it cost him eighty-five thousand to do it.' Natalie whispered to me.

Every morning after a two-hour soak in the tub, Dick would jump into the car, late for everything, and go on his rounds with Hennessy. I don't know if Blonda was a stop on the rounds. Neither Natalie nor I asked. We were glad to have him out of the house.

One afternoon I heard her speaking lovingly to someone outside the door.

'Come in dear. You look tired. Let me look after you. Have a wash and then a cup of tea.'

She sounded so solicitous, almost deferential, that I thought it must have been the Queen Mother calling. I peeped out of my room. She'd been talking to a retarded coloured man who emptied the dustbins.

There was also a big, blond ex-sailor, shoulders out to there, who came round twice a week to do heavy jobs. Natalie and I were mad for him.

Dick said, 'I wish you wouldn't be so familiar with these chaps. Next thing they'll be getting stroppy with the Countess.'

I didn't know whom he was talking about. Eventually I worked it out. He didn't want to marry Natalie because she'd lose her name and title. The Potockis had been the richest landowners in Europe, owning castles, even whole counties in Poland. She was a cousin of the Ciartoriskis, the Poniatowskis, the Sapiehas and the Radziwills, this, at a time when Jacqueline Kennedy's sister, Lee Radziwill, was in the news daily. He wanted a Countess Potocka not a Mrs Hayim. Natalie on the other hand begged him to marry her.

I discussed it with Dick one day. 'If you were to die, wouldn't it worry you to know you had left her without money? Rich Jews don't leave their daughters-in-law penniless. I'd fight Father for her.'

A year later he did marry her.

Some Poles living in the same block promised to supply the caviare.

'Grains like ping-pong balls,' they promised and they were. Huge, great, green-grey caviare balls, tasting like ping-pong balls too. I even dropped one on the table to see if it would bounce. After the wedding he left Natalie and spent the night with his latest girl-friend.

I had tried everything to get Natalie accepted by Father. I wrote. Natalie wrote. He replied in unfriendly terms, addressing his first letter, before they were married, to Miss Potocka, which was silly. After the marriage she wrote again.

Dear Mr Hayim,

I am sad you will not accept me. I love your sons and was hoping one day we might meet.

Dick was on bad terms with Father then. He owed the bank a fortune and when I reproached him for being deep in debt, Dick quoted Father, 'The more you owe them, the better they trust you.'

But Dick never had collateral.

At home Dick and Natalie entertained. The table, the silver, the linen were always exquisitely laid out. The conversation was Dick, Dick and Dick. After dinner, and during dinner, Natalie and I would escape to the kitchen.

In the late morning Dick went to work, whether it concerned the

207

pepper guns, the printing business, a girl-friend or the paratroop regiment which he always claimed he'd belonged to – until faced with a parachutist. He then introduced himself as a special serviceman. He was obsessed with guns and war and throwing people over his shoulder and when we'd been through all that he'd come out with some new scheme and machine to scrape the algae off the bottoms of boats.

I continued bringing lovers back to the flat. If they were ex-soldiers Dick'd button-hole them and even sometimes do me out of my screw. If Natalie was alone, she'd get sloshed with them and unwittingly do me out of another screw. But what's a screw between friends . . . or family?

It was sad to face the fact – Natalie drank. What had hidden her drinking was that when she behaved oddly she didn't smell of drink and was always impeccable and clean, but she did have something of old Pamela – pills or tranqillizers, I didn't know which. When she was eighteen she had driven Red Cross trucks all over France. She could cope with the dangerous moments of life, but not with life itself. She was adorable with my toughs, particularly with my last one, Ron, a man tattooed from wrist to foot and with blue lines on his eyelids. As the six-footer came into Natalie's dainty flat she took his face in her hands and kissed him on both cheeks, called him 'dear' and then shared a stiff whisky with him, after which I took him to my room for an hour. By the time he was ready to leave, Natalie must have had another six whiskies. She was wandering around the flat smiling amiably, fully dressed above the waist, but without a skirt.

'Come again dear,' she said as he was about to leave the room and then planted another kiss on each cheek. The same happened the next time he came. One day, Dick was there when Ron arrived and Dick cornered Ron and talked explosively until he had to leave on an errand. Ron remained and, again, when he was due to go, there was Natalie, woozy and vague, wandering about skirtless. I went off to the kitchen to make tea. When I returned Ron was lying on top of her on my bed. I didn't want to interrupt but was scared Dick might return any minute, which in fact he did. He called out from the passage, 'I've forgotten some things in the car.'

I dashed into the room making wild signs that Dick had returned. Ron didn't see me and Natalie smiled inanely into space. Dick returned just as Ron had settled into an armchair in the sitting-room. Dick had no idea what had been going on, nor had I, even though I'd seen it. Ron was a good sort, even though he was a hustler. I only reproached him for his lack of fire.

'Natalie,' I asked later that night, 'don't you find he lacks "bite"?' I made a face like a beast snapping its jaws together.

'No bite, no bite,' she repeated, without expression. She really was dotty. The next time Ron called, we sat together in my room. Natalie kissed him goodbye as she got up to go, asking him to return whenever he wanted. Ron sat silently unravelling a ball of string; we were now alone in the flat.

'Ron, you're a great guy, we all love you, but you don't have much . . .' and I repeated my jaw-snapping act, 'bite – you know, grrrrr bit, snap, snap, snap.'

He didn't answer but later when I was quietly reading, he suddenly attacked me. A minute later I'd been made helpless. I was bound and gagged, a pillow-case over my head. In the distance I heard drawers being opened and shut. Panic seized me. I didn't even know his surname. I could see Natalie coming home, finding me tied up and her few jewels gone. I managed to hop to the sitting-room where I wriggled the pillow-case off my head using the door handle, muttering through my gag about sportsmanship, honour and the law of hospitality in the desert. He wasn't listening. He wasn't even there but I caught a glimpse of him through the hall mirror, stripped naked in Natalie's room. But his legs! Something about his legs! Then he again slid out of view. Then he dashed into the sitting-room shouting.

'Wait till she gets home, I'll fuck her right under your nose . . . I'll tear the pants off her.'

At the word 'tear' he grabbed at the white tights he was wearing, tearing them off and freeing his rebellious cock. Two jerks later he'd shot his bolt and collapsed on the floor. Only then did I realize he was wearing Natalie's underwear. When I finally got free I was so grateful he hadn't ransacked the house that I pushed all the money I had into his pocket.

'I can't rip off a sweet guy like you,' he said and shoved the money back into my hand.

When Natalie returned after he'd gone, I was still shaking. I told her the whole story in detail and to prove it led her to the bathroom where her panties lay in shreds in the waste basket.

'I bought them in Zurich,' she said.

Hotel prices in Paris had soared and maid's rooms like mine were being phased out; I was better off remaining at Tony's in Brighton or Dick's in London.

Dick was constantly in contact with security firms about to blow up a bridge, a river or a man. This particular morning, as he lay in his bath, I reminded him that he'd been forbidden to soak his feet due to a fungus he claimed was incurable.

'They're not in the water,' he contradicted, taking his dripping feet out of the bath and resting them on the rim. It was a Wednesday and earlier that week he had told us the police had asked him to go down to Basingstoke to advise them. It was now one o'clock.

'When are you going to Basingstoke, Dick?'

'Basingstoke? Why on earth should I go to Basingstoke?'

'For the police. Remember?'

'Oh yes, of course. Of course.

'But it's Wednesday today, Dick.'

'Oh yes, of course. I forgot, I mean I forgot to tell you it's been cancelled.'

I was determined to nail him.

'Dickie, what do you think about that new Corioplasticization?'

He thought for a minute.

'I was reading about that just the other day.'

'Another thing that interests me, Dick, but I don't understand it, is the Illyratic combination.

'I know about that one, it's hard to explain. I'll get hold of that book I was reading and give it to you.'

'Dick! None of that exists. I've invented the lot!'

'No, no old boy, I read something about it. What's it called again? Yes, mmm, something like that, I do remember.'

Shortly after the Yom Kippur War, I phoned him from Paris.

'Dick, this is your chance. Go and help. I'll pay your fare.'

'What about my darling Natalie? What if something should happen to me? You'll look after her won't you?'

If she was 'his darling Natalie', then why was he breaking her heart with dreary Sarah? I replied that I'd look after Natalie, Father would look after Natalie, the whole of the Jewish community would look after Natalie. Dick left some days later, by which time the fighting had all but ceased. The first people he called on there were Natalie's very close friends, the Sokolovs. Old man Sokolov had been one of the founding fathers of Israel. Dick immediately began complaining to him about Natalie using too much washing-up liquid; how she left the meat for days in the fridge; how she was useless and that he was nothing but a crutch for her. It was, of course, all true but that story could perhaps wait until the war was over!

Later I heard that Dick had set out to drive a truck and had told the Israelis that they were doing everything wrong. After a short time they kicked him out.

When calm returned and Dick returned, Natalie, he and I agreed to spend a month in the South of France the following summer. She was like a little girl at the idea of being with us both. She threw her arms about me time and time again saying, 'We'll have such a happy time, like Mimi and her boys, we'll be Tala [Natalie's shortened name] and her Jews.'

When summer finally came Dick let us down. He'd been short-tempered for months, all to do with his girl-friend. To be fair Dick had married Natalie at my urging to ensure she wasn't left high and dry if he popped off. He'd never been really in love with her.

At least when I was with her, Tala was able to talk and even when she was sad, we could laugh. I'd encourage her to tell me about her past and about Poland. Her cousin, the last Count Potocki, had died virtually a prisoner of those around him. Apart from the castles and counties and millions of horses he owned in Poland, he also owned what is now the huge Polish Embassy in Paris, surrounded by acres of garden. Natalie had asked me to chase up a lawyer who was fighting to get some of his properties back for Natalie, her father being the rightful heir to the old Count's estate. The old Count had been surrounded by people who would let no one near him during his last days. Natalie and her cousins, the Sapiehas, had sufficient grounds to take their case to court – alas, without success. How strange that this heiress to vast territories, this tiny Countess, bearing an illustrious European name, should be a poor, fragile baby married to a nut like my brother, with a minimal monthly allowance. No wonder she was unbalanced. At least she'd found us. She and I talked of her lovers and adventures: she neither hid them nor bragged about them. She had loved all those men, but none like her Dickie. I had met her mother in London; she'd been a famous actress, now eighty. Natalie was her only child. She had lived through all Natalie's dramas, always expecting something awful to happen to her daughter. Yet, despite her maternal devotion, Natalie didn't love her mother. Sometimes the evenings we spent together ended on a sad note so she'd take a few pills. When tears did come to her eyes as she went to bed, knowing Dick was not going to return, I'd tell her, 'It can't last long, she hasn't a title and she isn't pretty.'

211

Now fed up living in my maid's room or dossing down in other people's homes, I demanded from Father a place of my own. All the rage and energy I had against him for having snubbed Natalie was channelled into my own new fight – this time for a flat.

'I want a place of my own,' I wrote. 'A room to sleep in and one to eat in – even if it's in your name. Do you want another confrontation which might do us both harm?'

While awaiting his reply, I had a call from Klosters to care for a sick friend. I stopped thinking of my own self-inflicted problems and drove through Paris on my way to Switzerland, only to have my car stolen on the way, so I arrived in Klosters 'on foot'. As I told my friends there, bewailing my fate, a man next to me said, 'Come and look at my car. It's a Fiat-130 coupé and you might like it.'

It was love at first sight. I could think of nothing but owning that beautiful car. When I baulked at the price, the man said, 'Go to Milan, look in the *Corriere della Sera*. Since the oil crisis started you'll be able to pick one up cheap.'

On arrival in Milan, I answered an advert and sent a friend to inspect the car for me.

Natalie then rang me from London in a very low state of mind, so much so that I forgot about my flat, my car, everything. It so troubled me that I called Dick.

'I've never heard Natalie so bad. She wasn't drunk, she was heartbroken. Be careful, she's so vulnerable and in a moment of depression she might do anything.'

'Oh shut up and mind your own business or I'll hang up on you,' was his reply.

'I'm warning you,' I said.

I rang up to cancel the car. I would leave for London that night. But perhaps I was being over dramatic. Perhaps Natalie had, indeed, been drinking. Anyway the car-owner eventually persuaded me to buy his car, so I stayed.

No sooner had I returned home from the purchase than the phone rang. It was Dick.

'Natalie's taken an overdose. She's lying in hospital in a coma with brain damage.'

'Oh God! I told you, I told you! Is there any hope?'

'She'll never be anything but a living vegetable. You'd better come now if you want to see her alive.'

I wanted to bash Dick's head. What right had he even to live in the

212

same room as so sweet an angel as Natalie? God strike him down!

I drove to London hating my new car, blaming it almost as much as Dick for my not having listened to my instinct and flown over right away. When I reached London I refused to stay at Dick's and only saw him at the hospital where Natalie was lying, her right hand twisted into some grotesque position, her eyes closed, occasionally letting out a snort as she breathed.

'I knew it was coming Dick,' I said.

'It's easy being clever after the event,' he replied arrogantly. 'Anyway, she was suicide prone. She'd tried before.'

'Then why the hell didn't you treat her with more care? Your wife is dying. Do you realize what you've done?'

Then the nurse came in full of sympathy for 'poor Mr Hayim whose wife has taken pills'. That was the limit. I noticed a bottle of Guerlain scent she loved. I thought perhaps if I put it to her nose it might make her recall something and return to life. When Dick left the hospital I sat down and wept.

Then I got up, brushed her hair, stroked her and kissed her. I knew nothing was ever going to help.

I visited her often, and tried to make her look as if she was asleep, but there was a constant frown on her face and always that terrible twisted hand glaring at me. In the end, as her hair grew out and the grey started to show, I had but one thought: to pull out the wire tubes feeding her intravenously and let her die. I had no compunction about doing that but I was afraid I might be caught, so like a coward I stopped even going to see her.

Dick had succeeded in persuading her mother not to see Natalie. He said there would be no purpose in torturing herself further. I bought a fresh fish in the market and took it over to Natalie's mother for lunch. She received me with calm and dignity. She had not quarrelled with Dick and the only way she showed her feelings was when I was leaving and she held me in her arms and said, 'I wish she'd married you.'

It was terrible to see a person who was once a famous theatrical star in Poland, now nothing but a broken, wizened old lady living in a modest apartment, after a life-time of gigantic splendour. She was alone. Her only child had gone.

She also told me that a few months before, Natalie had telephoned her in a curious state. She had been suspicious and had called the police to open the door after running over to Natalie who hadn't opened to her. The police transported her to hospital and saved her. Natalie had taken pills and then told Dick, who had ignored it, thinking she was just demanding attention.

Although Natalie was still breathing she was, I believe, considered legally dead. The mother now asked Dick to return to her a portrait of a Potocki ancestor seated on a horse.

Instead of carrying the portrait himself to her flat he complained to me.

'Natalie isn't even dead yet and the mother's asking for her portrait back.'

Subsequently, Dick had a jumble sale of Natalie's clothes. Two pounds for the shoes; three pounds the bag; five pounds the dress. It was so revolting I rang him.

'Perhaps her mother would like to sleep on Natalie's clothes like you and I did on our mother's nightdress after she died.'

Next he threatened to take legal action against her if she didn't return Natalie's mink coat.

'I bought all Natalie's clothes and paid half for the mink coat,' she told me. 'The other half is still owing. He can have the coat, I only want my daughter back.'

'Your brother's "barking mad",' their friend Dosia Young said, and I remembered that expression.

I rang Dick yet again.

'You've lost your wife. You're about to lose your friends and your brother. You've disgraced your name, your nationality, your honour, your race. You are shit. I'm informing Father just as you informed him about me. Hope you follow her to the grave – the sooner the better.'

I lay in bed and imagined myself saying to Natalie, 'Call him to join you,' like the gods did in mythology. 'Drag him into the realm of death. He must atone.'

Natalie continued to breathe for a few more weeks and finally stopped.

Much later, her mother told me what happened at the Polish funeral service. Dick had refused to stand where the widowed husband stands and kept shouting out that he didn't understand what was being said in Polish and just stood there scowling.

Several months passed and he telephoned me in Paris. 'Hi Georgie,' he said using the name 'Georgie' which he used when he wanted to be friendly. 'I'm off to the South of France and taking Mrs X with me.' 'X' was a well-known British actress. He couldn't resist telling me he was fucking a famous lady.

I hoped he would never call again.

214

23

The nightmare of Natalie now over, I drove down to St Tropez to enjoy a good summer. I arrived at night, unpacked and walked into the market-square. It had started to drizzle and there was almost nobody there. Next to me stood a red-faced man about thirty-five in overalls, thin wisps of red hair falling over his face, revolting except that both his arms bore tattoos and I have a thing about them.

We got talking and he told me he was Pierrot the plumber. I admired his tattoos and a few minutes later I got him to invite me to his home.

He drove his truck just out of town and stopped at a cottage down a dead-end. I followed in my car and together we walked to his front door, beside which stood a big board with keys hooked on it. He chose one and opened the door of his garden flat.

In a hurry to make love, I put my arm around him which he ignored. Instead, he went off into a corner and rummaged around in a cupboard. I was sure that he would come out with chains or handcuffs. Instead, he returned gun in hand, sat opposite me and lifted the muzzle to an inch from my right eye and said, 'I don't like people like you. They should be shot. I'm taking you to the police right now.'

There was a big bang. I felt something in my eye but all these things happen in a second and I hadn't been hit.

'Don't pretend,' he said as I put my hand to my eye, 'you're scared aren't you.'

'I like real men. Any cripple scumbag can be a man when he's holding a gun.'

'Come with me,' he ordered holding the smoking gun to my temple.

I was scared but quite excited. What a story for me to tell when I got away – if I got away!

'Careful George, it mustn't end in tears. Keep calm, keep calm.'

As we walked in the dark to the two parked cars, I thought that if I'd been James Bond I'd have done a kick that would have sent him flying.

I was sure I'd left windows closed so when I entered my side of the car and he went round to the other side, I'd do a sudden reverse movement and manoeuvre myself out. No luck! I hadn't closed the window.

Pierrot stood there, his right hand pointing the gun at me through the open window, the left fiddling about with the door handle.

My engine already running, I shot into reverse. The gun went off. I saw through the mirror the man tearing around like a chicken. I thought of running him over. I'd get away with it, but it would spoil my holiday, and it all flashed through my mind in a split second.

Once away, I felt something wet in my crotch – I must have pissed with fear. I undid my fly and touched my cock – it was bone dry. I stopped the car turned on the light and saw black liquid – blood. Where on earth from? I took off my trousers and a trickle of blood ran down my side. I was bleeding from a flesh wound at the waist.

I drove straight to the hospital. I could not believe I'd been shot without feeling a thing. I tried to get some attention at the hospital but no one cared about this assassination attempt. They led me to a room and laid me on a bed to take X-rays.

'First get the police,' I said.

A few minutes later and a woman doctor arrived muttering angrily, 'This can't go on, I've no time myself. I won't work like this.'

She wouldn't shut up, not even when two policemen arrived. I tried to calm her.

'You are a saint! What a thankless profession. Can you sleep without pills? Doctors should have mausoleums built to them,' I babbled away.

Eventually, they said there was no bullet inside me, but I should stay the night. I wasn't going to waste an evening in St Tropez. I signed myself out, changed at home, covered my new dressing with a plastic bag and drove off to the police station to make my statement.

Inside the building I heard laughter. Pierrot, my plumber, was drinking away with three or four policemen.

'There he is, the faggot,' shouted Pierrot, pointing at me.

'Is this a bar for clowns? A man has shot me and you, the police, appear to be enjoying it. I'll go to the County Court in Draguignan and report the facts and all of you drinking on duty.'

The laughter stopped. Pierrot was told to 'pipe down' and I made my statement.

'And where is the bullet and the gun?' the policeman asked.

'What are you talking about?'

They asked if I'd come in my car. Then they went down returning with both bullet and gun.

Three days later the plumber and I had a confrontation before a woman judge. Pierrot had been in prison since that first evening. He now looked sober and ashamed and behaved reasonably. There were no discrepancies in our story accept that he claimed I'd forced my way into his room and jumped on him. The woman judge then turned to me.

'It's so hot,' she said. 'Pierrot is only dangerous when he drinks. We can let him free until the trial.'

'What's there to stop him getting drunk and finishing me off?'

'We'll have him under surveillance,' she replied.

I lost my temper.

'You, Madame,' I sneered, 'are going to see he doesn't drink, with fifty thousand tourists invading St Tropez? I am a journalist, Madame. I shall see that every paper in England publishes the name of the judge who lets a madman loose because, "poor sweet, it's so hot".'

She kept him in jail.

Before I left, she asked me to pass by the Clerk's desk. There I was given seventy francs.

'What's this for?' I asked.

'You've lost a day's work.'

And people say I've never earned a penny!

My second confrontation there was with a pretty woman – Pierrot's lawyer. Again we went over the details until I said that Pierrot had not been able to open the door to my car. This she would not accept.

'It was dark and he was drunk. Now it's midday and you're sober. We shall see if you can get into my car here and now.'

'What car is it?' she asked.

'A Fiat-130 coupé. So come downstairs with me, try and get in and complete the idiot you are making of yourself.'

She gave in. I went to the desk and collected another seventy francs.

On the day of the trial the courtroom was crowded. There were five judges of different sizes, sex and ages. Not one ever smiled as sentence after sentence was passed.

Eventually, my name was called, followed by Pierrot's. We stood in different parts of the dock. Turning to me, one of the judges said, 'Is it

217

true that you tried to pick up this man?'

At that moment Pierrot's face was the colour of a beetroot. He stood there, ugly almost deformed.

'Believe it or not,' I giggled, 'some people actually like . . .' I paused, then pointed, 'monsters!'

Pierrot lurched furiously to his feet shouting,

'Faggot, faggot,' and pointing an angry finger at me.

'There is nothing illegal about being homosexual,' the judge replied. 'One year in prison.'

'And I want compensation. I have a hole through my side and my holiday's been ruined,' I said.

'Compensation granted.'

I then sat down next to a journalist who was reporting trials. He told me that, two years before, Pierrot had received a bill for one hundred dollars from the tax office in St Tropez. He had paid it his way – by dynamiting the building. St Tropez had considered him a hero. He had been given six months in a loony bin and two years' probation. While there he had won a lottery ticket for $20,000, all of which he had spent on a whole new arsenal of guns. He had never had a gun licence.

That summer in St Tropez was to be a great season for me. I covered my face with gauze, painted another face on it; I'd find a piece of chain lying about, stand on a street corner, loop it around my wrists and offer myself as a slave. I'd start at a high price – like twenty dollars – terrifying people at the sight of a bald, chained man, desperately failing to sell himself. No one suggested I wasn't young or pretty, they said it wasn't a seller's market.

Later, I offered myself for free. When that failed I said, 'Take me as a slave – I'll give you ten bucks.'

'An old thing like you is going to have to pay more than that,' some old woman replied as she passed by.

Then I bought a shrivelled plastic hand, stained with blood and stuck it into my fly. I went to a party in a black mini G-string, stuck a meter of corrugated rubber pipe in it and tied a blue ribbon round my neck to hold it up. Every time I turned, it followed me. Bardot, who was there, screamed, then caressed it. I became a star. I was on the cover of *Blick* magazine, 'Capricorn goat rising to the top.'

The weather broke. End of holiday.

24

When my book *Obsession* came out to a great review in the *New York Times*, I felt born again. I'd become someone at last. I always knew I could amuse people and say things like, 'It's disgraceful to take a job from someone who needs one,' or 'I'm helping my father. How else could he spend all his money?'

But to appear in the *New York Times* week after week under 'Best Reading' did give me standing, even though nobody bought the book. The review, which advises libraries all over America, said that the two discoveries of the year were Kurbahn Said, who had written *Ali and Nino* and myself.

I went to New York and talked on a few radio shows but was so polite about the work of the others on the show that I forgot to plug my book. Also, I'd come to detest everyone in the media, particularly those who had read my book and had understood nothing of it. I was to go on television but instead I left the country as quickly as possible.

Uncle Albert, who was in New York at the time, cut out the reviews from all the papers and sent them to me. He was proud of me, though embarrassed.

My father wrote: 'Congratulations. I only wish it had been on some other subject.'

In the meantime, I wrote to friends in Hong Kong telling them to order copies of *Obsession* from the bookshop frequented by all Hong Kong, but when they went to get a copy they'd all been sold. Uncle Albert had bought the lot. He then bought a shredding machine and shredded every single copy.

The previous year, before returning from Hong Kong, I received a telegram saying that a girl-friend of mine was dying of cancer in New

York. I agreed to go and look after her.

'How can you afford these things on your allowance?' my Father asked.

'It's cheaper to live in someone else's house than on my own, even though I do live in a maid's room,' I replied bitterly.

This had become my latest gripe. In the months and years that followed, I again suggested to Father that I should have a place of my own. I was met either with refusal or silence. I decided his refusal to get me a place to live was blocking my way to happiness, even if I was already happy enough. It became an obsession.

'Prices are going up, maids' rooms don't exist any more, I haven't an address. I'll soon have spent Mother's money. Your six hundred dollars a month allowance is less than a workman gets. I'm sick, I'm old, I'm a fag, I'm Jewish, I'm a cripple. I gave my life to England. I can't ask anyone home. I have no home.'

I began a barrage of letters to Father – all without response. I now shuttled between Toe's in Brighton, which cost me nothing, and St Tropez. In London, I was fortunate to meet, through Alex Szogyi, the Hunter College language professor who had written the best review of my book, Eliane Reinhold, a pretty New Yorker who had left the States after a painful divorce and was now living in London. We must have needed one another. She let me live in her home. I gave her company, introduced her to friends, lent her my car and arranged for her to stay with friends in Paris. Subsequently, when she went on a trip around the world, I gave her Father's number and wrote to tell him she would be calling on him and that she had given me a home, that she had family living in Israel and that her father was rich. I hoped it might shame him. I also knew that it flattered his vanity to have pretty women from Europe calling on him.

'That father of yours,' Eliane said when she returned, 'was flirting with me. He was out to seduce me.'

She told Father I had potential as a writer, that I should have a place of my own. She flattered him and shamed him. She told him his own immense power had unintentionally and inevitably stunted my psyche for life. She hadn't had pins stuck into her mouth by Father, so she wasn't afraid of him. As a pretty, independent woman of thirty-five with a New York background and fluent Jewish rhetoric she was able to say a lot in a short time. I'd also warned her never to say he looked well as he only wanted sympathy for his condition. Though genuinely crippled with arthritis and unable to walk upstairs or anywhere alone, he was forever the showman.

That winter I telephoned him from Brighton. I'd never phoned him before from Europe and was trembling. No sooner had he answered than I read out my text: 'I've got nowhere to live. I'm sick of maids' rooms. I don't care that you're going to leave me money one day, that day may never come. I've got to have a home and if I don't . . .' I hung up.

I hoped he might be worried about what I was gong to do next. I didn't know myself.

I remember little of the following months except hours and hours preparing letters for family and friends. One set was a circular letter with all my demands, another set was the one to be posted after my suicide. I got an artist to make a sketch of a hawk-faced Levantine sticking a needle into a child's lips and had it photocopied fifty times. After that burst of hate, I had no more contact with my father for the next six months.

I arrived in St Tropez the following year with a raging toothache. The woman dentist who looked after me had long white hands and blood-red nails. She said it would cost twenty dollars to get my molar extracted, more to treat the tooth. How could I make Father responsible for my plight? It was easy.

Where could I find the money to treat my tooth? I'd have to have it out for lack of funds. I actually wanted to damage myself irrevocably so I could blame him. But it was hard to make him responsible for that as the woman and her husband found it impossible to extract my huge molar. In the end they got it out. I lay in bed bleeding for the next few days, and blaming Father. I was not interested to know how much credit I had when my bank statement arrived from Switzerland. Probably enough to have two thousand molars treated or four thousand extracted.

On my return to London, I found a letter from Uncle Albert. He had finally succeeded in convincing Father to get me a home. They thought of involving Uncle Reggie, but in the end rejected the idea fearing he might get a cut. They would trust only Salach.

I sent some real estate literature to Hong Kong relating to apartments to fit my standing. I am not pretentious, but, at the same time, I felt entitled to a standard of living befitting the son of my father. I also

221

believed him to be very rich. He must have at least ten per cent of Wheelock Marden's shares; he originally floated the firm's share-issue and was its financial director. The company was then worth a hundred and fifty million pounds. Uncle Albert wrote: 'Never mention the word kitchen to your father. He says you'll be cooking for everyone.' (He was right.)

But it was all to no avail. Father now refused to buy me a place to live after all that excitement. So what now, make a scandal . . . Father's Achilles' heel?

I wrote and re-wrote those letters I was intending to send all over the world. The threat of my actually committing suicide in Hong Kong and leaving notes, sending letters to all the Tia Pans and bank managers, scared them.

To Father I wrote: 'In my present state of mind, I cannot answer for what damage I might cause you, myself, the family' – and I threw in the Jewish community as well while I was at it.

Where would I kill myself? In Father's office. It would be difficult to keep me out of it. I couldn't see the Chinese office boys spinning around and landing a karate kick on the jaw of the director's son. I'd have my scene with Father, then I'd go down to that woman on the floor below – the one Father insisted Albert took me to see years before. I would take half a bottle of sleeping pills in front of him and the other half in front of Marden. Before actually taking them I'd tell Father that if he refused me a home, I'd swallow the pills. At this point, I'd wave the sheaf of envelopes in front of him reading out big Hong Kong names: the Keswicks of Jardines; Butterfield and Swire; the Governor of Hong Kong; the manager of the Hong Kong Bank; Hutchinsons; the manager of the Bank of China, and tell Father what was written inside them. I'd have to post them then return to die in his office. I couldn't work out in what order to do things or when to post the letters. Before or after the pills? How long would the pills take? And should I take them out of their bottle so no one would know what I'd taken?

I did not want to die at all. I wanted a flat. I pictured myself lying with brain damage in a Hong Kong hospital. My Father would put me in the best room of the best hospital and have the sympathy of everyone in Hong Kong for what had happened to *Him*. But everyone would also have read my circular letter and everyone would know I was a cripple – crippled by him before the war, and now again after the war.

'Good God! Ellis Hayim's turned out to be a Jekyll and Hyde. He sticks pins into his baby's mouth. They do it in Baghdad, don't you know.' That's what I intended people to say.

It would be scandal and, worse still, poor Father would have no one left to torture. I'd put in my letters that Dick had lost his wife in an abominable suicide due to poverty and my family's brutal refusal to accept her. What I'd say would be so cunning and so shocking that even if Father succeeded in defending himself people would say, 'There's no smoke without fire.'

I left Heathrow airport on a bright summer morning for the great confrontation with Father. The last one – eight years before – had helped and it had brought me close to both Uncle Albert and steely Aunt Maisie.

Something was pushing and pushing me to have this flare-up. I wasn't starving. I could even run a car, but none of that prevented me from carrying my mission to the end. I thought I was poor. I thought I'd been wronged and I wasn't interested in reason. I wanted blood – anybody's blood – even my own.

In Hong Kong I took a bus to Kowloon side and stayed in a cheap hotel. I was shaky on my feet – nothing to do with the flight, just nerves. I must get into a rage, rush to Father's office, bang on his door in front of everyone and scandalize him into submission – not that he would avoid me. Father never avoided anything.

I spent two days trying to get into the right mood but the mood never came. In my room I actually, physically kicked myself saying, 'You're fifty years old and you're too scared to face an eighty-year-old man in a wheel-chair.'

I knew that I first had to have a wild night.

After Mother had died and Father and I had played at peace, I used to fly out every year, stay at the Singapore Hotel in Wanchai, and make out every night. Soldiers and sailors filled the area. The Union Jack Club was three minutes away and sailors would get drunk every night and pull off their pants to the shrieks of joy of all their mates. Now there was no one in the streets. The army had left. Hong Kong was no more a naval base and the club was empty. Having made this fantasy contract with myself, I knew I'd never get my flat if I didn't face Father and I couldn't face Father if I didn't get this adventure. Four nights had now passed and nothing had happened. So I changed hotels and returned to live in Wanchai.

223

I was wandering around at my lowest ebb one evening when suddenly a tall, great body came crashing down upon me in the middle of the street.

'Wanna shit, wanny shit, man. Where's a —?'

'Right here,' I said, grabbing him by the hand, then the arm, then steadying his whole tottering body as I led him home.

He was a sailor off an Australian merchant ship but I hadn't actually seen his face in the dark. I got him into the hotel, into my room, then pushed him into the bathroom.

I wandered round my room humming as one does when one is embarrassed and can't sit down and wait.

'Thank heavens he's drunk,' I thought. 'Please God, not too drunk. This is my last chance. Help me God, and I'll give you half the flat Father buys me. Please, please, please.'

Nothing seemed to be happening in the bathroom. He might have collapsed, then woken up in a rage and finished by beating me up. Still humming, I passed by the half-open door to see what was going on inside.

My Aussie sat naked on the throne, head falling off to one side. He was everything I'd ever dreamed of. Tall muscular, protruding cheekbones like those dead soldiers on a war memorial and on his chest sat the most enormous tattooed eagle in vivid colours, its wings stretching from one shoulder to the other.

'If I don't get this one,' I thought, 'I shall kill myself so I won't even need a flat.'

I was interrupted with a stern command.

'C'mere you. Wash me!'

Trembling, my hands cold with excitement, afraid I'd drop the soap, the towel, slip on the bathroom floor, I ran to him, remembering how I'd stood in St Tropez offering myself as a slave, and began to soap and rub him down.

'Harder. That's it. Lower. Rub. Wash my hair.'

The orders rolled out. Everything I've ever dreamed of and hoped was happening at last. I was totally and absolutely fulfilled.

In the morning I leaped up and down for joy, I thought I was levitating and might never return to earth. I gave him my watch, my shirt, my electric razor, everything he could carry.

And now for the office. Quick. Quick. Before I lost the impetus! I ran into the street, grabbed a cab and burst into Father's office. I'd flay him. I'd kill him. I'd . . . I didn't know what I'd do but I'd do it.

'Hello Father,' I said, walking in firm and strong. He looked shocked but quickly controlled himself.

'I had a feeling you were near,' he said.

'Of course you knew I'd come. I had to. No more sleeping and eating and pissing in the same room while I have an eighty-year-old millionaire father. I can't even have anyone home for a cup of tea. Here, I have some letters,' I said, waving them at him. 'And here,' I said bringing the Mogadons out of my pocket and waving them before him, 'are the pills. I've had enough. Enough! Enough! Now it's up to you, Dad.' I said the word 'Dad' sarcastically. He paused.

'I'll have the police move you out.'

'And I'll have the press in. Hong Kong Tai Pan, Baghdadian Jewish millionaire sticks pins in his child's lips. Ellis Hayim CBE let his wife drink ammonia, bedded all his wife's cousins, Anne and Nadia and Lilly, and all the British Tai Pans' wives.

Here I named the wives of prominent Hong Kong men who knew nothing of their wives' affairs with Father.

'I shall be dead, dear Father. Dead. But you, you have stuck pins in your baby's mouth like all good Baghdadians do, you who have turned me into a homosexual masochist who gets beaten and tied up, you dear Father will die of *shame*! Shame for the family. Shame for yourself. Shame for the Jews. Shame, shame, shame.'

I was doing a great job.

'Close the door,' he ordered.

'Leave it open. Let them all know. Let the world know. Think about it till it's your turn to die. In the meantime, before I take these pills, I'm posting these letters. Do you want to read them? Do you want me to? They're to everyone in every Hong Kong government office, to the Hong Kong Bank, the Bank of China, the Chief Rabbi, to Hutchisons, Keswicks of Jardines, Butterfield and Swire. They think you're such a dear old man.'

At that moment cousin Ezekiel came in.

'What's happening?' asked Ezekiel.

'Father won't get me a place to live, so I have chosen to take my life and bring the house down with me. Tell your mother, my father would rather I killed myself than buy me a home. I'm telling everyone else. You tell her.'

Ezekiel broke us up, and led me out of the office.

'I've only started, Ezekiel,' I said. 'I want a place to live and I'm going to get one.'

After walking out of Father's office and before leaving, I called on John Marden, a man about my age and now head of the firm, son of the man who had once said to Father, 'Come on Ellis, you silly ass.'

'I've come to get an apartment from my Father. You've bought flats for your daughters. I'm asking for twenty-five thousand pounds. Is that reasonable?'

'You'll never find one at that price,' he replied, 'but I can't help you. There's the question of religion.'

Religion! What the hell was he talking about? I shouldn't have spoken at all but Father'd find out I had, and Father knew Marden had bought all his children flats.

I didn't know what to do next, so I called on Nina, a secretary Ezekiel had always loved and who had become embroiled in the Hayim and Abraham dramas. We'd meet for drinks in Hong Kong's charmless hotel cafés and laugh and weep together. I'd always pick up strangers, which embarrassed but entertained her.

A few days later, Nina phoned me. Uncle Albert had asked her to go to Father's office. The family knew Nina and I had become inseparable and Uncle was trying to assess the situation.

'Nina, would George really go through with it and kill himself?'

'I thought for a moment,' Nina told me, 'and then told him, "If he does not kill himself, he will do worse. He will disgrace you, disgrace the family, disgrace the Jewish community, he will stop at nothing. All he wants is a place to live, for God's sake!"' She stood up and walked out of the room.

My back had given me pain on the trip out and had now become worse. I could walk about in the morning but by evening I'd be bent double. It had become so bad after my scene with Father that I had to get some relief and this I found at an acupuncturist's. He'd stick his needles attached to a battery into my back and legs, and after half an hour I'd be able to walk out free of pain, but by evening I'd be back where I started. Nevertheless, over the next four days, I found I was taking ten steps forward and only nine back. I was improving.

After my talk with Nina, I took a taxi up to the family house to see Maisie. Pitiless, iron dictator though she was, she'd always had a soft spot for me. It was so painful to sit in the cab that I was forced to do the journey on my knees.

'What exactly do you want?' she asked me as soon as we started talking.

'A place to live. It's as simple as that.'

Just then Ezekiel walked in, white as a sheet.

'I've been talking with your father. He has agreed to give you twenty thousand pounds for a flat. I know you wanted twenty-five but accept the twenty. He's a business man and its only a game. Let him feel he's beaten you.'

An agreement was drawn up by Father's lawyer and I signed a statement agreeing not to demand any more sums from him. These formalities over, I had no reason to remain in Hong Kong, and would have loved to fly through the air to Australia, and end my days with the sailor who'd transformed my life with a single shit.

'If your father does cut you out of his will,' Salach had warned, 'there's still hope. Hong Kong is considered a domicile for the purpose of making money and not a basic domicile. Your father was born Iraqian and his legal domicile reverts to Baghdad. In which case, you'd inherit most of it although every single relative would also have a claim.'

I'd been stirring myself into a fighting rage over the last two years in order to get this flat out of Father but now that I'd got what I wanted something was still missing. I felt cheated but finally it became clear. Father had been spared a scandal. He'd escaped unscathed. There'd been no pills, no body on his office floor, no ambulance, nothing in the newspapers. Father's face had been saved and I'd been robbed of my other purpose: to expose him. Father had been one of Shanghai's leading citizens, righteous and rich. Now thirty years later what was he? A dignified old Tai Pan, Commander of the British Empire. He was an eighty-year-old cripple, living in a wheel-chair with two children he was ashamed of, and his wealth was non-existent compared with today's Hong Kong millionaires. It was his vanity, his sense of his own importance that had made him give in to me.

I said goodbye to Albert and Maisie and thanked them for what I believed to be their silent support. I would never see them again. I wanted no more to do with the Hayims. I felt like Mother leaving her tragic note in her jewel-box. I hugged Nina and Ezekiel goodbye.

'Who knows,' I said, 'one day I may be able to help you both like you've helped me.'

It was a good thing that the plane back to London was empty. I could never have sat upright all the way.

Once back in London, I continued writing to Father. I thanked him in each letter for the flat, but requested he increase my allowance so that I would be able to run it.

'Even more than the flat or money, Father, what I really need from you is kindness – a kind word, some loving thing to show your human side so that if you die I will be able to weep for you.'

He did not reply. I was never to get another communication from my father.

Albert wrote that he hadn't delivered my last letters to him. Father had had an attack of shingles and was now in hospital. I didn't know what shingles were but someone told me they were painful.

Here was a sick old man, perhaps even a dying one, and all I felt like saying was 'now its your turn. Suffer, suffer, suffer and die.' I don't know what I'd have done if he'd called me to his bedside and said, 'Forgive me before I die. I've been so cruel. I love no one. I'll make it up to you with money. Please.'

A month later when I was at Eliane's the telephone range at four a.m. It was Nina.

'Your father died this morning,' she said.

I turned over and went back to sleep. The camp-bed I'd been sleeping on had suddenly become embracing, like when you're in pain and they give you a shot of morphine.

I awoke early and shuffled down Montpelier Street in my pyjamas to the paper shop.

'Hello mate. What's 'appened. Won the lottery 'ave you?' said the paperman, looking at me strangely.

At the butcher's, the fat wife got up from her cash-desk and said, 'Whatever's happened to you? You look ten years younger.'

Postscript

In 1970 I received a letter from Pamela in Portugal. It went something like this: 'Swine bastard my Parker pen, usurer Jewish queer'. On and on for two pages. That was the last any one ever heard of her.

Garith Windsor, my best friend and mentor for forty years, is also out of my life. He didn't write me a nasty letter from Portugal: I wrote him one in Paris after an outburst of his rudeness to me:

Dear Garith

Although you are all the enchanting things you always were: witty, learned, mischievous and cultured, I don't want to see you again.

So ended forty years of friendship.

Mother's 'Marie' is still married to Phillip Sopher in Geneva, where they own a sumptuous lakeside apartment furnished with a dullness only they could have achieved. But they do have exciting moments as when they booked seats on a train to Zermatt from Geneva, three hours away, five months beforehand! I have been told her sharpness and wit no longer exist. She sparkled in her tit-for-tat quarrels with Mother. With Mother gone, only 'tat' remains.

Brother Dick, together with Natalie's friend Elaine, bought a penthouse in Majorca. When boredom set in, Dick started elaborating on his adventures full time – his role in the Korean War, his advice to the Israeli Secret Service, how he and his boxer dog each jumped out of their respective planes and landed on the same sixpence.

'If I hear that last one again I'm leaving,' Elaine warned.

She did hear it again so she left him and married a lawyer in Singapore. To get even with her, Dick married a serious New Yorker who left her first-class job to join Dick in the South of France.

Later on Dick and Elaine met in Majorca to sell their apartment, but instead fell into each other's arms. So together they left for Las Vegas where they divorced their respective spouses.

I asked him what Las Vegas was like.

'Can't get a decent piece of bread in the whole place,' he replied.

They were duly married but life became increasingly difficult for Elaine. Dick's behaviour became more and more erratic. He'd have fits of rage and make scenes in airports and hotel lobbies. He'd go into banks and demand money, refusing to understand that they'd never seen him before.

Elaine could no longer cope so I found her a saintly male companion who dealt wonderfully with Dick, going along with whatever he suggested and humouring him until his passing fancy fizzled out.

Dick then started putting on his shirts over his jackets or disappearing from wherever they were living for the day. His face became green and he stopped eating. A cancer was diagnosed and he was forced to stay in a nursing-home in the country which Dick said was the home of an ex-girl-friend.

From there he rang friends in a normal voice, suggesting trips to Spain, France and America. They did not realize he was off his head.

His mind wandered contentedly. He behaved like a dotty old monarch, amiably suggesting this lot be shot or that lot have their heads chopped off.

'There are only two things worrying me,' he told Elaine, 'the regiment and my mother.'

'Your mother died twenty years ago.'

'Yes, well we won't go over all that again, will we?'

He died of cancer of the pancreas and was kept out of pain till the end. I wept as his coffin was lowered but I would have wept for anyone's.

Uncle Reggie is still bumbling around half-deaf. Young people who come to my London apartment find him adorable. When we are alone he's always talking of old times.

'I was a good husband and a good father, wasn't I?'

I sometimes forgive him for having ripped me off with those jades but when he claims I only gave him two instead of nine pieces, then I don't forgive him. Monolith nurses him like a saint.

He wears a hearing-aid but rarely remembers to switch it on. I once said in front of a bunch of kids, 'Uncle Reggie, shall I blow you?'

He replied with a friendly nod, 'You're such a good boy.'

Whereupon I held both his hands in a vice like grip and shoved my head into his crotch.

'Do you live in England?' interrupted a young girl.

'No, I live in Hampstead,' he smiled back.

I kept old Toe in comfort in his Brighton flat, and took him abroad once or twice, but he had become disagreeable. At his home he'd shut himself up, blocking out the air and smoking fifty cigarettes a day so that whoever entered would stink of stale tobacco until all their clothes went to the cleaners.

He insulted my friends on his trips up to London and hogged the TV to watch billiards, even when Horowitz was playing on another channel. He died aged eighty after having spent his last months living on chocolates and whisky.

Auntie Maisie lost her mind, her memory and her voice. She didn't speak for the last four years of her life except once when I visited her. She let out a cry of joy: 'George', which staggered the household. She died, followed by Uncle Albert who was ninety-seven.

During his last year spent in hospital Ezekiel used to read out stock prices daily though Uncle Albert could no longer talk. On the one or two occasions when Ezekiel skipped a couple of share prices, Uncle Albert carried on until Ezekiel went back and read them out.

I've given up my social life. Stars and aristocrats have been exchanged for passers-by outside my London flat. I haul them in through my ground-floor window where I sit watching most of the day.

I own a ground-floor flat in Paris's busy Montparnasse, bang opposite a cinema complex. As the audience leave down the exit ramp they can peer into my uncurtained home. Occasionally, when I feel naughty, I do a little number like getting someone to pull down my pants and flagellate me. But it *is* dangerous – not for me, but for the huge crowd on the ramp which could collapse at any moment.

I also live in Sydney, Australia, where I have two dogs, an abandoned

German Shepherd and a Harlequin Great Dane, both of whom sleep on my bed and bully the cat. I plant basil and dill and parsley and pull in people from the bus stop opposite my front door, offering them ice cream I make in my machine.

I don't miss either of my parents. Mother looms in and out of my memory like a glorious dream with floating robes but never totally real.

I shall never forgive Father for the past. Yet never is a big word. The income he left me has so corrupted me, I might one day think of him as a saint. I haven't forgiven him the molar he made me extract in St Tropez.

This morning I discovered a shop selling Manna from Heaven, the Bak bak Kadrassi from Baghdad. Right now my problem is 'Should I get another Great Dane pup, and if I do will it outlive me?'